The Theory and Practice of Landscape Gardening

THE

THEORY AND PRACTICE

OF

LANDSCAPE GARDENING.

THE

THEORY AND PRACTICE

OF

LANDSCAPE GARDENING.

BY JOSHUA MAJOR,

KNOWSTHORPE, NEAR LEEDS.

LONDON:
LONGMAN, BROWN, GREEN, AND LONGMANS.
LEEDS: REID NEWSOME.
1852.

NAB
250
M 28   "La

TO THE NOBILITY AND GENTRY

WHO HAVE HONOURED ME WITH THEIR PATRONAGE.

MY LORDS AND GENTLEMEN,

It would be ungrateful in me not to embrace any suitable opportunity of returning my most sincere thanks, as well for your present patronage, as for your numerous favours during my long professional career; and I gladly avail myself of an author's privilege, to dedicate these pages to all who have thus honoured me.

I have the honour to be,

My Lords and Gentlemen,

Your most obedient Servant,

JOSHUA MAJOR.

Knowsthorpe, near Leeds,
December 1, 1852.

INTRODUCTION.

MUCH has been already written on the subject of Landscape Gardening, and by men of high reputation; but it has generally appeared to me that, having been either professional or amateur painters previous to directing their attention to this art, many of these writers have been so strongly imbued with special principles, or with the desire of producing a picturesque effect suited only to the pencil, that they have almost overlooked what I consider to be one of the essentials of Landscape Gardening, namely, the finer finish of Home, or Dress Scenery. It is partly with a view to supply the omission, that I offer this work to the public; but also, because there is, I consider, abundant room for another contribution on a subject so fertile as the formation and improvement of Scenery, on the principles of which many diverse opinions have been given to the world. Perhaps the vast variety of tastes which Floriculture produces, may be another apology for this attempt to develope new ideas, and improve on those which have been long known and followed.

I admit that the production of a Picturesque Landscape is, or should be, a primary object with the Landscape Gardener; and that, in order to copy Nature as closely as possible, he, like the Landscape Painter, must study the principles and elements of picturesque beauty. But this is not all. Whilst to both belongs the art of producing a generally pleasing effect, to the former it exclusively appertains to give the detail of that which the latter only gives, as it were, in outline. The Painter sketches his ideas;

the Landscape Gardener not only sketches, but attends to the filling-up and carrying out of his designs.

I have followed Landscape Gardeners, indeed, whose practice has been merely to give rough sketches of their projected improvements, and then to leave their execution to others. But such is not my idea of a Landscape Gardener's duty, for in this way the Home view, or Dress Grounds, which ought always to be brought to the nicest finish, because they are constantly under the eye, are often left in the most slovenly and inartistic state; thus exposing the artist to censure, and occasioning disappointment and vexation to those who consult him.

It is thought by many that, if the art of Landscape Gardening were more generally studied, the result would be materially to injure the profession, by destroying its emoluments,—that landed proprietors and others would design their own plans, lay out their own estates, and superintend their own alterations. But this is not my opinion, for I have generally found persons of the most cultivated taste peculiarly anxious for improvements, and most ready to employ a professional man to execute them. And this is reasonable; for the same good taste which shews them what is wrong, also convinces them of their own inability, from want of practical experience, to rectify it. However, my object in this work is to assist in promoting a general taste for Landscape Gardening, and I hope my readers will find considerable assistance from a careful perusal of its pages. In them are suggestions for the Laying-out and Arrangement of both Park and Villa Grounds, and for the Planting of Forests, down to that of Flower beds. They will find, also, what methods to pursue and what to avoid,—what constitute harmonious beauties, and what discord.

In matters of taste, there have always existed, and ever will be found, great differences of opinion; but I am content to submit my ideas to the ordeal of public opinion, and to abide its decision.. Some of the views herein expressed may excite censure, for I have spoken freely of what I consider errors in taste,—no matter whose the demesne, or whose the hand that planned it; but my thoughts are given to the world without any unkind intention to any one. They are offered as the result of forty years' experience. From boyhood,—through life,—at all times, I have been extremely fond of Landscape Gardening, both as an amusement and as a profession, and have looked for reward only in an improved public taste for so delightful and interesting a pursuit.

CONTENTS.

	PAGE
On Consulting the Landscape Gardener prior to fixing the Site for a House	1
The Site for a House	3
The Style of House best adapted to particular situations	6
The Formation of the Lawn or Ground in immediate connection with the House	9
The Old and New Systems of forming the Dress Grounds in connection with the House	18
The Disposition and Form of Shrub Beds in the Dress Ground	25
Flower Gardens, considered in their various departments and under various characters	27
The Shrubbery	42
Dress Wooded Scenery in connection with Tender Trees and Shrubs	45
Rural Walks and Drives in natural Wooded Scenery	46
Trees and Shrubs about the House and Pleasure Grounds	49
Ornamental Trees and Shrubs	56
Arrangement and Position of Plants of peculiar character	72
Walks	74
Water	79
Bridges	90
Seats and other Garden Ornaments	93
Fountains	96
Plant Houses	101
The mode of Fencing between the kept Ground and the Park	103
The Approach	107
Lodges and Gates	114
Dress Scenery	118
Rural Scenery	132
Picturesque Scenery	133
Romantic Scenery	134
Park Scenery	137
The Outline of Plantations	150
The Arrangement and Grouping of Trees	151
Prospect Scenery; or Scenery beyond the Park	163
Trees best suited to Form the Aerial Line	165
The Management of Ornamental Trees and Screen Plantations	167
Fences for Park and Forest Plantations	169
The Time of Planting Trees, with a few Cautionary Directions	172

x

	PAGE
Sea Side Planting......	176
Removing Large Trees..	178
Town Gardens	183
Suburban Villas..	185
The Kitchen Garden	187
A few Observations on Villages	189
Public Parks connected with Large Towns	193
Miscellaneous :—	
Shrubs suitable as Undergrowths for Thickening Plantations	197
Climbing Plants	198
Plants for Beautifying Trees which are not of themselves pleasing objects............	198
Compost for Plants	199
To Protect Tender Plants	199
To Destroy Weeds in Walks	199
To Destroy Worms infesting Walks and Lawns	200

REFERENCES TO PLANS.

	PAGE
Plate I.—Ideal Plans for Town Gardens	184
Plate II.—Ideal Plan for a Villa Residence, upon One Acre of Ground	185
Plate III.—Ideal Plan for a Villa Residence, upon Four Acres of Ground	186
Plate IV.—Ideal Plan for a Winter Garden	34
Plate on the Grouping of Trees........................	159

The following Plans are inserted at the end of the Book, viz. :—

Plate V.—Ideal Plan, shewing the General Arrangement of a Country Residence.

Plate VI.—Ideal Plan of Park attached to a Country Residence.

Plate VII.—Ideal Plan, shewing the General Arrangement of a Palace or Mansion Grounds.

THE

THEORY AND PRACTICE

OF

LANDSCAPE GARDENING.

ON CONSULTING THE LANDSCAPE GARDENER PRIOR TO FIXING THE SITE FOR A HOUSE.

WHEN a gentleman has made up his mind to build or alter a house with appropriate grounds, and intends to consult the Landscape Gardener, he should do so in the first instance, before taking further steps. I confess I am surprised that this is so little regarded, because it is the very object of the Landscape Gardener's profession to fix the different views, and subject the varied scenery to his own command. In his mind the house is but a mere speck, and yet so important a point that every thing else should be made to contribute to its grandeur, beauty, comfort, and convenience. Nor am I alone in the opinion which I have thus expressed. Mason says—"I am of opinion that, when a place is to be formed, he who disposes the grounds and arranges the plantations, ought to fix the situation, at least, if not to determine the shape and size of ornamental buildings." Loudon also remarks—"In most cases an Architect is almost as ill qualified to decide upon the proper situation for a house, as a Landscape Gardener would be to build one."

By these remarks I mean no disparagement to the Architect, nor do I wish either to supersede him, or to interfere with his particular province, viz., that of building the house and its appendages; but to determine the position of the house and its principal entrance, with the sites for stables and other outbuildings, is unquestionably the province of the Landscape Gardener. The Architect himself would acknowledge the propriety of my suggestion, and the justice of my remarks, had he witnessed, as a Landscape Gardener, the numerous miserable (and not unfrequently irremediable) errors that have come under notice in the course of my practice, arising from either not calling in the Landscape Gardener till the house, &c., was built, or until some operations had been commenced. In some instances it has been necessary for the approach to pass through and interfere with the repose of the pleasure grounds, and even disturb the privacy of the living rooms; and in others, the kitchen garden, stables, and out-offices, have been glaringly prominent, in consequence of the entrance requiring the approach to pass them: all which nuisances might have been avoided by an earlier consultation with the Landscape Gardener.

ON THE SITE FOR A HOUSE.

In determining the site for a house, several things have to be taken into consideration.

1st. The Aspect—which should be south-east, if possible; if not, then south or east, or north-west. North, west, and south-west are all objectionable, on account of the cold and boisterous winds; and particularly the latter, on account of both winds and rains. South and south-east aspects are decidedly the best; they are the driest and the most cheerful, and therefore most suitable for the principal living rooms, while less important rooms may have a cooler aspect, and serve as a retreat during the hottest parts of summer.

2nd. Shelter—which also is a matter of primary importance. In choosing a site for a house, we should, of course, not fix it upon the summit of a hill, (I do not mean gentle rising ground, for in that case the summit may often be most suitable, not only for the sake of effect, but in order to avoid damps

FIGURE 1.

and fogs,) nor the highest point of the domain, unless it is well clothed with trees, as an edifice in such a situation would not only be very much exposed to boisterous weather, but prominent in the extreme, and at variance, therefore, with good taste; and a plantation of young trees would be at least half a century in either producing effect, or in affording sufficient shelter in high exposed situations. (*Fig. 1.*)

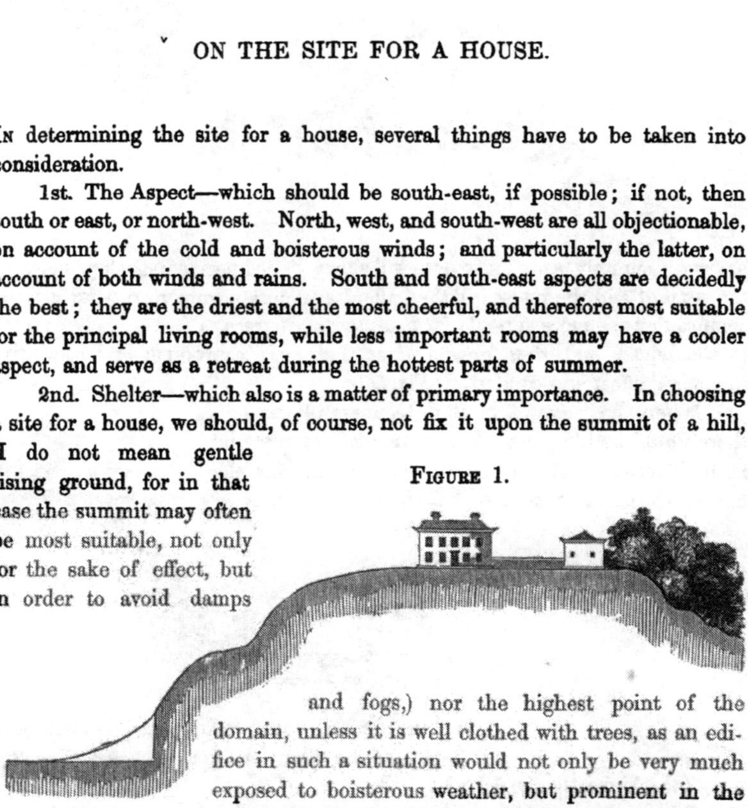

If, however, it is thought desirable to fix the site on a high situation, advantage should be taken of any moderate level that may occur in it, as far

FIGURE 2.

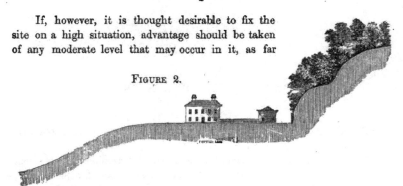

below the summit as circumstances will allow. The intermediate slope between the summit and the house will then afford a favourable opportunity for general composition, be more suitable for the growth of trees, afford a readier access to the house, and, therefore, be altogether more convenient and conducive to general effect and comfort. *(Fig. 2.)*

When, on account of the steepness of the hill, there would be too great an accumulation of material in the formation of one continued platform for the house, offices, yards, stables, &c., two platforms may be

FIGURE 3.

made: one for the house, offices, and kitchen yard *(fig. 3 a)*; and the other for the stables, &c., the latter taking the higher level *(fig. 3 b)*.

Whenever practicable, the site for a mansion should, unquestionably, be selected in the vicinity of old trees, whether they form groups in parks or fields, or are found singly, yet numerously, in hedgerows, or collectively in the shape of massive forests. Spots commanding extensive and interesting prospects (though very pleasing) ought to yield to situations of this description; for a mansion thus associated, though new, becomes at once embosomed in shelter, and bears immediate marks of grandeur and dignity, which nothing but antiquity could otherwise have given to it. And although it may not command all the best and most desirable prospects, yet the absence of these may in a great measure be compensated for by judiciously bringing into view such scenery (where it exists) at various points in the pleasure grounds; a circumstance which would probably create more variety and greater interest than if all the principal scenery were commanded at one view. We too often find a disposition to build on high elevations, for the mere sake of an extensive view, which seems with some persons all-in-all, regardless of either comfort or health. But, in my opinion, the most desirable site for a mansion is that which combines the greatest amount of comfort and convenience within and around it, with the most interesting rich home and middle scenery. This is far preferable to a site exposed to inconvenience and stormy blasts for the sake of prospect. The house should be placed on ground composed of dry material, as damp situations are unhealthy. When the site is not naturally dry, it may be rendered so in a great measure by forming, in addition to the main drains, numerous rubble or tile drains, from eighteen inches to two feet or more deep, in the immediate vicinity of the house, and by mixing stones, gravel, or any other hard or shelly material, freely with the soil whilst forming it. In fixing the site, the most appropriate and interesting capabilities for creating pleasure ground are of the highest consideration, and it should also present a suitable situation for the kitchen garden.

ON THE STYLE OF HOUSE BEST ADAPTED TO PARTICULAR SITUATIONS.

As the style of a house should be, in a great measure, adapted to the scenery of its locality, I will give a short description of the principal kinds of scenery, suggesting at the same time the kind of house which I consider best suited to each.

There are generally reckoned to be five principal kinds of scenery, viz., The Grand; the Romantic; the Picturesque; the Beautiful; and the Rural.

Grand Scenery is distinguished by bold, striking, and majestic features of vast extent. Mountains, for instance, which swell boldly out; or rocks which rear aloft their gigantic heads, or stretch far into the ocean, or into the still smooth lake, which reflects back the dark shadows of overhanging woods. Examples of the Grand are generally to be found in lake districts, in Westmoreland, Cumberland, &c. A mansion to preside over such scenery should either be Italian, Gothic, or Castellated; but if the undulations of ground are abrupt immediately in connection with the site for the erection, either the Castellated or the Gothic style would be the most suitable.

Romantic Scenery is where we find nature in her wildest and most changeful mood; ever varying in bold and sudden contrasts, such as precipitous and shelfy rocks, the impetuous cataract, the rapid river, the yawning cavern, the root-bound and craggy steep, tangled woods and wild and varied undergrowths, as may be seen at Bolton Abbey, Yorkshire, and Dovedale, in Derbyshire. To such scenery the Elizabethan, or Castellated, style would be suitable.

Picturesque Scenery is nature in her simplest and most artless form—hill, dale, brook, thicket; the stunted oak and the bramble bush; the ash, the elm, the sycamore, and their climbing parasites; and whins, and thorns, and other indigenous bushes; a fountain gushing from some cleft into a little basin of moss-grown stones, and the wild rose and the woodbine intertwined, as we see it everywhere on the broken banks and craggy hills of Wharfdale, and in most mountainous or hilly districts. The Elizabethan style is best suited to scenery of this description, with its numerous gables, and projections, terraces, vases and urns, and other similar decorations.

Beautiful Scenery is that which is quiet and retiring, where everything is soft and blending, and where there are no sudden contrasts, but composed of bold and gentle undulations, and adorned with handsome and stately trees, with now and then a peep at some gentle water or glassy lake.* The Grecian or Italian style is most in harmony with such scenery as this.

Rural Scenery is, of all, the simplest and most common. It is that where there is generally abundance of hedge-row timber, and hedge after hedge in constant succession; where there is the busy farm, dotted and animated with sheep, and cattle wading through the muddy pools or cool shallow streams. Here should be placed a modest unassuming house, or cottage orné, either of which would be well adapted to it. Or, if the domain be large, (demanding a family residence), a manorial edifice might be suitable. Scenery of this kind prevails most generally on the Great Northern Line, from the junction at Knottingley, near Ferrybridge, to within a few miles of London.

Whatever the style of the house may be, the stables should always be in character, and be placed at a convenient distance from it: near enough to associate with the house, and appear to belong to it, but never so prominent nor on so extensive a scale as to be mistaken for the mansion itself; nor yet so completely concealed or planted out as either not to appear at all, or to seem but a very insignificant appendage. The various offices should always be above ground, and correspond with the style of the mansion, whatever it may be, and placed in close connection with it. Buildings of this description should be arranged in broken lines, and be of different elevations, and attached to the main building by ornamental walls of different heights: they thus not only produce variety, extent, and importance, but being broken and

* The scenery about Harewood House, in Wharfdale, and farther up the vale towards Bolton Abbey, as well as that viewed from the Great Northern Railway a few miles north of London, and the vale of Richmond, near London, are good examples of the beautiful.

finished with judicious planting, they form an interesting and picturesque whole, and, at the same time, obviate that square, compact, heavy appearance which the house assumes when destitute of such accompaniments.

CARRIAGE ENTRANCE.—With regard to the carriage entrance, I would in no case have this on the same front with the principal living rooms; an error unfortunately too often fallen into, but which ought most studiously to be guarded against, as it destroys all privacy, and—to say nothing of the impertinent gaze of strange servants, &c.—subjects the family to be taken by surprise by visiters suddenly approaching at an inconvenient moment. Again, the carriage entrance front should not, where it can be avoided, command the best and most interesting scenery : as, in the hurry of approaching and leaving the house, it would run the risk either of being overlooked altogether, or, to say the least, of not being sufficiently admired and appreciated. The choice scenery should unquestionably be reserved for the principal rooms, where it can be studied and enjoyed at all times in uninterrupted privacy and quiet. I remember an instance in which the principal entrance occupied the best front, commanding the most interesting scenery. In that instance the approach was actually obliged to pass close to the kitchen yard, and almost wholly round the stables, in order to reach the entrance front door, between which and a stupendous precipice there was scarcely room left to turn a carriage. It is scarcely credible that such an error should have been committed under the eye of a highly respectable Architect; but such is the case, and it goes far to prove the necessity of first calling in the Landscapist, not only to fix the site of the house, but also the position of the main entrance.

ON THE FORMATION OF THE LAWN OR GROUND IN IMMEDIATE CONNECTION WITH THE HOUSE.

PREVIOUSLY to erecting a mansion, the greatest care should be taken to obtain the proper levels. An error (for want of this precaution) is often productive of most serious inconvenience and expense. For instance, when called in after a house has been commenced, I have often found the bottom of the plinths, which is the point that ought to regulate the level of the finished ground, placed considerably too high; so much so, that an immense quantity of materials, not always available, and often to be procured from a distance, and consequently at great cost, has been required for raising the ground about the mansion, and bringing it into harmony with the park and the rest of the pleasure ground. Moreover, for want of materials to level with, the improver is compelled to form an otherwise unnecessary terrace or terraces, or raise a sudden artificial knoll (*figure* 4,

FIGURE 4.

dotted line *a*), which must evidently not only appear as such, but also produce the appearance of being inadequate to support the edifice, from its steepness at so short a distance from the building, which ought rather to appear bold and natural, as at *b*.

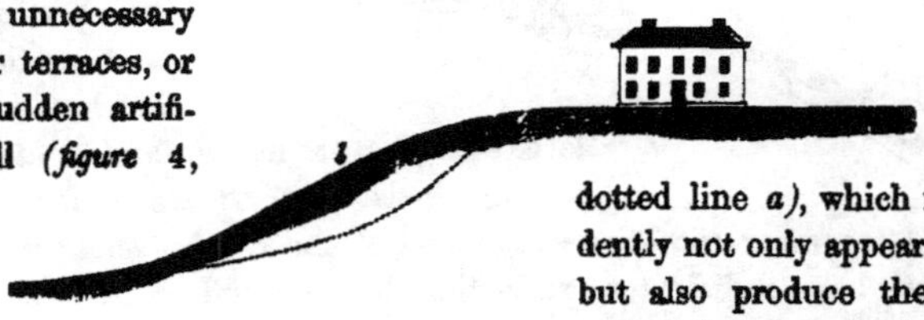

Although I approve of the terrace with its wall, (as will be seen hereafter), which would assist greatly in improving the appearance, yet it is not every gentleman who will either approve or be at the expense of it. Without it, however, the building would seem disproportionate in its elevations. A want of connection also arises, while the natural harmony between the ground on which the house stands, and the rest of the pleasure ground and park, is destroyed.

The levels should be so managed in fixing the house, as to produce, when the materials are removed, a platform sloping almost imperceptibly (say half an inch to an inch in thirty-six) for the first eight or ten yards, then declining more or less rapidly for the next fifty or one hundred yards or more, according to circumstances, and according to the nature of the ground, whether gentle or bold, which it has to connect, so as to blend gradually and softly into the adjoining field or park. The finish should not be limited by the line set out for the fence, for an abrupt finish would create too marked a distinction between the lawn and park.

In situations where the ground is of a bold or abrupt slope, I almost invariably find the bottom of the plinth of the house so placed as to clear the slope, or natural surface, the whole breadth of the house, to its back extremities, (as at *figure* 5, dotted line *a*), in consequence of which the foreground requires a great deal of raising,—a matter of no small difficulty when there are no materials to meet the demand; whereas, if the bottom of the plinth in the centre of the house had been level with the natural surface (as at *figure* 5 *b*), the materials taken thence as far as required backwards, together with the excavations of the cellars, would, in all probability, have been sufficient to raise the whole ground in front of the house to the proper level (as at *figure* 4 *b*).

FIGURE 5.

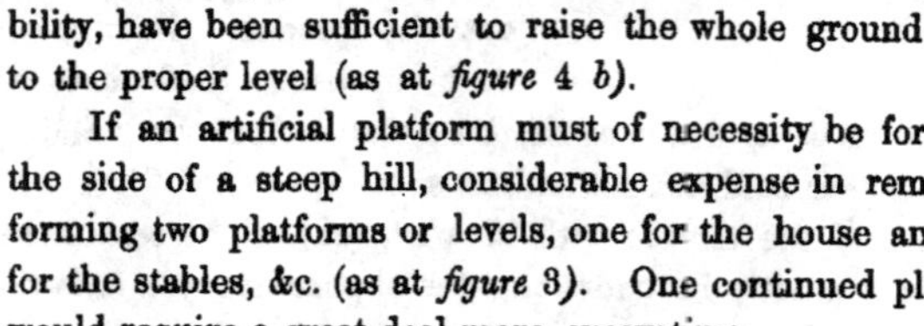

If an artificial platform must of necessity be formed for a residence on the side of a steep hill, considerable expense in removals may be saved by forming two platforms or levels, one for the house and yards, and the other for the stables, &c. (as at *figure* 3). One continued platform for all purposes would require a great deal more excavating.

In situations where the ground is naturally undulating or bold, I should, if possible, form and continue one unbroken bold slope to a considerable distance from the house, on the principal fronts, both to give the appearance of firmness and stability to the ground supporting the edifice, and to secure a sufficient breadth of easy surface for walking about the house. In other parts of the lawn, (after allowing the necessary platform, as above), where it is sufficiently extensive, the natural undulations should be studiously preserved, and, where considered deficient, improved as much as possible by art, care being taken, in levelling, to fill up all slight irregularities, or abrupt holes or hollows, so that whatever the nature of the ground may be, whether gentle or abrupt, the lawn may present one smooth and uniform verdure, and thus be mown and kept in order without inconvenience.

In situations where the ground about the house is very steep, the introduction of the terrace wall, or balustrades, is essentially necessary *(figure 6 a)*, and in all situations is far more appropriate than a sudden uniform sloping bank, which is frequently adopted in forming terraces, but is both at variance with good taste, and devoid of beauty. On private fronts the terrace wall should be at least eight yards from the house; but when the house is of considerable extent, and materials can be procured for filling-up the space between the wall and the edifice, a space of ten or twelve yards may be allowed. A palace should have from fifteen to eighteen yards. In all cases, from the bottom of the plinth of the house (which necessarily guides the level of the lawn) to the dwarf wall, or balustrades, there should be a very gentle fall, averaging not more than a quarter of an inch in the yard. At this point of level the wall must appear from about twenty inches to two feet above the lawn, on the house side of it. If the house be of such a style and importance as to require balustrades, their introduction will add much to the appearance, and in that case a greater depth will be necessary, say from two to three feet. The depth of the wall on the outside should appear in proportion to the fall of the ground; but rather

FIGURE 6.

than it should appear too deep, (that is, not more than six or eight feet, and for villas where the ground is not abrupt, from three to four feet), the ground at the base of the wall will have to be raised (as at *b*), so as to show the wall a proper height, and to appear of one level or depth throughout its length; otherwise a wall, if too deep and obliquely out of level, would have a tendency to destroy the due proportions of the structure when viewed in approaching it.

I have a decided objection to the house being so elevated as to require those lofty flights of steps which we so frequently find about them. They are exceedingly inconvenient to the invalid, the aged, and the infirm, and must be a constant nuisance to ladies, particularly in wet weather. The most glaring error of this kind I ever met with was at Beaucheif Abbey, a very ancient edifice, in Derbyshire. The exact number of steps I do not remember, but there must have been twenty or more, rising to the height of the first story, over the servants' compartments. The only effectual remedy for this was an extensive terrace, which I proposed. There is another example of this kind of error at Wollaton, the seat of Lord Middleton, in Nottinghamshire. Here there are several flights of steps one above another. The first (about twelve or fifteen in number) leads to a platform or landing; and this, again, is followed by other smaller flights leading to the door of the hall. In fact, there are numerous instances of the same kind in this country, but I mention these as most striking. Although there may, in the opinion of some, be a display of grandeur in these flights of steps, and they may appear to harmonize with the edifice, still I think an equal degree of grandeur might have been produced if the present living rooms at Wollaton had been on the ground floor, with only half a dozen steps to reach them, which is the utmost I would ever allow: and I am quite sure that a far greater amount of comfort in the interior, as well as greater extent and variety in the exterior of the edifice, might have been secured, had the compartments for the servants been associated with the west side, between the mansion and the stables, instead of being, as they now are, partially underground.

It is no uncommon thing to find houses injudiciously erected on sites from which there is no fall, and sometimes even on plots considerably lower than the ground contiguous to it, so that the fall is rather to the front of the house than from it. In such cases, in order to carry off the wet, and render the ground in the immediate vicinity of the house comparatively dry, (a point of the first importance), and in some degree to create an appearance of elevation, at least in the private or principal fronts, I would sink a gentle valley *(figure 7 a)* at a convenient distance, parallel with the front of the house. A fall of an inch in the yard from the house to the centre of the valley would be quite sufficient for the purpose, for, the more gradual and gentle the fall, the less likely would the valley be to present a ditch-like appearance, which would be very offensive to the eye, and therefore very objectionable. Should there be any natural valley near, this artificial one should by

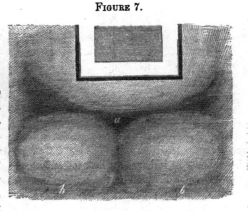

FIGURE 7.

all means be made to communicate with it; but, if not, two branch valleys might be formed *(b b)* to serve as outlets, and be allowed gradually to disappear or wear out in the distant rising ground beyond. But such terminations ought to be carefully concealed by judicious planting, in order that their termination may not be readily detected. In no case should the swells caused by sinking valleys be entirely planted, since a better effect will be produced by allowing the lawn to climb naturally and variedly over a portion of the rising ground. Artificial arrangements like these, skilfully managed, may be made to look tolerably natural and undulated, and at the same time they will give a slight appearance of elevation to the house.

Houses situated in sloping ground, or that which falls rapidly and obliquely across the front, as is sometimes the case, *(figure 8, line a)*, seem improperly balanced, and have a very disagreeable appearance. Such defects may in some degree be remedied by building a terrace wall eight or ten yards or more, according to circumstances, from the house, and levelling all the ground within it and on the outside, by sinking at the higher end, if required, *(b)*, and adding to the lower part in the direction of the dotted lines, making an exact level at the base of the terrace wall its whole length from *c* to *d*, then raising a swell *(c)*, and continuing it as far beyond the angle of

FIGURE 8.

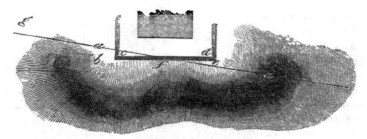

the house as will make it look tolerably bold and natural, and sinking a little in a circular direction on the contrary side, from *f* to *g*, so as to form a slight valley, and thus produce a gentle swell at *h* and *b*. This will create a somewhat corresponding appearance at each angle of the terrace; and although an equal balance will not be produced, yet the effect will be much better than that of an oblique slope. A still greater improvement might be made, if material were plentiful, by making another swell or two, of various extent, to group with the artificial swell above named *(e)*, at a short distance from each other, so as almost to unite and show a shallow valley, or gentle slack, between them. It will be necessary to plant that portion of the swell which is nearest the angle of the terrace, for the sake of breaking the angle, as well as for the purpose of dress, and further to destroy the deep part, and thereby producing a better balanced appearance to the house.

I wish it to be distinctly understood, that although the undulations I have been recommending are highly characteristic in particular situations for the purpose named, I am decidedly opposed to the formation of rude artificial undulated ground, either in a site naturally level, or on a gentle slope, especially if the adjoining ground is of the same character. Nothing but absolute necessity ought to induce the improver to undulate the lawn about a mansion, unless such undulations will be in perfect keeping with the surrounding ground. Some would-be Landscape Gardeners think that, whatever may be the nature and extent of the ground, nature is best imitated by sinking holes and raising mounds. I found a miserable specimen of this kind of error in the neighbourhood of an important city, where I was called in to fix the site for a house, which specimen was afterwards laid out by a gentleman who, it was said, had wrought wonders on a small plot of ground in the metropolis. The extent of space operated upon was about twenty-five yards broad in the principal front, and about thirty in the two others, from the house to the fence. In this confined spot of level ground, harmonising with smooth level pastures, a deep excavation was formed in one part, at the bottom of which, when the weather happened to be sufficiently wet, an irregular stagnant pool of water might be seen, little better in appearance than a common horse-pond, eight or ten yards long by three to five broad, and crossed by a rustic bridge. Of the material taken from this pond was formed a zigzag ridge, resembling a crooked canal bank, which abruptly destroyed the harmony between a beautiful smooth pasture and kept ground; the bank was for the most part planted with shrubs, which would eventually confine the eye, ever impatient of restraint, within the dress ground. The lawn between the varied part and the carriage road was laid out as a flat formal parterre, with a fountain in the centre. As the greatest portion of both these scenes, so totally different in character, was commanded from one point of view, the incongruity appeared glaring in the extreme, and completely at variance with all the principles of taste, and was calculated to strike even a common observer as a piece of absurdity. I have been the more particular in this description, for the purpose of showing the folly of attempting both rugged and smooth scenery within a limited space, and especially in one so contracted that the whole could be comprehended by the eye at one view. The foregoing remarks would seem to apply more particularly to new places, but similar operations will occasionally be found necessary in remodelling old places. In the latter work, judgment is required in rejecting what is bad, and retaining what is either really good, or at all events capable of improvement. In remodelling, it is by no means necessary to sweep all old things away indiscriminately; many things may be retained with considerable advantage. Great regard must be had to ornamental trees and shrubs, as well as architectural appendages. Thinning is one of the principal things to be attended to, and one which, if skilfully managed, will have a most striking and beneficial effect. Groups and masses may most frequently be much improved by clearing away many useless things, so as to display more fully the characteristic beauties of individual plants, and yet fully preserve necessary associations. Openings and vistas will have to be formed, so as to command objects of interest in the distance; but in all alterations, harmony with the edifice and surrounding scenery must be carefully studied.

The breadth of the kept ground between the house and the fence dividing the park from the kept ground, must necessarily vary according to circumstances, the foremost of which is the importance of the place itself; it may range from thirty to one hundred yards. When a park is kept tolerably close cropt by sheep or cattle, I consider an extensive breadth of lawn unnecessary, especially on the entrance front; I should much prefer a greater expanse of secluded pleasure ground. The level of the lawn, as it approaches the fence, should gradually blend into the park, so as to avoid any abrupt or marked distinction between them. Should the park not be cropt sufficiently close by sheep, &c., the coarser tufts may be mown occasionally to a short distance, and thus the harmony between the two may be tolerably well preserved.

In carrying out the finish of the lawn where it is difficult and expensive to procure sods, after the ground has been properly levelled down and well consolidated, the whole of the beds and walks may be lined out with narrow sods, six inches broad for beds, from that to twelve inches for walks, taking care that no bed be nearer any walk than two feet, so as to leave at the least two feet verge, except in very limited places, when the whole is lined and the sod laid sufficiently low for the earth to be quite level with the top of the sod.

The rest of the intended lawn may be sown down with proper lawn seeds, either early in Spring, or any time during the middle of Summer until September, in showery weather. Spring and Autumn are the best periods, as drought often proves fatal to the young sprouting seeds, the consequence of which is a broken bald verdure.

THE KIND OF SEEDS.—Poa pratensis, Festuca euvina, Styckney's rye grass, and Scotch evergreen, with a moderate supply of white clover. The two latter grasses, with a little clover added, quickly make a nice lawn.

17

As, in the operation of levelling and forming the lawn, some parts are often so impoverished as scarcely to grow the grass at all, when the seeds are sown, it will be well to give the whole a slight manuring with guano, or other decayed manure. Rolling, as soon as the grass is well up, and when the ground is not too wet, will be of great service; and frequent mowing, as soon as it can be done, will be necessary. But, at this stage of its growth, it will be proper to be cautious, in clearing off the cut grass, not to disturb the tender plants. Gentle raking will be better than sweeping, and rolling will be useful just after. In this way, a nice lawn may be produced in one year.

ON THE OLD AND NEW SYSTEMS OF FORMING
THE DRESS GROUNDS IN CONNECTION WITH THE HOUSE.

SINCE the days of Kent, Mason, and Brown, our first promoters of the English or natural style of Landscape Gardening, we have had a good deal of argument, both for and against the new and old systems; and, notwithstanding the able and celebrated men who have lived within the last century, contending for and endeavouring to establish the English or natural style, there still evidently exists a danger of true taste giving way to mannerism. There are some professors of the art of Landscape Gardening in the present day, who contend that the formal style should invariably be associated with the Castellated, the Elizabethan, the Gothic, or Manorial building; but why, I am totally at a loss to understand. They certainly have antiquity on their side, if that is their vantage ground; but will they tell us that Landscape Gardening, like Architecture, had reached the acme of perfection in ancient times, or that further improvement is impossible? Will they tell us that, because it was the fashion in former days to associate terraces, and balustrades, and flights of steps, &c., with the Elizabethan, the Castellated, the Gothic, or Manorial style, and to embellish the kept grounds with geometrical and formal parterres, bowling greens, oblong ponds, high clipped hedges, and fantastical bushes, it is, therefore, right to continue this practice, as if these were fixed and unalterable principles? They may, indeed, tell us so, but they will have difficulty in convincing us of the fact. Such principles, in new formations, are quite inadmissible at the present day. The fact of our finding Italian, Dutch, and Flemish gardens, indiscriminately associated with the old English, Elizabethan or Gothic, Grecian and Italian, styles of architecture, is sufficient to prove to any unprejudiced mind, that there neither are, nor ever were, any fixed principles in Landscape Gardening calculated to suit every style of architecture, and that the adaptation of Landscape Gardening to these different styles was always a matter of mere fancy and fashion, rather than of any fixed principles whatever. But, although the customs of the past, with their assumed true taste, are revived and imitated by some professors, yet let us hope that good sense and good taste will never allow its revival to succeed and supersede the free, cheerful, and flowing style of modern gardening, which has supplanted, in a great degree, the gloomy, harsh, and formal style of a few centuries ago. Let the proprietors who are about to lay out their grounds, not suppose that because they are building Gothic or Castellated Mansions, the grounds need be laid out in the formal style. No; as I have already said, that, in my opinion, would be a false principle. Before they adopt that course, let them visit the various noblemen's and gentlemen's seats which are supposed to be excellent specimens both of the ancient and modern styles, with their minds unbiassed; they will then be able to understand the difference, and judge for themselves; and I am satisfied that in ninety-nine cases out of every one hundred, their choice will be for the modern, and not for the ancient.

In the formation of a new place I should always have a straight walk of gravel or flags along the front of the house, whatever may be the style of the mansion. I have no objection to the introduction of the terrace wall, balustrades, steps, vases, and other architectural decorations, in accordance with the general style of the building. Indeed, to all good houses these accompaniments ought never to be wanting, as they not only apparently add to their strength, and form a base to them, but by seeming a part, they increase the extent, importance, and richness of the whole. In places of pretension the entrance court and stable yard should also be enclosed (as shown in the general plan for a palace or mansion grounds) by proper ornamental walls, embellished with vases, urns, &c.; and in arranging these accompaniments I should place the terrace wall (as I have stated a few pages before) from twenty-five to forty-five feet from the house, according to the extent of the building. But this must be apportioned with judgment and caution; for, on looking from the house, were the distance from it too great and the wall too high, the lawn beyond would on the one hand appear too contracted, and on the other, in approaching the house from the park, the connection of the two would be completely destroyed, for it would prevent the wall, with its decorations, and house from appearing as a whole with a variety of composition—a thing I am most anxious to secure. Midway between the house and wall I should have a straight walk, from seven to twelve feet wide, extending the whole length of the building, and in some cases even as far as the walls, enclosing the various offices or outbuildings, if the extent and magnitude of the residence should seem to demand it (as represented in both general plans). On each side of this terrace walk I would have formal flower beds for the reception of early flowers, and other pleasing plants, to be introduced from the greenhouse or reserve garden as they come into bloom.

FIGURE 9.

These beds should have an edging of rich ornamental cast-iron work, or stone, or clay, or terra cotta, from six to nine inches deep *(figure* 9); and for the sake of variety, especially in the round beds, strong wire basket work. Thus a gay, beautiful, and harmonious display would be produced. With the present cheapness of glass, the propriety of ornamental plant protectors, made to fit the beds within the baskets, suggests itself. These should be octagonal *(figure* 10). The frames would be best made of cast-iron, from four to five feet in diameter, and from two feet six inches to three feet

FIGURE 10.

high, and as light as possible. They should be provided with moveable tops, to prevent the frame having to be removed more than is absolutely necessary, and in order to be convenient for ventilation and watering—(a small lid would be convenient for that purpose when much ventilation was not required). In this way beautiful plants, too tender to stand without occasional protection, might be exhibited in the spring months in the beds in front of the windows. So far, then, I admit and entirely approve of the formal style, without at all taking into consideration the character of the edifice; but, beyond this, the formal or geometrical style has no right whatever to be claimed by any style of edifice; and to copy the stiffness and absurdities of antiquity in the formation of a new place, is not only erroneous, but absolutely barbarous.

In no case would I admit, either on the terrace or principal lawn in front of the house, those flimsy fantastical flower beds so improperly introduced by some of the supporters of the geometrical or formal system; for they not only betray want of extent in the ground, as if there were no room elsewhere, but detract from what there is. An instance of this injudicious laying out appeared in the grounds of a noble castellated place respecting which I was consulted. The terrace in front of the edifice, level with its base, is terminated by three, four, or five steps, I forget exactly how many. Ascend these, and you find yourself on a second terrace, with a parterre before you, geometrically formed with box edging, and displaying a variety of figures, cut up into such narrow stripes, and terminating in such long sharp points, that in some places for a considerable length there is scarcely room for more than a single plant in breadth, and that is in danger of being smothered by the box edging. These beds, together with a faintly dripping fountain, form altogether the most miserable specimen of ornamental work I ever saw. In comparison with the noble edifice they are intended to adorn, they are perfectly contemptible, and make one lament the barrenness of the taste which could either propose or adopt such absurdities. I have said above, that, beyond the terrace-wall, no style of house has any claim to formality. The principal or general lawn should never be subjected to the laws of the formal system. In short, all formality should cease with the terrace-wall (except where it may be necessary to associate with any other ornamental structure, or in compartments purposely set apart for that purpose). Beyond this, masses and groups, as well as single specimens of ornamental trees and shrubs, should be disposed so as to show various expanses of lawn, and thus deceive the eye as to the real extent of lawn from any given point. On one front, where practicable, the park may, with propriety, be connected with the terrace-wall, which will serve as a fence between the park and grounds.

Gilpin and others support the old system of high walls and close clipped hedges, especially in old places, as affording shelter and protection from the obtrusive eye; but in forming new places, at this day, I see no reason why the improver should follow such examples, at the sacrifice of good taste or true principles. Independently of this, however, shelter and retirement may, in my opinion, be better and sooner produced by a shrubbery than by a clipped hedge. The broad straight walk along the front of the mansion will generally afford ample space for walking exercise, when the weather is too unsettled for venturing out to a greater distance; and the winter garden (a site for which is given in the palace plan, and delineated on a larger scale, *plate* 4) will provide all that is requisite for comfort and retirement, without the introduction of harsh lines of high walls and clipped hedges into the landscape, which both offend the eye and mar the prospect, when arranged after the ancient style. Gilpin seems, also, to advocate the formal kitchen garden as a means of prolonging the necessary exercise, in which he says, "A succession of various objects imparts a pleasing variety of sensation to the mind." Now, to me, it is surprising that Gilpin, a man of otherwise great taste and practical experience, should have made such a remark. The kitchen garden ought never to be considered a portion of the pleasure ground, nor a place for recreation or exercise, although sanctioned by antiquity. The constant presence of workpeople, so destructive of privacy, is alone sufficient to prove my theory; if not, the unpleasantness arising from decaying vegetables, manure, &c., forbids it altogether, showing, at once, that visits there ought to be few and optional, and that it is not intended to be a place of general resort.

The interest we feel in ancient places arises more from the fact of their antiquity, and their celebrity for extraordinary events, than from the style in which the grounds and gardens have been laid out: and it must be evident that the stiff arrangements which are in the vicinity of the mansion, and especially those seen from the living rooms, can never inspire the mind with.

the interest and delight which are produced by gentle and graceful sweeps, with natural, or irregular and varied, masses and groups of trees and shrubs, blending softly and gracefully, with intricate glades of smooth lawn quietly and uninterruptedly retiring into distance. On the one hand, all is stiff, formal, and confined. Long straight walks, bowling-greens, vegetable gardens, &c., are ornamented with fantastic bushes, and bounded by high walls, and hedges clipped to an immeasurable height, as if art, conscious of its own inferiority, was making a gigantic effort to exclude the beauties of nature. On the other hand, all is easy, natural, and unrestrained. The eye, unimpeded by hard and restrictive avenues, and other lines of demarcation,—those frequently awkward and always objectionable features of the old system,—after pleasurably surveying the softness and harmony of the home scenery, passes freely and unrestrained to the park or middle distance, and thence over beautifully varied scenery, to the stiller and more distant landscape.

Allowing, however, that the antiquity of a place contributes much to its interest, I should proceed more cautiously in directing the alterations of it, in order to preserve that interest and importance which time and its connection with historical events have created. I should, in the first place, preserve the terrace and terrace walls, repairing them where necessary, and, if too plain, enriching them with vases, urns, and other embellishments in character with the building. The walls of the entrance court, with their decorations, I would also preserve. Good examples of avenues should remain, unless they produce a hard line so as to divide the park scenery when viewed from the living-rooms. The formal pond with its cascade, the fountain, alcove, statuary, dials, &c., should by no means be destroyed or removed, nor anything be done which is calculated to lessen the character of antiquity, on which the importance of an old place depends. The kitchen garden, however, with its old crooked walls, when in view of the living-rooms, I consider highly objectionable, and should remove at once, and convert its site into lawn, varied with rich shrubs, or, if too extensive, add a portion to the park, and plant it with groups of trees, so as to harmonize as much as possible with the adjoining natural scenery. Should the proprietor, however, prefer the formal character altogether, the lawn, at all events, should be bold, and not cut up too much into useless fantastical figures. Elongated and round beds (either with or without edgings of ornamental iron or stone), or baskets, would be best associated with straight walks, and I would leave large square portions of lawn occasionally without any beds at all. The bowling-green, occupying, as it generally does in ancient gardens, the principal front, and thus destroying stillness and repose, I should remodel in the manner described above, and choose a secluded spot elsewhere for the purpose, remote from the gaze of servants; for, although its boundaries might be varied with shrubberies, &c., yet being of necessity of a flat tame surface, and difficult to be brought into concord with the adjoining ground, it would be far better removed to a distance from the mansion.

ON THE DISPOSITION AND FORM OF SHRUB BEDS

IN THE DRESS GROUND.

I WILL next make a few observations on the form and disposition of shrub beds on the lawn about the house and pleasure grounds, which I propose making after the modern system. Shrubs, whether planted in masses, groups, or as single bushes, are not to be estimated merely by the elegance and variety of their forms, or the beauty and fragrance of their blossoms, but as embellishments indispensably necessary for completing the composition or combination of the home, middle, or more remote scenery, and as screens for masking out disagreeable objects. As shrubs naturally thrive best in dug compartments, the beds should be of the neatest forms and of various sizes; never formal and lumpy, but rather long than otherwise, and with deep hollow bends and bold prominent curves and juts, rather than with numerous indentations; and they should be so arranged as not to appear in a cross direction to one another, especially when near together. Although, too, they may not be exactly opposite each other, yet they should in some degree (as I have said respecting the flower beds) appear parallel, the convex bend of one seeming to fit into the hollow of another, and those beds that are near to the walks harmonizing with the walks. Moreover, all these beds should be so disposed as to associate with each other, rather than be at equal distances all over the lawn, but in a manner to create intricacy, so as not to show the real extent of the ground, and to exhibit some bold and free glades of lawn on which the eye may repose. *(See General Plans.)* Caution should also be used always to leave the narrowest part of the lawn sufficiently broad for the mower to work on freely,—a thing not sufficiently attended to by some of our celebrated professors of Landscape Gardening, as may be observed in various publications, as well as in places actually laid out, where in the forms of the beds (as well as. in the space between the beds) we find some of the indentations so narrow and deep, that it is impossible to mow them

E

without injuring the plants. As it is intended that the whole of the outlines of some of the beds should eventually be destroyed by overhanging or spreading growths, and the earth be completely concealed, these beds must be kept to their original shape (*figure* 11) for some time, until the shrubs attain sufficient size to do this naturally of themselves (*figure* 12). This varied outline cannot be effected by stiff upright shrubs, such as roses, spireas, arborvitas, junipers, mazerians, &c.; and, consequently, all of this stiff character which are required to remain towards the margin, should be fronted and mixed with some of the following, namely,—Daphne cneorum, Savins, Cottoneaster microphilla, Berberis impetrifolia, Mahonias, Arbutus regia, Erica herbacea, Erica multiflora, and other heaths, dwarf spreading cistus, dwarf evergreen St. John's wort, Gaultheria shallon, jointed, double, and other dwarf spreading brooms, Menziesia polyfolia, Andromeda polyfolia, and similar low reclining plants, which will cover the earthy parts, and yet not prevent the others beyond from being seen. But in order that neither these nor the larger spreading shrubs may spread out of bounds, they must occasionally be shortened in at proper places, so as to leave a natural careless outline. Beds appropriated to interesting shrubs of low growth, and such as, being of a stiff formal habit, are consequently not calculated to produce a broken outline—as, for instance, fuchsias, roses, azaleas, kalmias, andromedas, Rhodora canadensis, Rhododendron dauricum atro-virens, &c.,—these will always look better retaining their neat and original form. The kind of beds we have been speaking of may be said to be proper for all the dress-lawn, not only that connected with the house, but the more distant pleasure grounds also, where natural beauty of outline is a principal charm of the scenery. Those, however, which contain the more delicate plants, and require digging amongst, must always have their original outline preserved with neatness and accuracy. The foregoing directions can seldom be fully carried out in a place of the old school, but much may be done by cutting down, removals, grouping, and introducing interesting shrubs when necessary.

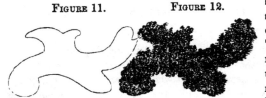

FIGURE 11.   FIGURE 12.

ON FLOWER GARDENS,

CONSIDERED IN THEIR VARIOUS DEPARTMENTS, AND

UNDER VARIOUS CHARACTERS.

I now proceed to the Flower Garden, the next compartment after leaving the principal Lawn, and which we must imagine to be separated from it by the masses and groups of shrubs just described; not, however, by a stiff belt, but so that the principal lawn may blend softly and gradually into the flower garden. The flower garden, as will be seen from my former remarks, ought never to be visible from the windows, (except in towns and small places, where the whole pleasure grounds are necessarily confined to the front of the house), as the appearance of numerous beds and walks, by interrupting the repose and extent of the lawn, has a tendency to destroy its boldness and importance, which ought to be studiously preserved: and the practice of huddling all the most interesting objects possible into one scene, in front of the windows, ought, unquestionably, to be discarded as a decided fault. In places that will admit of it, I invariably make a point of dividing the pleasure ground into different compartments, with the intention of exhibiting various scenes, and so enhancing the interest and prolonging the exercise of the visiter, as he proceeds from one scene to another: and, as bodily and mental exercise are highly conducive to health, such recreations as will at once attract the mind and exercise the body should be preferred. Nothing, I think, is so well calculated to soothe the feelings, inspire holy thoughts, and elevate the mind, as the retirement of a flower garden, judiciously and richly decked with beautiful flowers, filling the air with odour.

> "Welcome, fair scene! Welcome, thou lov'd retreat!
> From the vain hurry of the bustling great
> Here let me walk; or, in this fragrant bower,
> Wrapt in calm thought, improve each fleeting hour.
> My soul, while Nature's beauties feast mine eyes,
> To Nature's God contemplative shall rise."—DODSLEY.

The English, or Natural Flower Garden, which ought always to take precedence of every other style, is composed of lawn, and beds or patches of earth, in which flowers and flowering shrubs are planted. This garden should, in all cases, be arranged with returning walks, so that a visiter may return gradually into the principal walk homewards, when a more lengthened one would not be agreeable. A flower garden provided with only one walk, and that through the centre, is, unquestionably, ill-contrived; because it always obliges a person to return the way he came. And a flower garden on turf, without a gravel or dry walk, is worse. A walk is not only an interesting feature in the flower garden, but it is indispensable for the inspection of flowers, when the grass is wet. This kind of garden, when space will allow, may be subdivided into the following compartments, namely,—The General Flower Garden, American Garden, Florist Garden, Rosarium, Annual Garden, and Group Garden, which, though severally quite distinct and perfectly complete, need only be separated by walks, assisted by a judicious disposal of various masses and groups of shrubs and low trees, in order to produce one interesting whole.

Gentle and smooth undulations add much to the interest of the English Flower Garden, which, when the ground is an extensive flat, may be artificially contrived by sinking some portions of the ground, and raising others. The character of the flower beds *(see Plan for a Country Residence)* should generally be long rather than otherwise, of various elegant forms, produced by angles and graceful curves; all repetitions, except circles, and all such figures as ovals, hearts, squares, oblongs, queen cakes, &c., being studiously avoided.

I may here mention, that I disapprove of the common practice of raising the soil in beds much above the level of the lawn. These unnatural mole-hill-like forms, throwing, as it were, the lawn into sudden inharmonious slacks, are highly offensive to the eye of taste. When a bed is formed on level ground, the centre should never be raised more than from two to six inches above the turf, according to the size of the bed; but when formed on rising ground, and the turf appears to follow naturally, it will be in perfect keeping to raise the soil boldly to the centre of the bed.

In the disposal of the beds, the lawn must not be regularly spotted over with them, as we often see, exhibiting equal walk-like portions of grass between; they ought to be thrown into different forms, the beds arranged in some degree in groups, with naturally varied expanses of lawn, the narrowest parts of which should always be wide enough to afford sufficient room for the scythe,—say, five to six feet at the least. The beds should be made to harmonize with each other; the swell or convex part of one bed should appear to retire in some degree into the recess or hollow part of another, and should by all means run parallel to the walk, and not seem to start off at right angles to it. *(See General Plan.)* I mean those that are nearest to it. The small beds will produce the best effect when associated with the larger ones, and not when assembled together, the smaller beds in one neighbourhood, and the larger ones in another. I never introduce wire basket-work about any but round beds; with these, basket-work and iron edgings are strictly in character, and are an indispensable ornament to them.

Before commencing my observations on the various classes of the Flower Garden, I will take the liberty of addressing a few remarks to gardeners generally. From the little attention paid to the cultivation of plants by young gardeners whilst learning their business, one would suppose it a thing either altogether unconnected with it, or at least one to which it was a matter of very little consequence whether they attended or not. Hence it very often happens that a taste for flowers is never cultivated, and notions imbibed in youth are practised to old age, unimproved and profitless; consequently we find the same dull round of old flowers year by year fringing the shrubberies of the pleasure ground, and too often even the borders of the kitchen garden. This is a deplorable state of things, and calls for immediate remedy. The study and cultivation of flowers and plants generally are, in my opinion, among the most important and interesting branches of the gardener's employment; and I do not hesitate to say, that nothing would tend so much as a knowledge of these to elevate him in the opinion of his employer. Every gardener who can read and write, (and without a knowledge of these no man ought to be a gardener), should at least be acquainted with the names of plants, their native places, the time of their introduction and blooming, and the proper mode of culture. I need not tell a man possessed of these advantages how far superior he is to one who, on being asked about the names, culture, &c., of plants, is obliged to confess his ignorance in the common apology, that he has paid but little attention to such things, having almost exclusively applied himself to the kitchen garden and forcing department. Such a man will never be fit for anything beyond the kitchen garden, and is consequently eligible for but few situations; whilst one who, along with his various other avocations, has carefully studied the cultivation and management of plants, and has not lost sight of mental improvement, is eligible for any situation. As is sufficiently proved in our own day, he may even rise to a very high standing both in respectability and in fame.

GENERAL FLOWER GARDEN.

This is expected to be furnished with every possible variety of interesting herbaceous perennials and other flowers, and, therefore, every place with any pretensions to a garden should be provided with one of this description. It would be well if every proprietor would allow the introduction of all the most pleasing varieties of plants, rather than content himself with the monotonous repetition of the common kinds, so frequently to be met with in places where we look for choicer specimens.

AMERICAN GARDEN.

This is so termed from its being principally furnished with such American plants as bear our climate; and, as these plants are grown in peat or bog soil, many of our own English productions being grown in similar soil, the two are often associated together, and erroneously classed under the common name of American plants. This kind of garden may be said to be adorned, principally, with beautiful flowering shrubs, though several herbaceous plants also belong to it. Great caution is required in the arrangement of the plants, as it too often happens that the larger and smaller plants are crowded together in one bed. For instance, the common or large growing kinds of rhododendrons are frequently made the occupants of small beds, along with smaller growing plants, so that, when the former take to growing freely, the destruction of the latter is almost certain. Care must, therefore, be taken not to associate the large kinds of rhododendrons, azalias, &c., with plants of a delicate and more limited habit. All that is required is to grow the two sorts separately, according to their respective habits. The small ones will be best suited to small beds; and the large rhododendrons and azalias may form masses or beds, exhibiting only one plant of each of the most rare and beautiful varieties. The common kinds may, also, very properly be introduced into the shrubberies in connection with the American Garden, or any other part of the pleasure ground, with a portion of proper compost round each plant, to encourage, at least, its first growth.

I have often thought a very interesting feature might be produced by planting a permanent mass of tender greenhouse heaths; and, perhaps, this compartment might be the most suitable situation for it. I should form a stage of rock-work, composed of various specimens of spar imbedded in proper peat soil, in which I should plant the most select varieties of heaths, and form a walk round the whole. A proper structure would be necessary to afford partial shade in hot sunny weather, and also for protection during the winter months. An Arnott's, or Walker's, patent stove, would give out quite sufficient heat to resist frost in a frame of moderate size; but two would be necessary for a structure fifty feet long by twenty-one feet wide. No more fire will be necessary than barely to keep out frosts. The stove would be best heated with coke, as all the nuisance of dust would thus be avoided, and the injurious effects of the effluvia, &c., would, in a great measure, be avoided, being carried off by a short iron pipe at some convenient point: the cost of fuel would not be more than from one penny to twopence a day. In this way, the true character and beauty of this lovely family would be displayed. In this garden, if sufficiently extensive, I should introduce some of the most interesting low American trees, here and there, on the lawn, both for the sake of effect, and for the purpose of affording shady situations for such plants as require shade. Provision might here, also, be made for amphibious plants, or such as require a good deal of moisture, by forming a bog-bed in the lowest part of the ground, so as to be readily kept moist by watering, when a naturally damp situation does not exist.

FLORIST GARDEN.

This compartment is provided for the introduction of florist or show flowers, commonly cultivated for exhibition, viz., the dahlia, tulip, ranunculus, carnation, pink, hyacinth, auricula, iris, polyanthus, anemone, &c. Although some of these are considered to be grown better in pots for exhibition, yet beds of them, I think, are highly pleasing, and a private compartment may be kept for such as require potting. I should recommend the dahlias to be thrown into groups, each group forming a class, and each class comprehending all the flowers of the same colour in all its different shades,—care being taken so to dispose the beds in the several compartments as to produce the greatest possible amount of cheerfulness and variety over the whole. In order to re-embellish the bulb beds after the decay of the foliage of the bulbous roots, as the tulip, hyacinth, ranunculus, &c., a reserve bed, or, what is preferable, a considerable stock of annuals in pots, should always be provided, so as to be introduced the moment the bulbs are lifted for their summer's rest. In this way the Florist Garden might be kept a scene of gaiety throughout the season.

ROSARIUM.

This forms a very interesting compartment when the roses are in bloom. It is intended, of course, to exhibit a large collection at once, which is very necessary, both for the sake of a general display, and a ready comparison of the different varieties, now that they are so numerous, and in many the shades of different colour so faint as scarcely to be distinguished. I have an objection to masses of roses on lawns of small extent, for, although we allow the rose to be the queen of flowers, yet, when the plants have shed their blossoms, there are few shrubs which exhibit less beauty in their habit; and consequently, when the blooming season is over, such parts of the garden lose their interest. I have, therefore, generally preferred the formation of small groups of three, five, six, or more, in front of the shrubbery, to beds on the lawn. Where, however, a general collection is required, it will be necessary to provide a compartment for them, called, very properly, a Rosarium. This, as the roses lose their beauty, may be kept tolerably gay by the introduction of annuals between the plants, provision having been previously made for them at the time of planting. In arranging the Rosarium, it will be necessary to refer to some good catalogue for their classification. In all cases where we wish to preserve the natural style, I particularly recommend standards to be placed, so that their stems may be partially broken or concealed by either dwarf standards, and such as are on their own roots, or low-growing shrubs of various kinds. I think a stiff clustered head upon a small naked stem looks remarkably ill when exhibited on a lawn, or otherwise glaringly exposed; but when placed in small groups in a border fronted with shrubs of nearly their own height, their elevated blossoms appear very beautiful and certainly much more in character. Avenues and rows of standards may, however, be allowed in a formal Rosarium, which is a scene by itself : this is preferable to any irregular form, and may be planned something like those we designed for Mr. Paul's " Rose garden ;" or in the manner shown in the *General Plan* for a palace or mansion grounds; or the one we arranged in the Queen's Park, Manchester. Provision must also be made for climbing roses. The readiest plan is to fix poles in the ground here and there, or place five, six, or more, so as to form a circle of three or four feet in diameter, and let them all meet at the top. Cones of iron or wood trellis, or a circular arcade, may be formed in the centre of the Rosary, over a walk, for some of the most interesting varieties of pillar roses, and the enclosure serve as a pheasantry.

The Annual Garden.

The Annual Garden is a plot of ground set apart for the growth of annual flowers, the varieties of which are numerous, and many of them very beautiful. The plants should be selected for their harmony of colour and size, and should be set, or sown, in patches of from three to five of each kind. They would then present a very gay and interesting appearance in their proper season, which might, in fact, be greatly prolonged by plants or seeds in successional growths.

The Mass, or Group Garden.

The prevailing practice of growing certain kinds of flowers in groups or masses, seems to demand that there should be, in grounds of sufficient extent, a compartment or division in the Flower Garden for this purpose, which I have ventured to term Mass or Group Garden. For instance, different varieties of verbenas, petunias, fuchsias, salvias, calceolarias, geraniums, and mimulii, are amongst the kinds used for that purpose. Whilst we admire this fashion, we must guard against its predominance over the growth of the various and beautiful perennial flowers. I think that the beds for this kind of garden should seldom be large, and, perhaps, they should be most generally round, but of various dimensions, none exceeding six feet in diameter. Some, if not the whole of them, should also be edged round with iron or wire basket-work, as, otherwise, when the plants are trained down to the earth, they are liable to encroach upon the lawn, and to

F

destroy the form of the beds. The larger and variously formed beds which may be introduced, should be grouped either with various kinds of plants or of varieties in one family, blending into each other.

THE AQUARIUM

Forms a highly interesting feature in the General Flower Garden, in the shape of a natural rivulet, flowing in a devious course through the lowest part of it. Should there not be a natural dingle in the grounds, a suitable undulated course should be made, so that water plants may be grown, and that the sound of a rippling stream, however small, may be heard, with its refreshing and cheerful influence. *(See General Plan.)*

Supposing, however, that the formation of such a stream cannot be accomplished, a small compartment may be set apart, and provision made for such plants in round basins, or somewhat careless yet neat looking receptacles, margined with spar or fancy minerals, and cemented, so as to be water-tight. Water may be supplied to them, in any way most suitable or convenient, from time to time.

In all the compartments to which I have referred, handsome growing flowering shrubs and low trees may be introduced here and there, as shown in the *General Plans*, not only to produce an effect, but to give a varied imaginary extent to each. Of course, whilst the most agreeable kinds of shrubs are introduced for the sake of beauty and intricacy, strict regard must be paid to their not being introduced too numerously, or allowed to grow too large, so as to injure the flower beds.

THE GEOMETRICAL FLOWER GARDEN.

This compartment must stand separately from any of the rest, with which it is too formal to harmonize or be in character. I have therefore given specimens of this style of gardening, detached from the natural or English arrangement, but linked with the appendages of the house, *(see plate* 7), and to be used as a winter garden. In the plan, it will be seen that it is walled round, so, as it were, to shut it up and make it secluded, the walls being appropriated to various kinds of climbers. I have shown two modes of arranging this garden on a large scale *(see plate* 4): one, with dug beds cut out of lawn; the other, with walks and beds edged with solid cast iron, terra cotta, or neatly dressed stone, which I prefer to the Dutch fashion of planting

EXPLANATION OF PLATE IV.

IDEAL PLAN FOR A WINTER GARDEN,

SHEWING FOUR DIFFERENT GEOMETRICAL STYLES OR PATTERNS, FOR THE SAKE OF CHOICE.

FIGURE 1.

GLASS STRUCTURE FOR A WINTER PROMENADE, &c.

A, A. Plinth, twelve inches in breadth, and thirty-six inches in height, with shelves attached all round for plants.

B, B. Walks, four feet wide, independent of the shelf, which is to be level with the top of the plinth, twelve inches broad.

C. Centre walk, six feet wide.

D, D. Beds of earth nine feet wide, edged round with a neat curb stone, for plants to remain permanently. The surface of the earth to be grown over with tropical mosses and low-growing ferns; or, if it be preferred, the same space may be occupied by a stage for plants.

E, E, E, E. Basins, either with or without fountains, for the growth of aquatic plants.

FIGURES 2 AND 3.

TWO STYLES OF FORMAL PARTERRES ON GRASS.

FIGURES 4 AND 5.

TWO STYLES FOR A FORMAL PARTERRE, OR FLOWER GARDEN, EDGED WITH CAST IRON, DRESSED STONE, OR TERRA COTTA.

The square dots along the walk sides are sites for sculpture, or other garden ornaments.

F, F. *(Fig. 4.)* Sites for sculpture, dials, &c.

G, G. *(Fig. 2.)* Seats.

The walls are to be trained with roses and other interesting climbing plants. The masses of shrubs are to be composed of handsome, small-sized evergreens.

box or other live edgings. Live borders do not present so neat an appearance, besides both harbouring slugs and impoverishing the beds. In the laying out of either of these gardens the strictest nicety will be required; and as it is enclosed, and therefore sheltered, such may be appropriated to a winter garden. The walks should be made perfectly dry,—flags, indeed, being preferable to gravel; and the dug compartments should be furnished with early spring flowers, and small interesting evergreen shrubs, with as many winter flowers as possible. It would add materially to the comfort and utility of such a garden as a winter promenade, if one or more of the walks were covered in with glass, which, from its present cheapness, I may venture to suggest, will be more generally used for such purposes. Thus winter exercise would be afforded at all times when the weather might happen to be too precarious for out-door recreation. I have, therefore, suggested an idea in the annexed sketch. I would cover the winter walk by circular span roofs, supported by neat pilasters resting on plinths or dressed stone, with upright window-like sashes, of somewhat the following dimensions, namely, from the plinth to the top of the sashes from seven to ten feet, and the plinth thirty-six inches; the width of house thirty-two feet or more. If permanent plants are to be grown, a strip of earth between the walks must be formed, and the earth concealed by tropical mosses and small ferns; or, if employed as a greenhouse, stone stages are intended. In either case a stone shelf, twelve inches broad, next the glass, level with the top of the plinth, and all round the house, is proposed, on which to place plants in pots, as illustrated at *fig.* 13. Such a house will require to be furnished with all the early flowering plants possible.

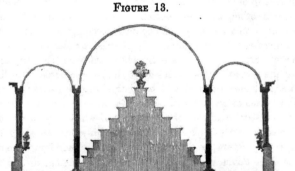

FIGURE 13.

Or, in place of a centre house, (shown in *plate* 4), the

whole of the boundary wall may be fronted with glass sashes, with a curvilinear roof, trellising the walls, on which to train climbing plants. In place of a glass promenade a covered colonnade or arcade may be erected, with open arches on each side, divided by pilasters of lattice or wire work, from twelve to eighteen inches broad, on which handsome climbing plants must be trained.

BOTANIC GARDEN.

The Botanic Garden should be at no great distance from the Flower Garden, but yet distinct from it, and approached by a shrubbery walk. It should be formal in its arrangements, and entered upon at one point, having either gently winding or straight walks; and should have its plants grown in their regular classes and orders, so as to offer the least interruption to the botanist whilst pursuing his studies.

I think that the borders should be sufficiently narrow (as shown in the *General Plan for a Country Residence)* so that the spectator, in moving along, may examine the whole of the plants without having to traverse both sides. It will be seen that I have only shown three lines of beds; therefore, in laying out the garden, a calculation will have to be made of the extent required, and, if necessary, strips must be added or made longer.

The walks may be five feet wide, with grass verges two feet wide, and one continued strip of earth, three feet wide, for the plants. Each family may be separated from others by large descriptive styles, or tallies, or by cast-iron edgings, or (what would be better still) by narrow edgings made of burnt fire-clay. Then there should be another strip of grass six feet broad, and after that a border of shrubs. When there are additional walks, the strip of grass should be of the same width on each side of the botanic border, and the last strip of grass, next the shrubs, should be of the breadth above-mentioned—six feet; or, in place of grass verges, the edges between the walks and beds may be of stone, slate, cast-iron, or fire-clay, all of which I prefer to box, or any other live edgings, which (as already said) not only harbour slugs, but, as the borders are very narrow, tend to impoverish the earth and injure the plants; or circuitous slips might be formed by this kind of edging, instead of the straight one, setting off from the boundary of the plot, and coiling round and round, until it closes in the centre with a seat, or some other kind of ornamental erection.

The Rockery, or Rock Garden.

Natural rocky scenes, although of themselves rude and uncouth, seldom fail to afford interest. They generally strike the mind with pleasurable emotions, whether it be merely as the sun peeps into bushes of rambling roses, which jut out from the crag beneath, or peers into the careless waving mantle of the lovely woodbine, or glances in upon some more mystic form, with shelfy projections, creeks, and recesses, adorned with indigenous heaths, foxgloves, crowberry, or other humble but beautiful flowers; or, mayhap, hovers by some dark boiling hollow, where mosses and ferns, and other amphibious plants, nestle and peep by the side of a murmuring stream, as it steals away to the adjacent river. Art must fall far short, however, of nature, in formations of this kind. It has seldom even a basis on which to construct a superstructure—often hardly an appliance suitable to the wishes of the artist; still something may generally be done, sometimes, even, a good deal, towards accomplishing the object.

When a natural rock presents itself suitable for this purpose, although it may be at a considerable distance, I should endeavour to unite it with the pleasure ground by a rural walk, graduating the scenery from the polished grounds till it harmonizes naturally with the rocky and wild composition : and, wherever practicable, advantage should be taken of salient points for the exhibition of various kinds of rock plants—always minding to keep immediately under the eye the simplest and most interesting kinds. This may not be done so readily as we could wish on bold and majestic rocks, but it may always be managed on smaller groups, which are nearer to view, and therefore more appropriate. I scarcely need observe, that preparations for such plants will have to be made by clearing obnoxious weeds, and supplying creeks, crevices, and all such places, with good soil suitable for their growth. It is quite practicable to form a highly interesting artificial Rockery, approximately natural, with proper materials, where expense is not much an object.

I should make choice, for instance, of some abruptly undulated ground, either near to the flower garden, or more remote, according to circumstances. In the *Plan for a Country Residence* I have shown it near the flower garden ; but it may be near, or further from it, at pleasure—linked together, first starting by a shrubbery walk, gradually approximating natural wooded scenery as it approaches the Rockery. The extreme outline of the plot allotted for the Rockery is the most proper situation for the principal body of rock, because the bank forms proper backing and support for the stones, and gives the idea of a natural rock protruding from it, as we generally find it in natural rocky ground.

Further, sometimes in sinking the lower parts of the given plot, and adding to the swells, when they are not sufficient of themselves, an opportunity is afforded of making rocky groups, in some cases to occupy the whole of the knoll, and in others only part.

The principal thing to be avoided in forming artificial rockwork is the appearance of a mere stone-heap, such as we too frequently see. The mass of the rock should invariably commence with the largest stones at the bottom, allowing the bottom of the stone to be just sufficiently covered, so that the depth of the rock cannot be detected nor even imagined. In order that the rock may appear massive and of importance, the principal stones should be of two or three, or even more, tons weight, and should gradually be diminished to about half a ton, and occasionally of less size, even to a few stones weight. The kind of stones most to be preferred are those which have become grey with lichen or moss, by exposure to the weather; but when these are not to be had easily, quarry stones may be resorted to, which in time will assume a natural hue. In placing these, they should be bedded as much as possible in seams, some parts appearing rudely perpendicular, now and then showing larger and smaller shelfy projections *(figure* 14). At certain heights, this upright part may be set back several feet, and sometimes yards, showing flats of earth mixed with large and small stones, where suitable shrubs may be

FIGURE 14.

planted. Broken or rugged platforms in extensive Rockeries afford the means of making an intricate pathway amongst the plants, over elevated parts, amongst bushes and rocky pyramids, so blended that the amount of rock-work cannot be comprehended. The extent of the Rockery must be lost by planting where the rock terminates with different shrubs, such as periwinkle, whins, heaths, rambling roses, hollies, blackthorns, &c., and by allowing groups of stones to appear bursting, as it were, from amongst the bushes and wild flowers, at different distances from the principal body of rock, so that its real termination cannot be detected.

Where Rockeries can only be conveniently placed on one side of a plot of ground, the side of a steep bank affords a good site for the simulated appearance of a natural rock, on which groups of different sized stones, in addition to the principal rock, might be so disposed as to give the appearance of a natural rocky bed, breaking through the precipice at different distances and of various magnitudes. Large stones should be placed in advance in some parts of the flat below, and here and there, as near as a few inches to the principal rock, so as to seem to have split off from the principal mass. Some of these principal stones should be furnished with low growing shrubs, as the spreading broom, heath, savin, cotoneaster microphilla, berberis, impetrifolia, whin, crowberry, bilberry, &c. These arrangements, judiciously managed, will, in two or three years, render it a difficult task for the visiter, especially if a stranger, to detect any art in the composition.

In situations where there is plenty of extent, a greater interest may be produced by forming caverns and subterranean passages (*figure* 14), presenting a rude, broken, rocky character inside. The passages should be large, and go through the bottom of the largest and deepest part of the Rockery, being so contrived by curves or angles, that, when entering at one end, there should be no light perceptible at the other, and they should lead to some other part of the grounds. These passages should be roofed by allowing broad flat stones to project by degrees until the whole is naturally covered in; and at the outside, at each end of the passage, there should be at least several yards of rock appearing on both sides, in order to destroy the idea of art as much as possible.

Conical Rockeries have a good effect when rising out of a mound, or conical hill, in rugged scenery. These, either naturally or artificially associāted with the general Rockery, and judiciously managed, are pleasing. Two or three groups of this kind, formed on the top of an extensive Rockery, would give variety to the general outline, the effect of which would also be heightened by mingling with them a few conical plants, such as junipers, savins, Irish yews, &c.

Conical Rockeries may be formed, or imitated, by grouping a number of large and small pointed stones, many of which should be placed as closely together as possible, nearly perpendicular, and of different heights. Then, in order that the divisions between these stones may not appear too great, smaller ones should be placed amongst them, so as to harmonize with the large ones, and, afterwards, scraplings and soil should be thrown amongst them, so as to prevent the base of the stones being seen at all, as that would destroy the appearance of their starting from a solid bed below. Lesser cones may also be formed in the same way, near to the principal ones, so as to form groups of cones; but the whole must appear to break out of the knoll, or artificial mound, that the idea may be given of time having wasted the softer material, and left the harder in its present state. In some cases, cement is used in fixing cones and other parts of rock-work, with a view to produce a natural effect, which is well carried out in some of the rocks at Chatsworth.

An old quarry, out of use for supplying stones, sometimes affords a fine opportunity for forming a Rock Garden. The various-sized knolls or hillocks produced by the refuse in working the quarry, will, in most cases, give the variety of undulation wanted. The whole of some of these hillocks will require to represent an entire mass of rock; others partly for rock and partly for planting; and others, again, for being principally covered with heath, whin brooms, honeysuckle, ivy, &c., with rude stones here and there protruding from amongst them. Against some of the larger mounds, perpendicular rock-work should be raised, to correspond as much as art will admit, and to harmonize with the principal rocky face left by the quarry-men. Perhaps in some parts the latter may want a little assistance to produce various flats or tables, projections, recesses, chasms, &c. Walks or tracks must be formed to wind naturally amongst the hillocks, sometimes advancing towards the principal rock, and at other times receding from it. These should be made dry, and instead of gravel should be covered with chippings of stone. Their breadth should appear unequal, and irregularly margined with indigenous growths, such as heaths, crowberry, bilberries, perriwinkles, dwarf spreading brooms, violets, veronicas, potentillas, &c. The rest of the ground will require, also, to be appropriated to wild growing plants, such as heaths, whins, spreading brooms, rambling roses, bilberries, foxgloves, primroses, wood anemones, blue bells, lilies of the valley, &c. &c. I remember having, upwards of twenty years ago, an extensive quarry to operate upon in the grounds connected with a gentleman's house. I laid this out with graceful winding walks and smooth lawn, planted the whole with corresponding flowers and cultivated shrubs, and erected suitable rustic seats. The whole presented a scene highly interesting and pleasing, and is considered such to the present time. Yet, I must confess, I was then in error;—congruity was overlooked, " smooth shaven lawn," and graceful winding walks, and cultivated shrubs, had no business in such a locality.

When water can be conducted to these natural looking Rockeries, and allowed to form trickling or dripping fountains, here and there, it would not only be appropriate for the growth of ferns, mosses, and other plants requiring moisture, but would also present an agreeable and natural effect.

THE SHRUBBERY.

THE Shrubbery is generally employed as a link connecting the Flower Garden, Kitchen Garden, and Forest, or wooded scenery, by a belt, or massive screen, on one or both sides of the principal walk, affording shelter, and often as a means by which to mask out unsightly objects. But this should not be the only object of a Shrubbery: it should be also considered and managed with a view to display the shrubs in their variety and true character, and with the greatest interest. We often meet with the most beautiful shrubs, either struggling for existence beneath a brawny tree, or, (if I may use the expression), gasping for air, amid a confined and suffocating mass of the more common or wilder growing kinds, instead of being managed according to their habits, and so placed as not only to afford them ample room, but to exhibit their true form and beauty. In order to effect this properly, the permanent plants, or such as are the most interesting, should be first placed in the compartment prepared for them, at such a distance from each other as they may be expected eventually to require, beginning with the smaller kinds nearest to the front, and going backward in rotational size, finishing with the large kinds. Then, amongst the whole, common kinds, as nurse plants, should be put in, for the purpose of producing an immediate effect, but with a view to their removal as the more valuable sorts advance in growth. Such removals, where proper space can be afforded, present opportunities for increasing or varying the lawn, which may not, in the first instance, have been sufficiently attended to; and thereby some of the more interesting plants may be brought carelessly to bound the additional lawn, or, in other words, by sodding up to them, made to bound it. And here I would mention, that although limitation may sometimes compel the designer only to introduce a narrow belt, or verge, of grass between the walks and shrubs, yet it should never be less than two feet in width; which may always be preserved if the the gardener would only use the grass shears generally, and the edging-iron but once a year, and not fritter them away by improper management. The edge line of the grass and shrubs would eventually blend together and be lost in each other, and yet preserve pretty much the breadth of verge required, by pruning the shrubs occasionally, but not stiffly. When there is sufficient space, it would be better to vary, considerably, the breadth of the lawn between the walk and the shrubbery compartment, showing deep and bold bends, rather than numerous small indentations, so as at the same time to make the broader part of the lawn convenient for exhibiting individual plants. *(See General Plans.)* I should, therefore, introduce such kinds of shrubs as are naturally handsome in form, as well as those which produce beautiful and fragrant blossoms, each of which, if judiciously managed, would greatly tend to vary the outline of the general strip, or dug border; whilst space would be afforded for each plant to display its true character, exemplifying what Loudon designates " the gardenesque style." Nevertheless, they should not be scattered, or dotted, but be planted in uncrowded groups, allowing, here and there, some of them to associate with and grow into each other.

In forming the kinds of Shrubberies of which I have been speaking, no large trees should ever be introduced. Although they may appear unobjectionable whilst young, yet, in a very few years, they become predominant and over-bearing. Yet here and there, in the back part of the Shrubbery, some of the most ornamental kinds of thorns, the double flowering cherries, magnolias, mespolis, laburnums, Hemlock-spruce, Gleditschia triacanthos, &c., may be planted, as they will prevent a monotonous outline, and produce a good effect.

Valuable shrubs should never be planted immediately under large trees which are already existing—a mistake which often arises when walks are made to pass under such trees for the sake of their shady canopy. They should be placed in groups upon the lawn in open spaces, whilst common laurels, box, variegated hollies, yews, Acuba japonica, rhododendrons, Gaultheria shallon, mahonias, &c., would give the required covert under the trees, when thickets or masking out is necessary.

When the shrubbery connected with the principal walk is employed to mask out a boundary line, or any unsightly object, I think the best plan is, to form a thicket of from a few yards in width to any extent required, of some or all the following kinds of plants—laurels, privets, yews, elders, hollies, dogwoods, allaturnus, lilacs, and filberts; and, if necessary, these thickets may be planted with groups of pines, firs, and other ornamental trees, fronting the whole with better shrubs. There are shrubs which are highly desirable to be grown for their showy and fragrant blossoms, but their habits and general features are otherwise uninteresting. Such are Deutzia scabra, Budleaglobosa, lilac, spindle tree, Garrya elyptica, Corchrus japonica, Tartarian honeysuckle, Guelder rose, brooms, Spirea areafolia, Spirea douglassii, and Spirea lind-leyana, barberry, standard roses and Pyrus japonica. Such must be planted so as to exhibit their tops and blossoms only, behind those of more pleasing habits.

DRESS WOODED SCENERY

IN CONNEXION WITH TENDER TREES AND SHRUBS.

In extensive domains the dress grounds often extend amongst ornamental and forest plantings, which are thrown into groups and masses, and blended with free and bold expanses of lawn. Here, in some degree, we ought to extend the shrubbery also. Masses and thickets of common shrubs are essential to produce variety and intricacy in the outline of glades, as well as to shut out wilder growths; and, in combination with suitable trees, to afford or produce nurseries for interesting tender plants. When grounds more in the vicinity of the edifice are not calculated to afford protection to tender plants, these preparations are important. Well-sheltered glades in wooded scenery, where the situation is dry and sufficiently open to the morning and mid-day sun, are undoubtedly better suited to tender trees and shrubs than an open south aspect in front of walls or buildings,—on which I think too much dependence is often placed,—because the winds are broken, and do not play upon them so violently as amongst walls unaided by trees, and they are also more protected from frost.

Of course, proper compost soils are necessary, and should be adapted to the various kinds of plants to be introduced; and in many cases a year or two's protection by basket-work or hurdles, branches of fir, or other devices, is important.

RURAL WALKS AND DRIVES IN NATURAL WOODED

SCENERY.

HAVING reached the termination of what may be considered the " Dress Ground," I scarcely need observe that a lengthened walk through wooded or rural scenery would not only afford protection from the heat of the sun, or shelter from boisterous winds, but would also afford stillness and quietude to the contemplative mind whilst reflecting on Nature's beauties and Nature's freaks, so beautifully expressed by our charming poet, Dodsley, who says—

> " Come, then, ye shades, beneath your bending arms
> Enclose the fond admirer of your charms ;
> Come, then, ye bowers, receive your joyful guest,
> Glad to retire, and in retirement blest ;
> Come, ye fair flowers, and open every sweet ;
> Come, little birds, your warbling songs repeat ;
> And O ! descend, to sweeten all the rest,
> Soft smiling peace, in white-robed virtue dressed—
> Content, unenvious ease, with freedom joined,
> And contemplation calm, with truth refined.
> Deign but in this fair scene with me to dwell,—
> All noise and nonsense, pomp and show, farewell."

Here, in our ramble, would also be observed the humble but odoriferous violet, primrose, cowslip, anemone, campanula, hyacinth, and the lovely lily of the valley, peeping out of their grassy beds ; the indigenous rose, too, would present itself reclining on some neighbouring bush, and the honey-suckle reaching to entwine some loftier tree, filling the air with delicious perfume ; whilst on every side the warblers of the woods would be swelling out their sweet solos, or pouring forth in full chorus notes which never fail to charm the ear and cheer the soul: sweet sounds ! harmonizing so well with the idea of Omnipotence and Omnipresence ! How beautiful in their plumage are the songsters also, as they hop from twig to twig, or fly from tree to tree, striking the eye with delight. Here and there, too, we may catch a glimpse of the noble golden pheasant strolling in our path. At the burst of his whirring flight the whole harmony of the grove becomes disturbed. The timid hare limps across the path, and steals away in fear. The frightened rabbit skips to hide itself in the thicket; the squirrel leaps from branch to branch, and away. And then we have the murmuring of the gentle streamlet stealing upon the ear and on the eye hither and thither in its winding course, now rippling over a pebbly bed, now leaping over some rugged steep, and—murmuring no more, but roaring impetuously to the river, on its way to the boundless sea—

> " Through groves sequestered, dark and still,
> Low vales and mossy cells among,
> In silent paths, the careless rill,
> With languid murmur, steals along.
> Awhile it plays, with circling sweep,
> And lingering leaves its native plain;
> Then pours impetuous down the steep,
> And mingles in the boundless main."—HAWKESWORTH.

Through such secluded and alluring retreats I would take the most interesting and varied course with my walks. Art must be employed, but with a careful hand, so that Nature's beauties may be presented with as little alteration as possible. In parts where the ground is of a general sameness, by reason of its being covered with one kind of wild undergrowth, a portion should be cleared, so as to form various-sized and natural glades of grass, blended with groups and masses of wild flowers and clustered native bushes.

In this kind of scenery the walks need only be made dry, and from four to five feet wide, always taking care to have shorter bends on abrupt ground than in that in which there are gentle undulations. These walks ought to take a natural and varied course, having no other margin than that of some indigenous growth. They must also be kept invariably clean and tidy, still preserving pretty much their width in a careless form. In very abrupt ground they would be more in character to be narrower than the width which has been named.

In new ground, when the mansion is so unfortunate as not to be associated with existing woods, but dependent on the dress of new plantations,

I should still form necessary walks in such plantations, which would be likely eventually to produce shelter and interest; for if they do not at once afford such gratification, they will at least afford scope for recreation and exercise.

In woods or plantations in which there is sufficient extent to form drives and rides, the roads must be made from ten to twelve feet wide, and firm and dry, with level glades of grass attached here and there, of a sufficient width for carriages to pass and repass each other. The roads may be made of stone or gravel, and grassed over, to appear more natural. The curves must be sufficiently bold, and of easy sweeps, so as not to be troublesome or perplexing to drivers. Seats here and there along the walks will also be needful for pedestrians ; and a neat cottage might be advantageously introduced,—to be used either as an alms-house or as a defence, with a spare room, to afford a retreat against storms.

ON TREES AND SHRUBS ABOUT THE HOUSE
AND PLEASURE GROUNDS.

As it will be necessary, in the course of this work, frequently to use various terms for planting, in order that they may be better understood, I am desirous to lay down in advance a sort of rule for such terms. I consider that trees arranged in numbers together—say, from two to ten,—should be designated as " a group;" from ten to twenty, " a massive, or large group;" and upwards of twenty, if standing unbroken, " a mass." When the plantation covers a few acres, we will call it " a wood;" and " a forest," when the wooded scenery is extensive. A continuity of scattered trees is generally termed " a grove;" a mass, composed of trees and bushes, so as not to be readily penetrated, is termed " a thicket;" a round, or oval, compact number of trees is termed " a clump"—Sir Uvedale Price says, " a better thing would be to pronounce the word without the first letter."

I have before stated, when treating on the situations adapted for residences, that trees are of the utmost importance for shelter and effect. Wherever it is practicable, a wood, or a considerable wooded mass, should be planted behind the house, so as to produce a good background, and also in such other places as will interfere as little as possible with the principal views to be obtained from it. But where shelter is of consequence, prospects, or views, must be of secondary consideration; and, therefore, whether there are existing trees, or trees to be planted, in order to preserve comfort, we must content ourselves with telescopic or partial views from the windows, along narrow vistas, so as to bring into immediate view the most interesting objects, and yet command the rest from various parts of the walks and pleasure grounds, as we best can. In some cases it may be enough to clear away the lower branches from some of the trees which interrupt these views, so as to command the prospect underneath them. This may be done without materially decreasing the shelter which we ought to preserve. The woods, or masses, so essential as a background to the buildings, are equally important as principals, with which the smaller masses, and various sized groups of the dress grounds, are to be associated.

In arranging these principal plantations on elevated ground, or hills, the practice of planting scattered trees just on the summit only, should be avoided as much as possible. They must be so managed as not to appear thin, or grove-like, or to show the horizon through their stems, when viewed from any public point *(figure 15, a)*, as that at once suggests the idea of a want of

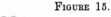

FIGURE 15.

extent, and, in appearance, at least, lessens the magnitude of the wood and importance of the place, whilst a dense block leaves the mind to imagine more. This error exists at Temple Newsam, near Leeds, and in Methley Park, the seat of the Earl of Mexbrough, and many other places, when viewed at some distance, and facing the front; and it might readily have been avoided if the wood had been lower down on either side of the summit *(figure 15, b b)*, but especially on the remote side. A further effect in the variation will be produced, and no less extent of magnitude of wood appear, but the mind be rather led to imagine a continuity of forest, by a glade or two of grass being, now and then, allowed to glide over the summit, so that the eye only catches the tops of the trees beyond *(c)*.

I should in no case allow trees or shrubs, particularly those of the large growing kinds, to stand so near the edifice as to touch the building, except in limited grounds. Such trees ought to be planted, at the least, ten yards from it; but considerably further off in an extensive place. They not only show a want of extent, by assuming the character of a suburban garden, but I am of opinion that they produce an unhealthy state of atmosphere, by causing dampness, and by excluding both light and air from the house.

When masses have to be planted, I propose to place them in groups, or masses of kinds as directed below; and when they are already in existence, to group them, at the time of thinning, as nearly so as possible. The most profitable kinds should form the most massive assembly, as the beech, wych and other elms, and oaks, sycamore, and ash. For example,—ten, twenty, fifty, or more (according to the extent of ground to be planted,) of wych elms, may be planted together at proper distances from each other; twenty, thirty, or fifty oaks; twenty, thirty, or forty beeches; and so with ash and sycamore, with smaller groups occasionally thrown in of spruce firs, Lombardy poplars, mossy-cupped oaks, limes, pines of sorts, larch, mountain ash, birch, two or three purple beeches, three or four weeping willows, &c. When these varieties are once distributed, they will have to be repeated till the whole space is planted, taking care that each kind of group varies in size and form from its neighbours, and is not stiff and round, but that all blend naturally and softly into one another. For instance : by letting two or three of the oaks run well into the group of beech, and a few of the beech blend into the oaks, and so on with every variety *(figure* 16*).*

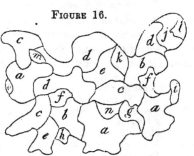

FIGURE 16.

a a a, oak; *b b,* ash; *c c c,* elm; *d d d,* beech; *e e,* sycamore; *f f,* pines; *g,* spruce fir; *h,* Cedar of Lebanon; *i,* Cedrus deodarus; *j,* Spanish chesnut; *k,* mossy-cupped oak; *l,* birch; *m,* locust tree; *n,* larch; *o,* silver fir; and so on.

When thus arranged, a distinct variety and spirit of colouring, as well as a broken and irregular sky surface, is obtained; the groups outgrow one another, and the most striking and imposing wooded scenery is in this manner produced. Besides, by this mode, there is not that danger of the most luxuriant varieties outgrowing and injuring those of a slower growth, which attend the old system of mingled planting. This natural style of arrangement applies alike to shrubs and flowers. For instance, on passing along the shrubbery, an occasional group of rhododendrons, laurestinas, azalias, roses, &c., produces a forcible and pleasing effect; and the whole being carried out in this way, the eye becomes relieved by falling upon fresh objects as it proceeds; while, otherwise, it becomes perplexed and tired by the same object presenting itself at almost every step we take.

Previously to planting the fore and other parts of the dress ground, the designer ought to consider what planting is necessary for shutting out unsightly objects, as also for the general composition; and let it always be remembered at the time of planting, that such principal trees or shrubs as are to remain permanently must be arranged first, and their future size and character taken into consideration, so that the effect hereafter may not be left to chance; for how often we find some beautiful view is shut out by some favourite tree, and others planted close to the edifice, as if, because they are pretty little plants at first, they were never to become larger! I remember meeting with a fine cedar of Lebanon, having a trunk four feet in diameter, growing within ten yards of the entrance door of a mansion, and spreading over the whole front with its magnificent branches and dense foliage. Thus the injudicious planter sees not the hidden power; as Mason has it—

> " A hidden power, at once his friend and foe.
> 'Tis Vegetation! Gradual to his groves
> She gives their wished effect, and that displayed,
> O! that her power would pause; but, active still,
> She swells each stem, prolongs each vagrant bough,
> And darts with unremitting vigour, bold
> From grace to wild luxuriance."

Again, in many instances, do we find trees and shrubs so indiscriminately arranged, that two, three, or more of the most valuable kinds are placed nearly together, rendering it extremely difficult at the time of thinning to know which is to be spared. Under such difficulties, the whole are pruned, in order to preserve all of them, and consequently the whole are spoiled; whereas, if such were planted at proper distances at first, so as to display their perfect form and beauty, and filled up as required with common kinds with a view to their future removal, we should at once be relieved from the painful task of having to displace trees which we should wish to stand, as well as easily preserve the true character of the whole of the adopted plants, or such as were appointed to be permanent.

The improver must be very particular in placing his principal plants so as to preserve views, thereby avoiding the unpleasant duty of removing them when they become obstructive. In doing this, he must take his views from the principal windows, and from the most important parts of the pleasure grounds, (remembering at the same time that the windows ought in preference to command the best prospects.) It will be necessary to have the assistance of a person with long rods, (made as conspicuous as possible by having the tops of them painted white or red), to fix as may be directed. These rods may either have the names of the trees to be planted written upon them, or be numbered, and a book be provided with corresponding numbers opposite the names of the plants to be introduced, stating at the same time the kind of soil or compost required by each. Perhaps, while so placing these trees and shrubs, we may interfere with the prettiest view elsewhere; but I think this sometimes advantageous, by producing different scenes from different windows, and thus producing variety in the general composition of the dress-ground and the scenery beyond. It must be always borne in mind that these adopted trees and shrubs are to be planted in various-sized groups of two, three, four, five, or more, according to the extent of ground and other circumstances. Sometimes a single tree or two may be planted near the fence which divides the kept ground and park, so as to form a unison with contiguous trees in the park or field, always remembering that a solitary tree or shrub in the midst of a glade is bad, since it destroys repose, and never gives that force or expression to the landscape which it has when trees are associated together, or with buildings or other objects. A tree or shrub placed thus singly can only be appreciated as a specimen. The chosen trees which are to remain amongst masses of shrubs should be cautiously arranged in groups, allowing necessary views, and also so as to vary the surface of the shrub mass. In planting the groups, whatever may be their extent, equal distances and straight lines must be studiously avoided. A group of two trees only always looks the best, growing close together, mingling their branches into one handsome top or head, but displaying two trunks; therefore there should be no hesitation in planting two trees now and then in one hole. In a group of three, the third may stand five, six, or more feet from the other two. In a group of four, six, nine, or more, the trees may vary in distance from two to thirty feet apart or more, according to the size of the group, always making it a rule for two, three, or more to be placed near to each other, so as to form a principal, if I may so speak. In large groups, two or three of these principals may be formed: for their being clustered together gives far greater spirit and effect both in stem and top, and produces a far more natural and pleasing group, than one wholly scattered, though it may be arranged variously. *(See Park Plan.)* It is essential also that the outer trees of a large group should stand at a greater distance from each other than the inner ones, so as to have a loose straggling effect, rather than a stiff lumpy one; and though some of the plants, arranged as I have directed above, may be thought too near for each tree to exhibit its true character, yet we often find these, when their outer branches are allowed to expand freely, forming noble clustered heads, and, as a group, their stems being near together and sometimes touching one another, they constitute a more natural, important, and agreeable feature in the landscape, than if the whole were more scattered or equally dotted. We sometimes see a most beautiful object produced by three, four, or more rising from one root, and forming together one handsome head. The groups we have described are, however, not to be so placed as to divide the lawn equally into parts, but they should seem to be parts of the principal masses of shrubs or trees, and therefore be assembled pretty near to them. It is important to observe, that the best effect will be produced by planting them near to a prominent bend or jut of a bed or mass, inasmuch as it adds to the projection and depth to the bay. Occasionally one or two plants may be planted in the recesses, by which the outline of the mass becomes softened and more varied and intricate; while, at the same time, open expanses of lawn are left free for the eye to repose upon. This arrangement also gives greater force, variety, and beauty to both. Of course there will be parts where groups may be planted with proper effect, when not exactly in connection with a mass; but it ought not to be general. We frequently find ornamental trees introduced into small beds of shrubs, which ought not to be the case, unless they are planted together for present effect, and with the view of eventually allowing the trees to remain, and of clearing all the shrubs away, except such as are necessary for association with the trees, letting the lawn take possession, or obliterate what was the bed or earthy part. Such large trees in a small dug bed, may be compared to an overgrown geranium overbalancing the small garden pot it first occupied in its infantine state.

In the case of shrub beds on the lawn, or other shrub masses, which are intended, eventually, not to show a hard line, or earthy part, but to blend softly and naturally with the lawn, there are many shrubs of stiff unpleasing habit ill calculated to effect this object, and which, certainly, ought not to take the front, though they may be deemed desirable, in consequence of their showy or odoriferous blossoms. Such are the lilac, Deutzia scabra, budlea, brooms, roses, spireas, and all plants of similarly uninteresting forms or habits; but they may be introduced with good effect, if judiciously fronted by other shrubs, of better outline. The following are well calculated for that purpose, and yet so dwarfish in habit that the interest of the shrubs I have named will not be lessened, but improved, by their occupying the front ranks (as shown in the chapter on Shrub Beds):—Mahonia aquifolia, Arbutus regia, spreading savins, dwarf St. John's wort, Cottoneaster microphilla, Berberis impetrifolia, perriwinkle, spreading brooms, Daphne cneorum, heaths of sorts, Andromeda polyfolia, Rhododendron ferrugineum, and hirsutum. These will cover the earthy part, and form a natural, soft, harmonious connection with the lawn.

ORNAMENTAL TREES AND SHRUBS.

For the benefit of those who are not acquainted with plants generally, I have named, below, a few select ornamental trees and shrubs as suitable to introduce into the dress-grounds, where they must be so arranged and adjusted .that they may remain permanently, and have the intermediate spaces filled up with common kinds, to be taken away when required.

The following trees are adapted to situations requiring large growing trees, as grass plants, or otherwise, in masses, viz. :—

The Purple Beech *(Fagus sylvatica purpurea)*, whose noble and wide-spreading branches, and peculiar foliage, are particularly striking and interesting. It should have plenty of room in which to show its form and beauty, —I believe quite as much as the common beech,—but should only be here and there introduced, for variety's sake.

The Cut-leaved Beech *(Fagus incisa)* is another, rather more formal and upright than its relation, and branches more from the stem in tiers, but becomes, in time, a large and most beautiful tree, having numerous feathered twigs on its stiff arms, and beautiful long serrated leaves. These beeches, being large growing trees, are most suitable for a situation in the centre of others of lower growth.

The Horse Chesnut *(Æsculus hippocastanum)* is a large, pendent, and handsome tree, when aged; but, till it is so, it is stiff, and not much to be admired, excepting for its large cut leaves and long spikes of cream-white blossoms in spring. So with the Scarlet Chesnut *(Æsculus rubicunda)*, whose habit and growth are similar. Its large spikes of scarlet blossoms, however, make it extremely showy. Both kinds may advantageously be planted on lawns in front of a mass, or in a group of trees of more open and lofty growth.

The Spanish Chesnut *(Castanea vesca)* is a majestic open growing tree, whose handsome serrated and glossy foliage, and green-yellow blossoms in summer, and spiny fruit-case in autumn, make it an object of general admiration : being, also, a lofty growing tree, it is well adapted for a back ground.

The Turkey, or Mossy-cupped Oak *(Quercus cerris)* is a large, handsome, and rather upright, but loose and free growing tree, suitable for back ground, or for rising out of a group of round-headed lower trees, or for planting where ready effect is required.

The Plane Tree *(Platanus occidentalis)* is another handsome tree, though of rather formal habits. It has large and noble indented foliage, and thrives best in a sheltered situation, as it is liable to be injured in very severe winters. It forms a handsome tree on lawns fronting a mass of other trees, or when taking the pre-eminence, or centre, of a group of lower growing trees or bushes. Similar observations apply to the *Platanus orientalis*, which is also a handsome tree, with deep lacerated foliage.

The Cedar of Lebanon *(Cedrus Libani)* is a majestic evergreen tree, of formal symmetry, throwing out from its trunk ramified arms, which produce, in turn, regular tiers of massive horizontal branches, and a *tout ensemble* noble, dense, and most imposing. Unfortunately, it is, in most situations, of slow growth. I think a cold soil and moist atmosphere suit it best. Some years ago, I noticed several good specimens in the grounds at Byerley Hall, near Bradford, which were growing in strong soil and clay bottom; one in particular, on the entrance front of the house, was truly grand, stretching out its majestic limbs over a space of upwards of forty-five yards in circumference, while its trunk, at three feet from the ground, measured upwards of four feet in diameter. And a few years since, I observed, in a gentleman's grounds in Westmoreland, (where I was professionally engaged,) a young plant of the Cedar of Lebanon, about eight feet high, growing close to one of the lakes, and, apparently, quite as freely as the common larch. Here, again, the soil was strong and naturally damp. As we have proof of this tree attaining to a large size, we should be cautious about planting it as a grass plant, too near the front of the mansion—twenty or twenty-five yards being near enough. Neither should its form be lost or deteriorated by bad associations. No plant, in fact, ought to be placed near to it that would rise above its lower branches, and these should be at least several yards from it. This very interesting tree should not be planted in too great numbers. Its character is peculiar and striking, yet more calculated to be subsidiary to a scene than to form a principal object. Too many, therefore, within one range of view, would mar the effect intended to be produced. I do not object to a few groups of two, three, or four being introduced, and, in extensive grounds, would recommend several larch, or spruce fir, or white cedar, being intermixed, in some instances, for the sake of variety. But I mean, that a numerous repetition of the Cedar of Lebanon over the whole ground, would tend much to lessen its interest, as is the case at Warwick Castle, where, I think, they prevail too extensively.

The Larch *(Larix Europœa)* is a tree commanding admiration, and is, I am sorry to say, not duly appreciated by many persons, which may be owing to a certain monotony of character which it exhibits. It is to be found rearing its head in almost every modern plantation, and is generally so crowded as rarely to have room to assume its true shape. But I do not hesitate to say, that a fine old-grown larch, displaying its elegant, sweeping, and recurvant branches, and delicate drooping spray, and, in spring, its red-brown blossoms and light-green tints of foliage, is an object truly beautiful, and its occasional introduction into the kept ground is indispensable. A group of three, or more, at unequal distances, has a fine effect indeed, independently of whatever kind of tree may be their neighbour. A more striking effect is produced, however, when one larch takes the centre of two or more spruce, or silver firs, Cedrus deodara, or some other evergreen trees, or where two or three of each are blended together. A larch, or, indeed, a formal fir of any kind, should always be closely associated with other trees. They are too formal to be isolated. It may be made more picturesque by stopping its leading shoot when ten or fifteen years in growth, and by repeating this operation when the tree attempts to regain its lead; but such specimens should not be general, as, by this course, the true form or character of the tree is destroyed.

The Silver Fir *(Picea pectinata)* is a fine, broad-based, pyramidal tree, throwing out, from its smooth stem, regular tiers of horizontal fan-like branches, furnished with light silvery-green thick-set foliage. It is of rather tender habit, and ought to have a sheltered situation in front of masses of round-headed trees; or it may be mixed with such masses, with room to display its character.

The Weymouth Pine *(Pinus strobus)* is a highly ornamental conical tree, with a beautiful smooth-barked stem, and soft, long, thread-like foliage of a light bluish-green colour. Its whole appearance generally gives it pre-eminence over most of its family, and, with the silver and spruce fir, it forms a very pleasing group. Three or more pines placed at various distances round a larch, or three larches blended with four or five pines, produce an imposing effect. I think it thrives best in a cool soil.

The *Pinus excelsis* is a large, handsome, quick-growing tree, of recent introduction, with foliage similar to the Weymouth pine, but more silvery. Its habits assimilate to those of the last-named tree, but it is more robust. *Pinus cembra* and *Webbiana*, and many others of the same family, which have been more recently introduced, are highly ornamental. None of these, however, should be over-planted, as they would produce too much gloom, and mar the landscape.

The Common Lime *(Tilia Europæa)* is a handsome, ovated, closely-formed tree, with pendulous branches, which in some fine aged specimens re-curve from the ground. Groups of limes exceeding three in number may have their sameness broken by one, two, or three larches, according to the size of the group, or by one or more evergreen trees, rising out of the midst of them. A single lime would show its character and be in harmony, if placed in front of some two taller and loosely-formed trees, such as the Turkey oak, Fulham oak, or Spanish chesnut. It would also be in harmony if placed as a principal, with three or four low-growing trees, planted at unequal distances, and sufficiently distant to avoid interference with its form: as, for instance, with some of the fancy thorns or hollies, and even with still lower growths, when it is necessary to vary the ground-line, such as the rhododendron, laurestinas, pyracanthos, Mahonia aquifolia, &c. The broad-leaved American, yellow, and red twigged lime, are desirable species grouped together.

The Spruce Fir *(Abies alba)* is an interesting evergreen spiral tree, and, like the larch, too lightly esteemed; but to me it appears strikingly beautiful in groups of two, three, four, or more, or when grouping with two or three larches. It harmonizes well with the various pines, or in the midst of a group of English elms; but, in consequence of its sombre appearance, a numerous repetition of it should be avoided.

The *Abies menziesii, morinda,* and *douglassii,* are considered handsome species, and should be similarly treated.

The Acacia or Locust Tree *(Robenia pseudo)* is an open, long-jointed, thorny or spiny tree, of quick and large growth; but it is more to be admired for its foliage and white blossoms than for its general appearance. Certainly its blossoms and foliage are very beautiful; but its long naked branches and general form, when stripped of its foliage, forbids its being introduced numerously or as a front plant. It ought, in fact, when planted, to have its top only seen above those of lower growth.

All the trees now named attain to a considerable size, and should therefore, of necessity, be planted at a sufficient distance from the mansion to allow room for their own expansion, and to permit a free circulation of air; and it should be particularly remembered, that all large evergreen trees should be sparingly planted, lest their deep-toned foliage should become too powerful or predominant. The following are a few trees generally of lower growth than the preceding, but useful for the production of variety and effect :—

The *Robinia microphilla* is similar in flower and foliage to the locust tree, but altogether handsomer, and groups well with the Gleditschia triacanthos and hemlock-spruce.

The Three-thorned Acacia *(Gleditschia triacanthos)* is a low and slowly-growing ovated tree, of elegant pinnated foliage. It is somewhat tender, and should therefore be planted upon a lawn in sheltered places. This and the deciduous cypress group well with the hemlock-spruce.

The Deciduous Cypress *(Taxodium distichum)* is an upright, elegant tree, also of slow growth, and thrives best in a moist and sheltered situation. The unripened young shoots, like the Gleditschia triacanthos, are liable to be injured in severe winters. It also groups well with the spruce, larch, pine, and white cedar.

Taxodium sempervirens is likely to be a hardy, handsome, and rapid-growing evergreen tree, and should have a choice situation on the lawn.

The Leucombe Oak *(Quercus Leucombeana)* is a handsome sub-evergreen tree, with large bright foliage, and in sheltered situations assumes the character of an evergreen oak. It groups well with the Turkey oak, or it would assist in forming a handsome group, placed as a principal in the midst of a few low-growth evergreens, such as hollies, phillyreas, arbutus, &c.

The Hemlock-Spruce *(Abies Canadensis)* is a very elegant and ornamental evergreen tree. Indeed, its pendant branches of light feathery spray charac-terize it as one of the most graceful grass plants we have. Three, four, or five, judiciously placed on a lawn, would form a most agreeable group, or with any of the following, taking a central position amongst them, viz. :—The Weymouth pine, spruce fir, silver fir, red cedar, or larch. I believe that it thrives well on moist soil; and it bears the shade very well, but is all the better for shelter.

The Cembran Pine *(Pinus cembra)* is a handsome and compact tree, calculated for the middle of a group of low trees, or for two or three, taking the outside of a group of larches.

The *Cedrus deodara* is of rather modern introduction, but promises to be one of the handsomest evergreen trees we have. It seems to partake much of the character of the larch, having very similar twigs and foliage, but of a bluer green, and differs materially from it in being an evergreen. In habit it is elegantly pendant. It is likely to be as hardy as the Cedar of Lebanon, and of quicker growth. Indigenously it attains a very considerable size, and scarcely ought to have been classed amongst low trees. It should have a prominent situation on lawns where three might form a group; or the red cedar or upright cypress, or perhaps both, rising from amongst them, would have an agreeable effect, while a larch would look still better. But there should be nothing placed before the cedar that would be liable to obstruct the view of the whole of its graceful form.

The Saddle-leaved Tulip Tree *(Liriodendron tulipifera)* is peculiarly interesting, and greatly to be admired on account of its singular and beautiful leaf, which is large and of a cheerful green, something in the shape of a saddle, (from which I have no doubt its name has been partly derived, and partly from its blossoms being in the form of the common tulip flower). It attains a fair size in some situations, and has all the characteristics of the Spanish chesnut when without foliage. It should be planted in sheltered situations, and in some good loose soil. It groups well with the plane tree.

The Thorn family *(Cratægus)*, of which species and varieties are numerous and highly interesting. We may select the following:—Cratægus grandiflora, punicea, punicea flora plena, douglassii, præcox, tanacetifolia, glabra and celsiana, spathulata, orientalis and sanguinea, all of which may be thrown into groups of two, three, four, or more. Some of the groups may have their massive outline varied by introducing amongst them one, two, or more, of any of the following:—the larch, spruce fir, hemlock-spruce, silver fir, Weymouth pine; or two red cedars and a cypress would produce a pleasing and a broken outline in a massive group.

The Magnolia is a highly interesting flowering family, but is scarcely hardy; and though some of them become trees, yet, in our cold climate, they seldom assume more than a shrubby character. They are principally grown against walls, for the sake of shelter. The grandiflora, and grandiflora exoniensis, succeed moderately well in warm and moist situations; consequently, a well-sheltered bay of lawn, with a south-east aspect, should be chosen. The exoniensis is a fine evergreen species, of noble, thick, shining light-green foliage, similar to the common laurel, but much larger. *M. conspicua* is deciduous, and produces showy white blossoms early in the spring. These, with lanceolata, rotundifolia, glauca, and tripetala, form suitable groups—tripetala taking the centre, being the largest grower, and, in some instances, making a good-sized tree; and one or two, or more, may take part in a group with the Laurestinus, Acuba japonica, or Mahonia aquifolia or intermedia.

The *Cryptomeria japonica* is a tree of modern introduction. It is a very beautiful, formal, evergreen tree, with a straight stem, studded with regular tiers of branches in a horizontal position, similar to the silver fir. It makes a fine lawn plant in a sheltered situation.

The Evergreen Oak, *(Quercus ilex)*, though generally seen as a low dense evergreen, often becomes a majestic tree. During one of my visits to Wollaton Park, the seat of Lord Middleton, I saw some noble specimens on the lawn at the south front of the edifice. One of them measured upwards of four feet in diameter a few feet above the ground. They are quite hardy, and while young they are well calculated to mask out any object, or to prevent the eye from tracing the whole extent of lawn.

The Silver and Gold-edged Holly, Snowy Mesplus, Arbutus, Weymouth Pine, or Hemlock-spruce, would, any of them, afford variety, and harmonize, if introduced in some of the groups of oaks.

The Chili Pine *(Araucaria imbricata)* is a singular and strikingly noble evergreen, of compact upright form, with regular tiers of stiff limbs, heavily clustered with branches thickly clothed with small rigid foliage. This must have a select situation on the lawn: though moderately hardy, shelter is essentially necessary, as it is somewhat top heavy, and therefore liable to be injured by winds. It might with propriety be associated with the pine family, phillyreas, or hollies, but should not be interrupted by them.

The Holly *(Ilex)*. The various fancy hollies are exceedingly handsome and useful shrubby evergreen trees, and ought to be planted in large and small groups on lawns, as well as in the shrubbery, and so as to exhibit as much as possible the different varieties. I may mention the gold-edged, silver-edged, dark smooth-leaved, opaque, balearica, green and variegated hedgehog, small or willow-leaved, with the latifolia, as being distinct and pleasing, generally suitable for forming blocks and producing intricacy, so as to deceive the eye as to the real extent of the dress grounds which they may adorn.

The Maiden-hair Tree *(Salisburia adiantifolia)* is another tender tree of slow growth, more singular than beautiful. It has peculiar, thick fungus-like foliage, and requires a sheltered spot. It may associate with the holly, white cedar, and China arbor-vitæ.

The Snowdrop Tree *(Halesia tetraptera)* is a low deciduous tree, having white snowdrop-like blossoms, in spring, hanging upon its twigs, which make it an elegant object, especially when mixed with the thorn family.

The *Cotoneaster frigida* is a low deciduous shrubby tree, of pleasing form and foliage, retaining its leaves longer in the autumn than many others. Its white blossom in the spring, and coral hawthorn-like berries in the autumn, render it an agreeable object. It groups well with the mespilus, or would be in keeping if interspersed, occasionally, with the Phillyrea ilex, alaternus, or scarlet and double pink thorn.

The *Ailantus glandulosa* is a stiff-growing deciduous tree, with obtuse, finger-like branches, and ash-like foliage of immense size, which renders it singularly ornamental. It groups well with the Robinia tortuosa and microphilla.

The following are a few useful and interesting kinds of larger and smaller shrubs :—

The Buckthorn *(Rhamnus alaternus)*. The broad, narrow, and blotched leaved alaternus all form loose, evergreen, shrubby trees, and are proper for hiding any deformities or improper objects, and form, of themselves, varied massive groups. When thought desirable, an agreeable variety may be produced by introducing into the group of alaternus, a larch, spruce fir, or Weymouth pine.

The Arbor-vitæ *(Thuga)*, whether the American, Chinese, or Siberian, is well adapted for grouping in confined portions of the pleasure ground, especially the flower garden, where spreading bushes might prove detrimental to the flower beds. The white, pink, and autumnal mazerian may, with propriety, be introduced into some of the groups.

The *Phillyrea.* The foliage and general habit of this family form interesting and moderate-sized evergreen bushes, and, generally, they are pretty hardy. P. ilex, P. oppositifolia, and P. angustifolia, are distinct, loose growing bushes, and are useful for masking out disagreeable objects, or varying the boundaries of lawns. The different species, of themselves, form varied and pleasing groups; but a striped holly, arbor-vitæ, or a deciduous low-growing tree, such as the double-blossomed cherry, crimson thorn, or double-blossomed pink thorn, placed amongst some of the groups, produces a good effect.

Portugal Laurel *(Cerasus lucitanica).* This is a hardy, noble, and beautiful flowering evergreen shrub; but, in consequence of its round, formal, and sombre appearance, it ought to be cautiously and sparingly introduced, that its marked character may not appear too prominent. It has a bad effect when placed prominently in front of a house. I remember an instance where there were two exceedingly large ones placed on each side of the front door, at equal distances from it, and receding from the mansion about twelve yards. These, when viewed from the park, produced a very gloomy and most inharmonious effect, having the appearance of two large blotches on the elevation of the edifice. In another instance where I was consulted, there were four placed on the south front of the mansion, only eight yards distant from it, which had attained to such a magnitude as very much to darken the rooms, and almost to shut out from them the principal landscape, which was truly beautiful. Although the plants of themselves were magnificent specimens of their kind, yet their injudicious disposition left the improver no other alternative than their total extirpation. How essential it is, then, that the planter, in giving the sites for his various plants, should consider well their form and beauty, and also the size which they are likely to attain, and so place them as to prevent the painful necessity of destroying them after their true form has been attained. I should recommend the Portugal laurel to be placed in front of masses, or massive groups of low-growing trees; on the lawn, at proper distances to allow room to display its *true character;* or in front of a shrubbery in some bold bend, there to be permitted to form its own boundary line on the grass. In this way, its deep tone and compact massive form would be a good deal softened, and be more admired than when detached so as to be backed by a building, or when seen marking out its formal figure on the horizon. I think it would be wrong to place associates near it, or, at least, in front of it, as that would lessen its dignity; but, occasionally, the laurustinus, holly, and Phillyrea ilex, Phillyrea oppositifolia, and Mahonia aquifolia, may associate with it well, if we are careful to place the Portugal laurel a little in advance, as the principal plant, and at a distance not to be encroached upon by its neighbours.

The Common Laurel *(Cerasus laurocerasus)* is a most lively, glossy, loose-growing evergreen, producing beautiful spikes of white blossoms. It is indispensable for forming thickets, and, now and then, detached bushes on the lawn; grouping with the laurustinus, alaternus, or rhododendron. There are two small-leaved varieties, which are also good bright evergreens; the very smallest make nice front plants, and are suitable for small beds.

The Strawberry Tree *(Arbutus)*, the unedo, and unedo rubra, make large, handsome, evergreen bushes, and are quite hardy. The former produces small bell-shaped flowers, of a greenish-white; the latter, of a pinky-red: both kinds bear strawberry-like fruit, which adds much to their beauty in the autumnal months. It would be proper to group three or four together, including both varieties; and one, or more, may be grouped with one or two rhododendrons, Azalea pontica, or Garrya eliptica.

The *Arbutus regia* is a hardy, spreading, dwarf evergreen, with small white flowers. It forms a nice bush, planted on the lawn, or is well adapted to front a thicket in a shrubbery, or form masses in wilder kept pleasure grounds.

The *Aucuba Japonica* is a fine, large, singularly showy, and hardy evergreen shrub. Its yellow-and-green marbled foliage gives it a striking and lively appearance, differing materially from any other shrub. It will thrive in almost any situation, and will bear the smoke of towns better than any other evergreen; indeed, I have seen it flourish well on a lawn at the back of a mansion, where the sun scarcely ever reached it. Consequently, it is most valuable for such situations, besides being an invaluable undergrowth, and forming thickets. It thrives well, also, in situations more fully exposed to the influences of the sun. Its associates may be the rhododendron, Mahonia aquifolium, Ilex balearica, and other varieties of hollies.

The American Honeysuckle *(Azalea pontica)* is a hardy, deciduous, flowering shrub. Its highly interesting large yellow flowers make it desirable as a grass plant near to the mansion; but, when out of bloom, it is uninteresting. It should, consequently, be united with the rhododendron, Mahonia aquifolium, Daphne hybrida, and pontica.

The *Azalea coccinea*, *Azalea alba*, and the other Ghent varieties, (all deciduous), mixed with Kalmia latifolia, Daphne hybrida, Mahonia glumacea, and repens, form a brilliant group; and all of them being early bloomers, are well adapted for a sheltered part of the lawn, near to the house.

The Berberry *(Berberis empetrifolia)* is a truly handsome, small-leaved, trailing evergreen, every branch of which is thickly studded with small waxy yellow bell flowers, making a delightful, but small, grass plant, when planted so as to rise out of the midst of a group of small stones, or spar, and to bear the spreading branches in a mass from the ground, two feet, or more, high. It is also a proper plant for pots, to place in vases, and especially low wire vases, or other low trellised receptacles, placed on the lawn. It makes an elegant pendant plant, arched upon the Berberis sinensis, or the common berberry.

The Berberis sinensis is a handsome, large-growing, sub-evergreen shrub: it may group with the Mahonias, Arbutus, &c. The Berberis dulcis is also a handsome variety, and may take a share in the group.

The Ash Berberry, *(Mahonia)*, the aquifolium, glumacea, repens, and facicularis hybrida, are handsome, low-growing, hardy, evergreen flowering shrubs: their showy tufts of yellow flowers rising out of reddish-green glossy foliage early in the spring, make them truly interesting, and well suited to form a group, so placed as to be viewed from the windows. Perhaps the group might be improved by the introduction of Rhododendron catawbiensis, R. Caucasicum album, and R. dauricum atrovirens. They are also highly proper for planting in front of shrubberies.

The Box *(Buxus sempervirens)* is a shrubby, evergreen tree; and being quite hardy, is better adapted for exposed situations than many others. There are several varieties, which together produce a pleasing as well as a useful group for masking out. They bear the shade well, and consequently are good undergrowths. The B. balearica is a fine, bright, large-leaved kind, and although rather tender, it may be placed in a group in such a manner as to exhibit itself, and at the same time be protected by the hardier kinds. The round-leaved box *(Buxus rotundifolia)* is a handsome bush, of recent introduction, and is a very desirable kind. It may group with the balearica and others.

The Cotoneaster microphilla, C. uvaursii, C. buxifolia, and C. marginata, are pretty, small-leaved, evergreen shrubs, of low habits. They produce small white blossoms and coral-like berries, similar to the pyracantha. I think C. microphilla the prettiest variety. They make very pleasing grass-plants, trained over old trunks of trees from two to three feet high ; or they may be planted in the midst of a group of three, four, or more moderate-sized stones, in order to bear them up. They are also proper for wire vases, or other wire trainers. They make handsome grass-plants, about three to four feet high, grafted or budded on the cockspur, or seedlings of any of the fancy varieties of thorns. If worked on stems too long, the stems require to be concealed by other low-growing shrubs, such as the taller species of erica and mahonias, &c. All these kinds, when not grafted, are particularly adapted to destroy the edging line of shrub beds.

The Red Virginian Cedar *(Juniperus Virginiana)* is a formal, close, spiral, upright, evergreen shrub, or low ornamental tree, attaining to the height of from twenty to thirty feet. Its flamular form and dense pine-like foliage, make it particularly neat, and well suited to vary the monotony of a shrubbery. It will be useful also in forming a group on the lawn, associated with the Swedish and Irish junipers, or with the arbor vitæ, if care be taken to place the cedar most central.

The White Cedar *(Cupressus thyoides)* forms a pleasing group when associated with the red, and with another variety of the white species, the foliage of which is variegated ; and also with the juniper. Both these kinds are handsome plants. The Cupressus torulosa, or twisted cypress, is, I believe, also a handsome tree, as are also C. lambertiana and funebris. The latter is said to be very beautiful indeed.

The Juniper, *(Juniperus)*, both the Swedish and Irish, are low flamular-formed shrubs, of dense, small, spiny foliage, and very similar to the red cedar, but of less growth. Of the two the Irish is the hardier, and grows

K 2

the more quickly. The Juniperus Chinensis is a beautiful evergreen shrub, suitable for the centre of a group of these plants, and the recurved juniper *(Juniperus recurva)* is also a handsome pendant variety, and quite hardy. All this tribe form pleasing groups of themselves, some being placed very near together, and others at different distances, yet not so far as to appear straggling. They are also proper plants to place occasionally in small groups on lawns of limited extent, and now and then in the midst of a group of low-growing shrubs, such as the ericas, Daphne mezereon, &c. The Irish and Swedish juniper are indispensable for points of beds at the junction of walks, inasmuch as they do not spread so as to interfere with the walks, nor require so broad a space to grow in, as a spreading bush would do.

The Cytissus purpurea, alba, roseus and secundens, are pretty, deciduous, low-growing, flowering shrubs ; but, in consequence of the two former being of a dwarf habit, their interest is a good deal lost. When, however, they are worked upon clean and handsome stems of the common laburnum, three or four feet high, their pretty pea-formed blossoms show well, and are highly appropriate for grass plants, but, like all other standards, their naked stems ought to be partially broken or concealed by other low shrubs, such as ericas, savins, and mahonias. The above kinds, on their own roots, would be proper to be occasionally placed together in one group. The white and purple are highly suitable for vases, and well adapted for front plants near the edges of beds.

The Andromeda floribunda is a very pretty dwarf evergreen shrub, which flowers early—a proper grass plant near the house. It requires peat soil.

The Daphne mezereon, especially the purple and white varieties, are low-growing, early flowering, odoriferous, deciduous shrubs; and therefore a few should always be planted near the house, grouping with some suitable evergreen shrubs.

The Daphne autumnalis (or Autumn Flowering Daphne) is a valuable species. It commences blooming towards the end of autumn, and continues so through the winter months, in mild seasons, and, consequently, claims a place within view of the windows. I believe the seed, or berry, of the mezereon is poisonous; therefore, where there are children, they should be charged not to eat them; or the berries should be gathered when green.

The Daphne cneorum is a beautiful, sweet scented, early flowering ever-green, and may be used as an interesting grass plant in the vicinity of the house, or near to the principal or general walk, with the assistance of a group of fancy stones, to elevate it about half a yard, or two feet. It may be planted on the natural level, and trained amongst the stones, which, in time, will spread over the whole, and form a very pleasing mass; or, it may very properly be supported by wire vases, or other contrivances; or, at pleasure, be planted in pots, to be placed in vases. It is also suitable for the edges of beds. It is handsome, as a low standard, grafted upon the wood laurel, Daphne mezereon, or Daphne pontica, two or three feet high.

Daphne collina latifolia is a beautiful, odoriferous, early flowering, ever-green shrub. This, also, should be planted near the house, and grouped with those of its family; but, being rather more tender than the rest, it should be provided with as much shelter as the circumstances of the place will admit of.

The Japan Quince Tree *(Cidonia Japonica)* is a beautiful scarlet flowering shrub, exhibiting its large showy blossoms early in the spring; and there is, also, a white variety. Both make pleasing grass plants as low standards, worked upon the Area theafrastii, or trained to form a short stem on their own roots. Sheltered and warm situations are necessary to mature the wood sufficiently to produce blossoms. These should be grouped with other plants, in order to break the stiff and formal appearance of the stem. Bushes of these plants, on their own roots, are also beautiful objects when in blossom; but, at other times, they wear a confused and ragged appearance. With care, the shrub may be trained to have a short single stem, and pretty fair in form. As this species blooms early, it should be planted near the residence.

The Heath *(Erica)*, the stricta, herbacea, multiflora, carnea, and australis, are indispensable as dwarf grass plants, and especially useful when introduced as associates to small standard shrubs. The Erica carnea being a very early bloomer, it will be proper to place it near the windows and walk sides, and it will be all the better if supported by a few fancy small stones, or spar, to elevate it, as before named. It is also suitable for pots, to place in vases, &c. Most of the varieties of ericas are proper for concealing the line of shrubberies.

The Kalmia latifolia is an admirable evergreen, and beautiful flowering grass plant, but requires a sheltered situation, such as a bay in the lawn, bounded by a thick shrubbery, so as to shield it from very severe weather. It thrives best in peat, or bog soil.

K. glauca and glauca elegans are highly beautiful and early blooming shrubs. They form a pretty group mixed with Rhododendron hirsutum, and ferrugineum.

The Camellia Japonica makes one of the most splendid shrubs imaginable, when it succeeds. It does pretty well in sheltered situations in the south of England. It requires to be embosomed in a thick group of evergreen shrubs, or on lawn in a bay of shrubs. I have no doubt it may be found to do well, too, in select places in the northern counties. At all events, such as are in pots for late blooming, when plunged in the lawn, and both pots and soil covered with moss, make handsome objects in sheltered spots near the windows.

The Jasmine *(Jasminum nudiflora)* makes a handsome grass plant, supported by a device of wirework, or it may be trained to a strong iron rod, and occasionally pruned, to keep it within bounds, but not in a stiff or formal manner. It is the handsomest of all the family, and highly valuable, because it blooms at a time when flowers are so scarce. Its green slender twigs, studded with bright canary-coloured blossoms, make it a beautiful object.

The Rhododendron ranks amongst the most favourite shrubs we have; all of them are highly ornamental and beautiful flowering evergreens. Some of the hybrids of catawbiense and ponticum are hardier than most of our evergreen shrubs. Some of the more tender kinds, such as R. Russelliana, R. nivaticum, R. Nobleana, Smith's white, R. campanulatum, and Cunnyngham's white, with many others, are truly splendid and mostly early bloomers. They may be grown to great perfection in moderately sheltered situations, if planted in proper composts of sandy peat, decayed turf, and leaves.

The R. Caucasicum, although a shy grower, is nevertheless indispensable on account of its buff or light yellow blossoms, so distinct from other varieties: and the Caucasicum album is also indispensable, on account of its healthy habit of growth, and free blooming, for which it is unrivalled.

The R. hirsutum and ferrugineum are pretty small flowering kinds, and are highly proper for grass plants, for fronting beds, and for destroying the edges of such beds as are eventually to blend naturally with the lawn.

R. dauricum atrovirens is quite distinct from any of the other species. It has small box-like foliage, exhibiting its purple blossoms very early in the spring, in favourable weather, and is very beautiful. The above kinds, with many other varieties, make splendid grass plants, but should be thrown into groups by themselves, or with the azalea.

The Yew, *(Taxus)*. The Irish Yew *(Taxus Hibernica)* is an upright, dark, glossy, sombre, and hardy evergreen shrub. Its close compact habit adapts it well for the lawn in confined spots, in points of beds dividing two walks. There are several other fine varieties of yews particularly worthy of notice as grass plants, such as Taxus Japonica, T. devastonii, T. Harringtonii, and T. elegantissima.

The Common Yew *(Taxus Vaccata)* is a fine evergreen low tree, and makes a handsome feathery grass plant; but, owing to its sombre appearance, few only ought to appear prominent. It is suitable for masking out objects, as well as a valuable, indeed one of the best, undergrowths we have. Besides, it is useful in destroying the earthy parts of shrubberies. The gold and silver-leaved varieties make very pleasing associates for the common yew, as well as the savin and juniper.

The Laurustine *(Viburnum tinus)* is a highly beautiful, large, evergreen, winter-flowering shrub, forming a thick but loose irregular bush, fitted for blockading and varying the lawn, or destroying the edge-line of shrub beds. It is liable to be injured in very severe winters, and therefore should not be placed in bleak situations. A group of two or three will be in character with a red cedar, or an upright and spreading cypress, rising out of the midst of them. Small and larger groups may be formed without any other associates.

ARRANGEMENT AND POSITION OF PLANTS OF PECULIAR

CHARACTER.

In planting the points of shrub beds at the junction of two walks, the conical or small upright kinds are the most suitable, as they are not so likely to spread and interfere with the walk, or with spreading shrubs. Small conical plants are also better adapted for all points of beds than spreading shrubs, as the latter become too large and out of proportion for such situations.

In arranging all trees and shrubs, it should be observed that in a group where there is a conspicuous tree, or one very strikingly marked in character, that should be placed seemingly in the middle, yet still avoiding formality and their being planted at equal distances from each other. For instance, the purple beech, with its striking foliage, would be more harmonious in the middle than on one side of a group composed of four or five trees of limes, chesnuts, or elms, &c., or the same number of any one kind. The same may be said of the pointed conical kinds, such as the spruce fir, red cedar, larch, Lombardy poplar, cypress, &c. One of these would appear to balance better, and be much more in harmony, in the midst of various pines, than if on one side. And again, a spiral or conical-growing tree never properly harmonizes with only one of a different character: as, for instance, the spruce fir and the lime; but add another lime, keeping the spruce central, or *vice versa*, two spruces and one spreading tree, and though there would be a great transition in colour and character, yet a pleasing effect would be produced.

These observations in like manner apply to the arrangement of low-growing trees and shrubs. For example: it would not be in harmony for the dense, round, formal Portugal laurel to be associated with only one shrub, whether spiral or loose-spreading; but with two or more of either of the former kinds at proper distances, (letting the Portugal laurel advance rather than otherwise), the effect would be pleasing. Again, one or more of the arbor vitæ, or other shrubs of upright and pointed habits, showing out of the midst of an occasional group of rhododendrons, would be in good taste; but place these near to, or on one side of the group, and the group would (so to speak) be unbalanced, and thereby lose both interest and beauty; and so with other kinds. *(See Plate of Groups, shewing the difference.)*

WEEPING TREES.—Of weeping trees there are several kinds—the weeping ash, elm, lime, new weeping beech, larch, laburnum, poplar, willow, and especially the new American weeping willow, which is the most elegant of weeping trees: the common weeping holly, too, is a very singular and pleasing plant, and Fraxinus lentiscifolia pendula is an elegant drooping tree, very superior to the common weeping ash. These are not distinct species, but varieties only of their respective families. Their singularly drooping habit, and the canopy they afford over seats, have seldom failed to create interest, excepting when viewed with a painter's eye, which scarcely can be reconciled to them; but, perhaps, with judicious management, their formality and roundness may be made to appear not quite so objectionable. They should be placed singly upon the lawn, near to, and fronting a mass or group of trees, or of such low-growing trees as will appear higher than the weeper. In this way its formality will be a good deal broken by its associates rising higher than itself, and seeming to form a lead, or centre to it; and, at any rate, its stiff formal appearance will not strike so forcibly upon the eye as to become offensive.

L

ON WALKS.

Dry gravel walks are indispensable for the enjoyment of scenery in the pleasure ground. We should therefore begin by forming a good, firm, straight walk through the whole length of the retired fronts of the house, or the sides with which the carriage entrance does not interfere. Such walk should not be less than nine or ten feet from the house, and exactly parallel with it, so as to afford room on the side next the house for vases, urns, basket-work, or other ornaments, to be placed in correspondence with what may be on the contrary side of the walk. *(See General Plans.)* This walk will also afford an important promenade when the weather is too doubtful to allow of a more distant stroll. The walks ancillary to the above should commence about the end of the building, bending very gradually from it—indeed, almost imperceptibly, at least for a few yards. In all cases where it can be done, some part of the approach to the house walk should be thrown sufficiently out to admit of the edifice being clearly seen in perspective, especially when the approach does not scan the house favourably: this is too often neglected. In many instances we see the beauties of costly edifices entirely lost to the observer, unless the house walk is left, and the lawn traversed to view them. At the same time, it is of importance that the winding walk itself should be hid from the window view as soon as convenient; and in no case should the repose of the lawn in front of the house be injured by the walk passing through or round it. Moreover, it must be remembered that it is always in bad taste to look across two walks at one view; and, except in limited town gardens, or where the ground is sufficiently undulated to lose the farther walk from the windows, such an error must be avoided.

In forming the width of the general or principal walks, we shall have to be a good deal guided by the extent or magnitude of the place. A residence of great pretensions should have the terrace or house walk from ten to fifteen feet wide; the principal winding walks from seven to nine feet wide; and the episodical walks, or those which divide the various compartments of the flower garden, or others purposely set apart to afford scenes of themselves, of less dimensions. A moderate villa residence should have a house walk six or seven feet wide, and the principal winding walk about five or six feet. No pleasure ground walks should be less than five feet wide, except the house and grounds are very small indeed, or the grounds very precipitous, where a four or five feet walk would not only be more readily formed, but would be more in character than one wider. In very abrupt rude situations, they should appear more like natural tracks. The principal walks uniting with the terrace walk should become gradually narrower, until they soften imperceptibly into its proper width. But where a returning walk intersects the principal one, that would be a still better place for its change, provided the distance is not too great to continue the whole breadth. Walks in kept grounds of gentle undulations or of a level surface, should invariably be of long, gentle or graceful sweeps; not only because such are most beautiful and pleasing, but because they are less interrupting to the student or reading pedestrian, than those of more sudden and numerous bends. *(See General Plan.)* At the junction of two principal walks, each should diverge gradually in an opposite direction from the other, *(figure* 17, *a)*, which would be more in character

FIGURE 17.

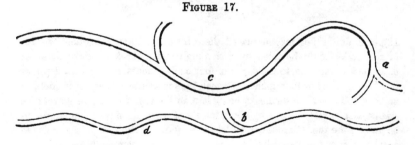

than if both inclined one way, *(figure* 17, *b)*. In many cases, a branch or subordinate walk should set off at right angles with the direct or general walk, of course rounding the sharp points off. Steep rugged ground, or ground of abrupt folds, naturally demands that the bends of the walks should be shorter and more numerous, for the purpose of obtaining the easiest ascents and descents. In woods or thickets, a short bend in a walk would be proper and quite in character, especially if there should be a fine tree, bush, seat, precipice, or any other object requiring a deviation. In all cases, the bends of walks must be sufficiently deep or bold *(figure 17, c)* to afford room for shrubs to be planted, so as to prevent the eye from looking over more than one bend at once. A walk taking, as it were, one direct line, with numerous zigzag or serpentine bends, *(figure 17, d)*, is objectionable in the extreme.

In the formation of a walk, the earth should be thrown out to allow a depth of stone, or gravel, of eight or nine inches; but, of course, if the soil is valuable, materials for forming the walk are plentiful, and expense is no consideration, there can be no objection to the soil being taken out to twice that depth. What I have named is sufficient to make a walk firm and dry, except in clayey and very retentive soil, in which case a drain should be made, six inches square, down the middle of the walk, and covered with a flag, *(figure*

FIGURE 18.

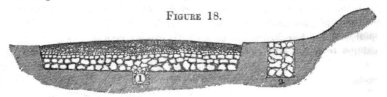

18), or draining tiles may be placed there instead. Then the whole breadth of the walk should be filled up with rough stones, broken bricks, dross, or other rough materials, to the depth of four or five inches, or to such a depth as to allow of three or four inches of small broken stones, averaging an inch, or an inch and a half, in diameter, being laid on the top of them; or gravel of a similar size would do, leaving room for about an inch only of fine gravel to be laid on the top. Care must be taken, in forming the level of the walk, to avoid the offensive barrel-like appearance which we commonly see; an inch and a half in the yard fall, from the middle to the side, will be quite sufficient. Previous to laying on the fine gravel, (if it is not of itself of a cementing nature), this foundation must be well rolled, and then have spread on it as much of scrapings from limestone roads as will just fill up the crevices; or, if this cannot be procured, very small dirty limestone or chalk scrapplings, or equal parts of lime, sand, and road-scrapings of any kind, may be substituted with pretty good effect. In all cases, rolling is essential to keep the whole firm and smooth; and this, if done in summer, will be best effected a few hours after rain. In most cases, rolling in dry weather loosens the gravel, rather than otherwise; therefore, at times, it will be necessary to have recourse to watering. I consider it a very important feature, in pleasure grounds, to have the walks firm and smooth, and quite free from loose gravel,—an evil much too prevalent. It is, indeed, too common a practice to hoe and rake the walks; whereas, if they are hand-weeded properly, (the weeds being on no account allowed to seed), and kept firm by rolling, the labour soon becomes trifling, in comparison with the slovenly and expensive practice just named. Hoeing and raking, by the way, never leave an easy, smooth, walking path. Deep edges to the walk sides must be carefully avoided. They should never at any time show a greater depth, from the top of the turf to the gravel, than one inch; neither should the edges ever wear the earthy appearance occasioned by cutting with the edging-iron, or spade, except more than, perhaps, once a year, to keep the walks to their true form and width; as it is quite possible to have them kept very even, and with the greatest neatness, with proper grass shears.

Where walks are formed on the sides of hills, they are liable to be damp; drains, therefore, should be formed on the upper side of the walks, and parallel with them *(figure* 18, 2). Grates should be placed at proper distances, close to the walks, with receptacles to catch the sand and refuse which are carried from the walk sides by the top-water caused by heavy rains. *(Figure* 19.*)* Each of these receptacles should be about fifteen or eighteen inches square, and about a foot deeper than the drain which is to take off the water from it, *(figure* 19, *a),* in order that the sand may lodge below the mouth of the drain. They must, also, be fre-

FIGURE 19.

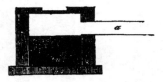

quently cleared out, so that the drain may not fill up. The drains which branch from the sump-hole, or depôt, may be taken to the drain in the middle of the walk, or to a principal drain elsewhere; or, in the absence of such principal drains, a suitable cess-pool may be formed at a little distance.

Grates, five inches by seven, fixed loose into a small frame of iron, wood, or stone, would afford sufficient room for cleaning out the pit; and this size would not be so offensive to the eye as larger ones. To make them still less objectionable, it would be better to fix them either entirely in the grass verge, or as close to it as possible, and only a very little lower than the level of the walk.

In situations where it is necessary for the walks to be very abruptly steep, small rises, like steps, should be formed, having the flats, or treads, three or four feet broad. This may be done by first placing a larch trunk across the whole width of the walk, to form the front of the rise, and then filling up the whole with fine gravel, or paving it with pebbles or very small paving stones, in a gradual ascent, until it is necessary to place another trunk, and so on. If this is not attended to, such steep parts left in the usual way are liable to be disfigured and greatly injured by rapid runs of water; they are, moreover, actually unsafe.

Grass walks are soft, cool, and inviting: a luxury in hot dry weather, but useless in wet weather. When room is plentiful, and the expense of keeping them in order no object, such walks may be formed through wooded scenery. In doing this, formality must be avoided: the walks should be of various or irregular widths—sometimes three or four yards, and at others ten or fifteen —fringed naturally with bushes, or shrubs and trees. In order to make a grass walk of this kind more generally useful, it must be kept closely mown and well drained.

ON WATER.

THERE are two styles of water to be considered, namely, that which is still, and that which is in motion, or even turbulent. Naturally, water, whether as lake or rill, river or sea, mere or waterfall, forms, in its various characters, an object most beautiful, captivating, and even sublime; and, certainly, it is an invaluable element in landscape scenery. Let us notice it particularly in the following forms, namely,—The Streamlet, Brook, River, Lake, and Sea.

The simple, yet cheerful Streamlet, rippling by the side of a rural, shady walk, now concealed beneath some thicket, now breaking again over shelfy stones, has been most poetically described by Doubleday:—

> " Now, moving scarce, with noiseless step, and still;
> Anon it seems to weary of its rest,
> And hurries on, leaping with sparkling zest,
> Adown the ledges of the broken hill."

The Brook pleasingly winds its devious way, calmly and smoothly, through rural scenery.

The River meanders through a beautiful fertile vale, having its margin fringed with sylvan dress, whose waving branches playfully lash its stream; or forcing its way furiously through rocky channels and abrupt broken ground, (as in the neighbourhood of Bolton Abbey),—each of these is ever to be admired.

The Lake lies among hills and mountains, and is of various extent, from a mile to many miles; sometimes screened with wood, at others, decked only with humble shrubs, yet having on its bosom fleecy clouds reflected, and an incessant variation of sun and shade, charms the soul; while the mighty Sea, with its restless billows, and the stately ships which traverse its waves, is an element in a landscape equally beautiful and sublime.

But in making alterations in water-courses, or in forming lakes or ponds, we must ever remember the true character which they ought to assume. A streamlet, for instance, may be improved in rude and wild situations by clearing away wild indigenous plants in proper places, so as to let the eye now and then catch a glimpse of it as it ripples over collections of roots and stones, &c. Sometimes a slight natural fall may be improved by raising it judiciously with stones, and sinking the course below, so that the depth of the fall may be increased, and the course made broader here and there, especially above and below where a bridge is to be carried over (in order to show a cause for a bridge); keeping, however, to natural and varied outlines, the water not too deep nor too wide, lest it should lose the character of a rill, and become a brook, which it would do if it were more than five or six feet in breadth, and densely deep. In thus interfering with the natural course of a streamlet, care should be taken to vary its course by bends and planting, so that the eye may not be able to see from the bridge narrow parts, and those which are barely covered with water, as such would give an idea of the bridge being useless.

A Rill may also be usefully and with very good effect taken through grounds of a more polished character. In such cases I should make deep and natural bends, varying its breadth; at the same time the margin should be kept neat, so as to be in harmony with the lawn, and the bottom of the rill should be covered with white pebbles, to give a cleanliness and cheerfulness to it. The deepest part of the water should not be more than ten or twelve inches. When a rill of this kind can be made to ripple cheerfully along, and at times glide silently through a flower garden, it may become available for the growth of interesting aquatic plants. Further interest may be afforded by introducing fancy fish into the water; but in this case small covered retreats will have to be formed in the deepest parts under the margin, to afford them shelter.

The Rivulet, or Brook, being a more extensive stream of water than a rill, and being sometimes rapid in its course, can scarcely be said to be in character in the flower garden or highly kept grounds; but it may often be made highly interesting, especially in cases where perpendicular precipices present themselves of materials adapted to form a cascade, or fall, and where the brook can be conveniently turned over it. Where the ground is steep,

81

without either rocks or stones, a fall may be formed by excavating a sufficient width out of the bank to afford room to lay, or wall, large rude stones, from a quarter of a ton to two or more tons in weight, as circumstances permit; and these should be placed (of course, the largest at the bottom) so as to form a natural, broken, and rough concave, appearing, as much as possible, as if worn by time. In an extensive cascade there should be slopes and perpendicular parts; and, in some parts of the slopes, the water should be divided by large blocks of stone, leaving cavities at intervals in the course, for bushes of ferns, or other low plants capable of bearing the spray. The streams must meet again before entering the principal perpendicular fall. In order to prevent the water from taking a wrong course behind the stones, cement should be used in the joints. A good clay-puddle will answer, if the stones are properly bedded in the clay, and well puddled behind them : clay and gravel, or small broken stones, must also be well worked together into the crevices. It will be important to observe, in walling the fall, that more than the breadth required for the watercourse will be necessary, and various breadths of rockery must appear. It is desirable, too, to place the stones in beds, showing natural seams, and forming lesser and greater shelfy projections. A small pool of water, a few yards in diameter, should lie at the bottom of the cascade. It should be of considerable depth just where the water falls, to give the appearance of its depth being caused by time, through the action of the water. This pool, as well as the watercourse,—at least in the vicinity of the fall, and from points whence the fall is seen,—must wear the same character, by being varied with larger and smaller stones, and thus harmonize with the principal rock. The fall should be viewed from a walk passing near to it, from a seat, or from a bridge crossing the brook. To give greater variety, if the ground will allow, the stream may occasionally be brought to spread into various breadths, fringed with indigenous bushes, presenting, as much as possible, a brook in all its natural character. These, with other interesting parts of the same rivulet, should be brought within the range of view of the continued walk, and, at other times, retire so as to be totally lost in thickets. The murmuring sounds, also, should at times be lost, and again the ear may be cheered by them, alternately distant and nearer, thereby producing variety and pleasurable interest.

A River.—To divert the course of a river, or form a cascade across it, would be a gigantic work, and a question of expenditure; but when this is not a consideration, sometimes a noble cascade may be obtained. To form a natural fall, secure against floods or heavy water, will be attended with more difficulty than one which is built with regular masonry. Still it is possible to form such a fall with massive stones, some tons in weight, judiciously and firmly placed in mortar; but to do this effectually, a considerable breadth of dam in all parts will have to be employed; and perhaps, in most cases, a wall will be required, as shown in the sketch on Romantic Scenery, where the river fall is again treated upon. The fall must not be formed in one straight line across the river, but varied by deep and rugged recesses and angular projections, letting the convex parts meet the stream, which must be broken by masses or considerable blocks of stone, rising in groups above the water here and there to give variety. When the river happens to run over the slope of a dam of masonry, it may be varied very much by groups of stones here and there being allowed to stand some inches higher than the rest.

When it is thought proper to improve the course of a river, either by varying its breadth when it is considered too formal, or entirely changing its course, so as to bring it more interestingly into view from the mansion, nature should be strictly kept in view and imitated. Its course should not be smooth and uniform, but its margins or banks should present deep bends and angular as well as bold projections, evidently producing various breadths of water: and it is important that its course should be so directed that the spectator may view as much of its length as possible, rather than look across it; and as we see the natural course of a river formed by interruptions of gentle and abrupt swells in the ground, with masses and groups of trees and bushes, by which the stream is driven to take the lowest and uninterrupted ground, so, in forming a new course, such examples will have to be imitated. Islands may be occasionally introduced in some of the wider parts. In planting the margins, which must be kept free in some places, so as to command the best points of view on the river, alders, willows, junipers, ferns, rushes, &c., may be employed. The dress must be least wild in those parts where the margin of the river and the adjoining ground are naturally smooth.

A Lake, or Pond.—In arranging a sheet of water, our best skill will often be called into exercise; and we must, therefore, always bear in mind that water seeks its bed in the lowest ground. It is, undoubtedly, proper that the lowest part of the ground should be made choice of for the formation of

83

a sheet of water. As a proof of this, natural lakes (which we ought always to imitate) are generally seen to rest in flats, or valleys. It is quite unnatural to look over a sheet of water into lower ground beyond. When the lowest ground cannot be made available, so as to bring the water into view from the house, or the pleasure ground, and a higher level must unavoidably be taken, the view beyond must be stopped by planting. The designer, therefore, after he has fixed the sites, and taken such levels as may be considered most suitable for the purpose, will at once see the necessity of judicious planting about the lower end of the lake, so as to fill up, and shut out, as much as possible, the appearance of the valley below, especially in the vicinity of the lake. In most cases this will give the appearance, in a great degree, of water resting on a natural flat. In lining out such lakes, natural, bold, and angular prominences, and deep bays, must be produced, rather than tame, zigzag, or small indentations. At the same time, these deep bends and prominences must not be of regular smooth curves, but broken occasionally by small, varied, and natural indentations. *(See Park Plan.)*

In kept grounds, lakes or ponds must be characterised by the same bold curves; but the margins should be kept neat, with smooth grass to the water's edge, rather than consist of deep, earthy, and broken banks. Yet gentle and abrupt grassy swells, rising immediately from the water, are important acquisitions; and some portions of the margins may be fringed with interesting and suitable plants.

Independently of the kept grounds, nature must be imitated by showing, as may be suitable, abrupt, broken, earthy, rooty, and rugged grassy margins, now and then embellished with bushes and trees.

It is of the utmost consequence, in order to prevent accidents by persons falling into the water, that there should be a shelf, or ledge, formed all round the lake, or pond, four or five feet broad, which need only be covered from six to eight inches deep with water.

Islands are indispensable in pools, or lakes, of considerable dimensions; they not only add greatly to the variety and interest of the scene, but are of importance in assisting to conceal the real extent of the water.

The greatest depth of water in a lake should never, if possible, exceed five feet, in order to render it safe from accident during sailing excursions, and winter amusements on the ice. This depth is, moreover, quite sufficient for fish, proper provision being made for their retreat, in severe weather, about the islands and in the deepest parts of the water. These retreats may be composed of roots of trees, or stones, reared together; or stones, sunk at intervals, with a slate across them. The water should also be clear and not stagnant, and kept free from rubbish.

Whatever may be the character the water is to assume, whether pond or lake, the site having been decided upon, we must first determine the levels. If the fall of ground is considerable, it will generally be better to lower the highest side, rather than to raise the head or dam too much. I would rather lose sight of a portion of the water nearest the point of view by the rising ground, than have a prodigious embankment; this would, in almost every case, not only be found to work better but please the eye more, especially with a judicious sloping of the higher ground, and with proper breaks in planting. The levels being taken, a better notion of the form of the water will be ascertained. But in staking out in undulated ground, advantage must be taken of the lowest parts of the ground, to give breadth or expanse to the water, and variety of form in its outline. Otherwise, cutting down the rising knolls would not only cause additional expense, but greatly lessen the variety of surface, which we ought ever to study to preserve. I have before stated it to be essential that the outline or margin of the pond or lake should exhibit bold prominences and deep recesses, naturally varied; therefore, where a bridge is to be introduced, two of these prominences should be brought near enough together to afford a natural site for that purpose, *(see Lake in Park Plan)*, and also that the space of the bridge may not be too great for the size and extent of the water,—say from five to thirty yards long. An extensive sheet of water will require a large bridge, and *vice versa* with a small sheet. Where a bridge is not required for convenience sake, but only for effect, one end of it may rest on an island; in which case, the latter must be sufficiently large to make a bridge seem useful for landing upon it. A hut for aquatic animals will render its utility still more apparent. In shaping the embankment or head, much will depend upon its depth and extent. If the valley, where the head is formed, be narrow, its construction will not be difficult; but should it be wide, great caution will be required, not only for security against the pressure of water, but that its outline may be as natural as circumstances will allow. This will generally be best managed, and the pressure of water best borne, by forming a large and bold promontory to shoot out a considerable extent into the lake, of sufficient surface to allow of an outlet for the water, and room for planting on each side of it, without interfering with the puddle. This will be most properly effected by raising the ground a little above the general level, (with the exception of the margin close to the water), and so providing depth of soil for the roots to work in. Further, in forming the embankment or head of a pond or lake, it should slope considerably under the water, *(figure* 20), starting from the edge of the plat-

FIGURE 20.

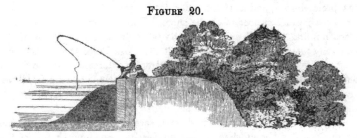

form I have before named as a safeguard against accidents. This gives great strength to the dam, inasmuch as the water bears upon the slope, and is not so liable to burst the bank as if the latter were more perpendicular. An equal, or rather greater, slope will be required on the contrary side of the bank; and it is indispensable that a firm wall should be built where the water passes over, to prevent its being washed down. But if an interesting fall is to be formed, (which certainly ought to be if water is plentiful, and if a walk can with propriety pass near it), it should be built in a natural, firm, rude form, with large massive stones. Islands, judiciously managed, afford variety, and assist to lessen deformities common in the construction of heads or dams of pools, and also indicate extent. One island near the head will generally be necessary; and, if sufficiently large and well managed, will be better than more. This should be placed ten or twenty yards from the outlet, and perhaps should be the widest across the pond parallel with the dam; letting the side next the outlet of the water form a broken or irregular concave, in order to harmonize with the convex or promontory stretching into the water. Then, a little above the island, the margin or outline of both sides of the pond should be made to project into the water, so that, conjointly with the island, the eye may be prevented from discerning the end, or outlet of water; thereby deceiving the mind as to its real extent. But in order to effect this properly, bushes and trees must be planted on the island and on the sides of the lake. *(See Park Plan.)*

In lakes or pools of considerable extent, groups of islands would be effective, and ought to be introduced, in preference to their being scattered singly all over the water. They must, further, be placed not as if by design, but rather to appear in connection with some of the smaller, or moderate-sized promontories, and as if the water from time to time, had severed them from the adjoining projection of the shore. Whatever may be the number of islands forming a group, care should be taken to have the largest of them about the centre. For instance:—on all the sides but that next the shore, the smaller islands will appear most in character outermost, and the distance from one another must vary considerably. These islands may be from five to thirty yards or more from the side of the water, according to its extent; but must be sufficiently far from the middle not to appear central.

In a lake of fifty or one hundred acres, several groups, composed of three, four, or five, of different shapes, may be formed; and one or two of these may be of considerable extent,—say, from a quarter of an acre to one or two acres. This will not only give importance and magnitude, but afford room and convenience for the erection of huts for aquatic animals, retreats for fishers, ornamental lighthouses, &c. In addition to these groups of islands, a few may be sometimes placed singly near a concave bend, or in advance of a promontory. It will be essential to vary the size of the islands, especially in the groups,—say, from a few yards in extent, to the larger above mentioned. They must be of irregular and natural forms, with broken margins, not lumpy, but lengthy, letting their length be most parallel with the shore. *(See Lake in Park Plan.)* Although I recommend the avoidance of formality in placing islands, yet I think the appearance on both sides the lake should in some measure be equalized, leaving the widest portion of water about the middle, but still naturally broken or varied with the islands. Were there a large island and numerous small ones on one side of the lake only, from some points of view the water would appear (if I may so speak) out of balance, leaving the eye dissatisfied. This effect must be guarded against.

. I have already referred to the prevention of danger as necessary to be observed in the formation of water. Such danger too frequently arises from the usual way of forming ponds or lakes, and the means by which it should be averted are these:—First, It is quite unnecessary to have deep water close to the margin; as there is the same breadth or extent of water, and certainly an equally good effect is produced, when the water is shallow, as when it is of considerable depth. I urge it, therefore, as of the first importance, that a shelf or platform, four or five feet broad, should be formed all round the margin of the lake, admitting only of water resting upon it to the depth of from six to nine inches, so that should even an infant fall in, its life would scarcely be in danger. *(Fig. 21, a.)* This platform may fall from the margin towards the water to the extent of four or five feet, at the rate of about an inch in the foot; the slope from that point must be much more rapid, until it

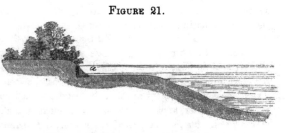

FIGURE 21.

ends in the deepest part. If white pebbles, or pebbles of any kind, or even small stones mixed with sand, could be spread all over the shelf, it would add much to the clearness of the water, and the general beauty of the water's edge. All the margin in natural and varied surface should not appear smooth and even, but nature should be studiously imitated; and this will be greatly promoted by allowing at intervals steep or deep earthy margins to appear, and large stones, and roots or stumps of trees, to present themselves in masses and groups. Of course the margins in polished or kept grounds must assume a varied appearance, without being rude.

In all ponds or lakes, it is necessary to use puddle of clay, or finely sifted earth, in places where embankments are made to dam the water, in order to prevent leakage. In such parts, I should propose the puddle-dike to be made in the ledge, or shelf above-named, where, I think, it would be the least liable to be injured by the roots of trees and bushes. The bottom of the lake, also, when the materials are not naturally retentive, will require puddling, especially about and under the dam, or other raised parts.

Trees and bushes are indispensable as embellishments to water. They are important for concealing the real extent of a lake, besides producing light and shade; and their shadows, moving playfully on the glossy water, never fail to afford pleasure. In planting near water, we must not interrupt the best and most lengthened views of it, as seen from the house and the principal parts of the park, or pleasure ground; neither must we make such a disposition of the elements at our command as entirely to shut out from view the whole of the ends, or boundaries, of the outward prominences, or some of those parts which project into the water. At the same time caution must be used not only to prevent the eye from catching the various bends of the outline of water from any one point of view, (which would be bad), but also so as to afford variety in the grouping of the trees and shrubs: indeed, the whole planting must be so effected as to leave the extent of the water undetected, and even unimagined, from any one position.

The following may be named as suitable for planting in the neighbourhood of water. Those to be employed as low growths in kept grounds, are the common heath, ferns, double Ayrshire roses, sweet gale, English juniper, dwarf spreading willow, Andromeda polyfolia, Ledum palustre, and other sorts. The alder, kept low by occasional cutting, makes a fine fringe, and a strong barrier for the margins of water when the current is liable to wash away its banks. The common thorn, bramble, hedge rose, red dogwood, honeysuckle, and blackthorn, afford proper marginal dress for water in all natural scenery. Trees suitable for embellishing pools, lakes, or rivers, are of various kinds. Those best adapted for positions nearest the water, where the ground is liable to be moist, are the common alder, various kinds of willows, (including the weeping and rosemary-leaved willow), Alnus cordifolia, Norway spruce, deciduous cypress, and hemlock-spruce. Such plants are also quite proper for the islands; but in order that the roots may not lodge too much in water, the parts of the islands to be planted should be raised irregularly, or in a natural manner, with stones, roots, sods, &c., mixed with suitable soil, a few feet higher than the level of the water. The five last-named kinds of trees are most appropriate for beautifying water in dress ground. Amongst the larger trees employed, not exactly fringing the margin, but at a moderate distance from the water, the wych elm is the most elegant, and should always be planted in extensive places: its elegant massive twigs and pendent branches entitle it, above all other large trees, to this distinction. Nevertheless, the English elm, lime, beech, weeping birch, and larch, will be proper. I do not mean to say that other trees would not be appropriate, but these are amongst the best. Every kind of poplar should be excluded, except, indeed, the

Lombardy, of which two or three may be planted so as to rise out of the midst of masses of other trees.

In planting, room should be allowed for walking on the water's edge; sometimes close to it, and at other times with a bush, or group of shrubs, interposing.

Small fancy boats are needful for recreation and pleasure, besides adding to the interest of the scenery. In the latter sense, sails would be an addition. Swans, by all means, must be introduced, as well as other water fowls.

A striking effect might be attained by introducing into the lake a floating island. While I was engaged in laying out a gentleman's grounds in the Lake district, a natural floating island was pointed out to me at the head of Esthwaite Lake, near Hawkshead, which was composed of low growths, matted firmly together, and studded with a few living, but stunted, low growing trees, which appeared to act as sails in moving the island from side to side, as the wind might direct. This phenomenon has suggested the idea of its being imitated, in the formation of lakes or ponds in pleasure grounds, to give additional variety to the scene. Nor would this be the only advantage, but the spectacle of trees, bushes, and minor vegetation thus floating, would have a singular and rare effect. The size of such an island may vary according to circumstances: we will suppose twenty-four feet by twelve. In the first instance, boards must be nailed together on ribs, or bearers of wood, four or six inches square, forming a boarded floor, or flat. This, again, should be boarded round, forming a ledge, or belt, ten or twelve inches deep, as a receptacle for the soil and plants, but, altogether, exhibiting as varied an outline as possible. The whole will require to be filled with soil, rising naturally from the sides to the middle, in different elevations of from two to four feet, carelessly and negligently sodded with ling, rushes, aquatic ranunculus, mosses, &c., and showing, at intervals, a few stumps and rude stones. About the centre of the island, two or three alders might be planted, and, occasionally, a patch of small growing willows, sea buckthorn, sweet gale, with rambling roses and honeysuckles to climb up the trees.

BRIDGES.

A BRIDGE is an important feature in connection with water, and seldom fails to give interest to the landscape. It ought to be placed to front the best point of view, or nearly so. In forming a piece of water, (as before shewn), a narrow neck must be contrived either between an island and the outline of the pond, or the whole piece must be so contracted that the bridge shall not be too long or extensive. *(See Park Plan.)* But as a bridge may tend also to give an idea contrary to the repose and privacy which a lake generally suggests, its position should be carefully chosen. At all events, it should be placed so as to give as much of the lake as possible on the side between it and the principal point of view from the residence *(see Plan);* because a bridge suggests the idea of a public road, and a public road would naturally fix, as it were, the boundary of the park or domain, and lead to the conclusion that the water beyond it may not belong to the domain. Perhaps the best position would be at some narrow part of the lake, as remote as convenient, so as to shew the principal body of water between the bridge and the place from whence it is viewed, and that, whilst crossing the bridge, the boundary of the water should be completely lost to the eye in various parts, as well by its position as by judicious planting. Thus the extent of a moderate sheet of water might be concealed, even from the stroller crossing the bridge. *(See Plan.)* I have frequently seen a bridge placed across the neck of a pond, so near to its extremity as to suggest to the spectator whether it could have been formed for any utility at all, and thus destroying the interest which might have been created had utility been more apparent.

Of whatever a bridge may be composed, whether of wood, iron, or stone, or of whatever extent it may be, it should be perfectly horizontal or level across. The effect is inharmonious when it falls each way from the centre.

A bridge of masonry is best adapted for a river, on account of the probability of its use by public conveyances; therefore, the appearance of strength would be appropriate. In this case, as in all others, a bridge will have its importance and usefulness increased when viewed from any principal point, by a connecting walk or road being more or less seen not far from it; at least so near as to seem to lead to it, and leave no doubt on the mind as to its utility.

The kind of bridge most suitable for a walk interrupted by a rivulet or brook, in a wood or other rural or uncultivated scenery, is one simply formed of rude wood work, as delineated in *figure* 22. When a walk can be carried across a rivulet in front of a cascade or fall, about ten or twenty yards distant from it, a bridge will add interest to the scenery, and afford convenience to the spectator in viewing the fall. A bridge crossing a rill in a flower garden, or other polished parts of the pleasure grounds, may be of iron; but one constructed of larch rods and poles stripped of their bark, and stained

FIGURE 22.

—not painted—though less characteristic, would be generally pleasing. *(Figure 23.)* This kind of bridge would also be proper for a lake, with a number of arches according to extent, unless the drive should cross an extensive lake; then a more substantial bridge of masonry, with stone battlements, would be more appropriate. When stone is scarce, stone piers may be finished with strong rustic wood battlements; or battlements of a more finished character may be substituted for stone. A drive interrupted by a brook in the park or elsewhere should have a bridge of masonry, as it harmonizes with any kind of landscape, whether rural or picturesque, or of gentle or abrupt undulations. In abrupt rocky scenery, a simple stone bridge

FIGURE 23.

would be better than any other kind. However, in lieu of stone, a solid bridge of strong larch of the above kind may be formed.

I should recommend that the wood bridges be made of peeled poles and rods, stained oak colour, or something similar. Iron bridges should be painted (perhaps bronzed) green, or iron colour; never light green.

The ends of all bridges must be finished off with trees or bushes. Those upon a large scale should have noble, round-headed trees for their decorations, such as the wych and English elm, weeping willow, lime, oak, and alder; but the best of all is the wych elm. All should be more or less associated with loose-growing bushes. For smaller bridges in kept grounds, the hemlock-spruce, deciduous cypress, tamarisk, Robinia microphilla, sea buckthorn, rosemary-leaved willow, English juniper, &c. For small bridges in wild scenery: alders, willows, thorns, hollies, honeysuckles, rambling roses, brooms, whins, &c.

SEATS, AND OTHER GARDEN ORNAMENTS.

Seats are essential to pleasure grounds. They may be of various forms and character. Open seats may be made of wire, some of lattice work, and others of round larch rods, or crooked oak branches. Latticed seats should be formed of four or five screeds of deal, one inch thick by two broad, and six or seven feet long, (leaving half an inch between each), and nailed upon three neat trusses or bearers, with or without backs. If backs are attached, they should be neat, light, and ornamental.

The Rustic Open Seats, of larch and oak, are formed similar to the other, or by nailing the rods across two long bearers, with or without backs, with feet at each end, in the manner generally practised; always minding to have the cross rods even and easy to sit upon. The two former kinds of seats should be placed in the dress grounds, and those composed of larch and oak in more rural scenery. Covered seats are indispensable structures to afford shelter from rain, sun, and wind. Some should be ornamental, composed of boards and lattice work, or wire, beautified in the inside with cornices and plain or fluted panels. Beautiful ornamental wood houses are necessary, having windows and doors made to lock up. These may be used as reading rooms: others may be of a ruder character, yet still architectural, composed of boards, varied by nailing straight rods of larch, or hazel, over them, inside as well as outside, forming panels, or other devices. Fir cones, also, may be used for embellishing the inside. These seats should have low, broad, or old English windows of glass, in diamonds of lead.

Grottos, or Mineral and Shell Seats.—These may be round, octagonal, octagonally ovated, or of other fancy forms; built first with brick, then coated over on the outside with small fancy stones, or sea pebbles, fixed in cement or mortar. They should have windows on each side of the door, either Gothic or old English; the inside must be panelled, beautified with rich minerals, shells, and pebbles, and mingled with different kinds of mosses, especially the blue, (such as are to be found amongst ling and on trees), and the knotted kind, which is white when dried, and which grows in moist or wet places.

The Moss House and Ling House are of a ruder character. The former may be circular, with three open entrances; the other parts may be walled with bricks, and the inside must be lined with rude boards; and, about two feet above the seat, short, crooked oak sticks, about an inch thick, may be nailed on in different sized irregular figures. These, and the rest of the back, may be lined in patches or masses of one colour, with various kinds of mosses blending naturally with each other. The roof may be slated and covered with ling, projecting nine inches or a foot over the erection. The inside of the roof should be lined with moss, either of one colour or of different shades, (that is, each division between the spars to possess one kind, or shade). The entrances should be formed by four rude trunks of trees, five to six feet long above ground, and from nine to fifteen inches in diameter, with low arches springing from their tops. The seats may be covered with platted silk, ling, or Egyptian matting. The front of the seats may be finished with a bordering of stick-work, four or five inches broad, and the seats themselves should be supported by trunks of trees.

The Ling House may also be round or an octagonal oblong, formed of six or eight trunks of trees sunk into the ground, or let into large stones. The spaces between them may be filled up with slips of wood, so as to allow the whole to be thickly covered, inside and out, with ling, leaving an entrance and two open irregular-formed windows. The top must be covered with slates, and ling over them, projecting nine inches or a foot over the whole building.

The trellis and wire seats (which ought to be of the most pleasing designs,) are suitable for the flower garden: rude seats should not be introduced into any of the dress ground. Perhaps the grotto would not be out of character placed in a massive shrubbery. The moss and ling huts will be best placed in wooded or rural scenery.

The Aviary.—An aviary is a proper object to be introduced into the pleasure ground. It should be an elegant structure, affording proper compartments for the different families of birds; and while there should be plenty of light, there should also be shady places for their retreat in hot weather. The aviary should be placed in some part of the dress ground, where the shrubbery will afford concealment for a small shed, in which to place a boiler and fire-place for warming the aviary with hot water. The portion of pleasure ground selected for the aviary should be planted with ornamental trees and shrubs, blended with lawn of sufficient extent to afford room for the erection or formation, here and there, of retreats for large interesting birds, cages for small birds, and perches or poles for hawks, owls, parrots, &c., when it is thought proper to have them in the open air. In this way the general combination would be varied and pleasing.

Garden ornaments of various devices, formed of wire, such as rods of iron topped with wire in the style of an umbrella, for creepers, wire vases, and numerous other plant-bearers, and basket work for round beds, may be introduced into the dress ground; but no rude device, such as tree roots, tubs, or other rude materials : such are more in character with scenery not so highly cultivated.

Dials.—Dials are very useful objects in pleasure grounds. They should be placed so as to let the sun's rays fall upon them throughout the whole of the day, and in frequented parts, where there can be a ready access to them. The junction of two walks diverging from each other would be a very suitable position; also in front of a greenhouse or of any other ornamental structure.

Vases and Urns are suitable ornaments for placing on the terrace wall of the mansion, in front of greenhouses, on each side of steps, and in any other places connected with buildings. Vases may be placed with propriety in dress ground, on the gravel, at the junction of two walks diverging from each other, in order to finish the point of grass dividing the walks. They should be furnished with plants in pots, placed inside, so that they may be replenished at pleasure; and the earth and pots should be covered with moss, which will give a neat and clean appearance, as well as prevent the roots of the plants from drying so fast as they would do if they were exposed to the sun and wind.

Statues are very interesting objects in kept grounds when introduced occasionally, and assembled in groups according to their relative characters. The obvious intention of such appendages is to recall to mind personages and events which transpired in bygone days, and they have, therefore, a tendency to withdraw the contemplative mind from other interesting objects which are to be found in a flower garden. On this account, recesses of lawn in shrubbery walks are the most proper places for their introduction. If introduced upon the general lawn, they should be so placed as to be a good deal embosomed in shrubs, that they may not present themselves prominently from every point of view, but rather burst suddenly upon the eye on its approach, and thereby create surprise and pleasure.

FOUNTAINS.

ORNAMENTAL FOUNTAINS are of various kinds. The two drooping fountains represented at *figures* 24 and 25 are neat, and amongst the most pleasing and suitable, especially for placing near the house, or in any dress scenery. Of course they will have to be finished in the style of the house, whether Gothic or Grecian. I should never recommend a fountain of any design to be lofty, but from six to twelve feet high, according to the body of the water. When too much elevated, the streamlets, which ought to fall regularly, are more liable to be thrown out of order. It is, indeed, the regularity of the streams from the basins, together with a perpendicular boiling jet, which constitutes, to my mind, the very essence of effect in a fountain. Water should never be permitted to fall from off the basins of a fountain, now in agitated splashes and then in more gentle streams. It is discordant either with order or design. An instance of what I mean was shown in the two fountains in Trafalgar-square, London, as they appeared in 1848. If the water of these fountains were only allowed to rise six or eight feet from the orifice with the whole body of water, and regulated in the pressure so as to avoid flickering or jerking about, I have no doubt a proper and good effect would be produced.

FIGURE 24.

Numerous devices may be made to screw upon the end of the outletting pipe of ornamental fountains. Amongst the best are the umbrella, convolvulus, tulip, and Catharine wheel. But, in my opinion, the grandest effect of all is produced when a column of water is allowed to boil or rise boldly and freely out of the whole width of the pipe, which should appear about six or eight inches above the upper basin or projecting rim of the column. The water may rise from two to six feet yet higher, according to the supply, only so as to preserve its density or boiling effect, and to keep within the limits of the basin without spreading into mere spray or mist. A fountain

FIGURE 25.

of half-inch bore is as small a size as ought to be adopted. One of an inch bore would produce a pretty good effect; but a magnificent one would require twice or thrice that bore.

A rude kind of fountain, or, more properly, a jet, might be introduced upon a rocky island in a lake or pond, or in grounds wearing an aspect of wilder character than the dress ground; the principal cone to be a rude stone, three or four feet above the pool, a hole being drilled through the middle of it to admit of a proper sized pipe. The diameter of the stone may be from twelve to eighteen inches at its summit, and proportionately thicker at the bottom, which altogether should present a rough uneven surface, having larger and smaller protuberances. This stone may be the principal one, rising out of the midst of smaller long pointed ones of different heights, placed so near or close to each other as to represent a natural splitting cone starting out of a rocky island. The rock or island should be formed sufficiently solid and extensive to allow of several smaller cones appearing from two to five feet above water, according to the magnitude of the design; or cones may be formed more conveniently without the centre stone above named, by a pile of pointed stones closely and connectedly placed, leaving a space for the column of water to rise from a pipe concealed in the centre. The scene will require varying by clusters of large stones rising just above the water at intervals, pretty near the island, to suggest the idea of extent under water. The margin of the pool in the same neighbourhood should also represent a rocky appearance. Old pendent trees near the pool would add much to the effect. If water is plentiful, a group of jets, three, five, or more, rising out of these cones, would have an imposing effect. I directed the arrangement of a group of five in a gentleman's grounds, and which are very pleasing. The centre one produced about an inch column, the other four were about five-eighths of an inch, and the whole from five to seven feet apart, rising out of small cones about two to three feet above the water, which could not well be raised higher, to allow a slack between some of the cones for the water or level of the pool to appear between. If the cones were much further apart, the group of jets might perhaps appear too straggling. Of course, if the column of water had considerable substance, from five to nine feet would be proper; the five rocky cones might then be made bolder and still more natural. Amongst some of the stones in the island, a few water plants, mosses, or other amphibious plants, might be introduced. The main pipe, conducting the water from the bottom of the pool or reservoir to the point for the jets, should be of iron, lead, or gutta percha, about four inches bore, according to the supply required. For a group of jets similar to those I have named, four inch bore will be necessary. Care should always be taken that the main branch pipes are wider than the outlet. Taps would be required to each branch pipe, with openings equally large, or at all events larger than the outlet or apex of the jet. It is always best to have both tap and supply pipe large enough, as all can be regulated by the tap. I scarcely need say that the whole of the pipes must be concealed under water in passing to the parts where they are to rise. All the pipes should be turned up at the ends, so as to cause the water to rise quite perpendicularly, with threads or screws fixed on, of proper widths to receive any device that may be required.

However, it is my opinion, (as I have before stated), that, in preference to any other device, a solid column of water is the grandest and most beautiful when it is allowed to rise out of a plain orifice only so high that its apex will appear solid, close, and perpendicular, and not to spread and fall in misty spray. Of course, the bottom of the pool or cistern of water required to supply the fountain, must be of a higher level than the height the jet is to rise. If the reservoir is near, a few inches will do; but more will have to be allowed in proportion to the distance, except the conducting pipe has a good fall, and is of greater width than is necessary for supplying the branch pipes. These considerations are requisite as a set off against friction in the action of the water passing through the pipes.

To my mind, a group of fountains issuing out of masses of stones similar to those before mentioned, and rising various heights, from a foot to three or four feet, in a boiling manner, has a more pleasing and natural effect than if raised higher. For these rude kinds of jet, I would take a position about the middle of the lake, if it is small; but efforts must be used to prevent the rocky island appearing formal, by placing other islands on each side of it, as well as promontories shooting into the water from the shore. This, properly managed, would allow a central position, without the appearance of formality. It is essential that so striking a character should appear somewhat central, or an unseemly balance would be observed. This will be obvious from analogy. Suppose the stiff striking figure of a weeping ash or elm, or an architectural figure or fountain, placed upon a naked lawn, near to and in a line, or almost so, with one end of a mansion; when this was viewed either from the windows or park, the eye also embracing the whole scene, a second object would be at once required at the opposite angle, in order to be harmonious. Not that I should place weeping trees in such situations—I have only named them for the sake of example. So with a striking object like a jet or fountain, if placed on one side of a sheet of water, the whole of which was at once commanded by the eye, it would no doubt appear inharmonious, unless another were placed on the contrary side, that the effect might be equalized. It is the same with every remarkable object; all require similar adjustment in order to produce balance. In a large lake, if the middle is too far distant for a jet or groups of jets there placed to be advantageously seen, it may be proper to choose as its site the midst of a deep bay, which might be formed into a sort of compartment by grouping three or more islands, (as background to the fountain), partly planted and naturally arranged, so as not to make it entirely a distinct compartment, or pool of itself, but still appear a portion of the large pool. A few yards space between the islands would prevent any such appearance, and the rocky groups composing the fountain would occupy (seemingly, at least,) the centre of the pool. A pleasing effect would be produced if the jet were placed to suit the point from where it is to be principally viewed.

Jets, as we usually see them, never seem to me calculated to produce general solid interest. They may astonish the citizen, or others who see them for the first time, and who are not in the secret of their action; but, I apprehend, they seldom afford general gratification, and yet we find them in places where we ought to expect better examples. We often observe miserable attempts made by introducing into a formal pool, or sheet of water, a simple lead pipe, and allowing it to appear just above the surface, throwing up a column of water to a prodigious height, but of too little substance to bear the necessary atmospheric pressure, and yet rise perpendicularly, or to support its great height without being dispersed into mist.

If there must needs be a jet in formal polished scenery, it ought to issue from an ornamental column in the midst of a basin of water, bordered with corresponding architectural masonry, sufficiently massive and extensive to correspond with the body of water, and to encompass the whole in its fall, so as to prevent wetting the ground about. The water should be allowed to rise only so high as to be kept within its compass, shewing a solid column; and instead of mist, to fall in silvery bubbles. A group of jets issuing from an assemblage of various figures of rich design, in a corresponding basin, would be in character, and still more pleasing.

PLANT HOUSES.

THE plant houses, which are employed for the protection of beautiful and interesting plants too tender to bear the open air in our climate, should be very ornamental, and situated either in the flower garden, or in a part of the pleasure ground connecting the flower garden with the mansion. Such structures, when tastefully designed and judiciously placed, add greatly to the beauty of the demesne. When they are to preside over the flower garden, they should be placed near the boundary, *(see General Plans)*, with a morning aspect of any degree from nine to twelve o'clock, which is much better than facing more to the west, though such an aspect would be allowable. Very often a proper site presents itself when a wall is employed for dividing the offices and yards from the private pleasure grounds, especially when it is in such a position that the terrace walk passes directly in front of it, as represented in the *General Plans*, or at the terminus of a terrace. Even in cases where the aspect is not so good, yet with plenty of light and good management, plants may do well. I have a strong objection to the antiquated practice of placing the plant houses in the kitchen garden, either in the midst of forcing-houses, or alone, as at Chatsworth, Harewood, Temple Newsam, and many other places. A great portion of the most interesting plants are there grown in the kitchen garden, far away from the house, and therefore comparatively unavailable as a resort to the frequenters of the pleasure grounds. The associations of vegetables and flowers are not the same. Every one feels this difference on visiting either garden separately, and this feeling is increased when orchids and cabbages come within the same range of vision. I have, if possible, a still greater objection to see, as I sometimes do, imitative wild dress, with rock-work, waterfall, stumps of trees, rocky staircases, &c., attempted within the limited space of an elegant stove or conservatory. The two sets of ideas which this combination suggests are really opposite one to the other; and I cannot but wonder when such incongruities are recommended by writers in our popular journals. Let me venture rather to recommend basins of water for aquatic plants, (with or without gentle fountains,) neatly margined with fancy spar, minerals, or beautiful shells. Handsome garden pots, urns, wire basket-work, or other fancy devices of a light kind, would be appropriate as recep-tacles for holding spar, pebbles, or pieces of wood, blended with mosses for orchideous or other plants.

It would be a striking improvement to our conservatories if the bald earthy parts we see everywhere were covered by various tropical mosses and low-growing ferns. Of these there are many beautiful kinds well adapted for the purpose, and which would not be materially detrimental to the growth of the permanent exotics. They would, indeed, be of double service, namely, in hiding the soil, and presenting a high degree of beauty. The following are the names of a few suitable kinds :—Adiantum pendulinum, Adiantum formosum, Allantodia australis, Pterris serrulata, Lygodium scandens, Lyco-podium densum, Lycopodium denticulatum, &c.

Where there is room, provision must be made, in connection with the greenhouse, for such plants as require placing out of doors in the summer months ; these should form convenient wings or appendages (see reference to Plant Houses in *General Plan,*) formed of ornamental trellis work, having pilasters for creepers, and having a flagged floor covered with moss or sand, or coal ashes faced with sand, so as to appear clean and neat, into which the pots are to be plunged in order that they may be kept cool, and the plants less exposed to the sun and wind.

When, however, such appendages cannot be conveniently erected in connection with the plant houses, then recesses or bays may be selected for this purpose in the flower garden, (protected from boisterous winds by shrubs) without any trellis work at all.

THE MODE OF FENCING BETWEEN THE KEPT GROUND

AND THE PARK.

THE best method of making the division fence between the park and the dress grounds in front of a house, has, for many years, been the subject of controversy among Landscape Gardeners. The Ha-ha, the Stone and Chain Fence, the Iron and Wire Fence, the Dwarf Wall, &c., have all had their advocates.

The Sunk Fence, or Ha-ha, has been very extensively employed, because it affords a free connection between the grazing land and the lawn. But there is always this objection to it, namely, that it is liable to be seen with its hard unsightly wall, and its ditch-like aspect, from many points of view, and even at a considerable distance. In most cases the eye may detect its divisional line, which renders the view imperfect. But it is especially objectionable for two other reasons—first, for its harshness as the spectator views it in traversing the lawn near to it; and secondly, for the danger of falling over it, to which children are subjected when playing on the lawn.

Wire Fences are of various kinds, and, perhaps, there are some which answer pretty well. This is the case when a straight line can be formed of a few uprights or bearers only, pierced with a small hole, through which the wires are threaded, and stretched tight at each end by screws. In straight fences, the number of wires used are much the same as the rods used in an ordinary iron one (five or six); and such a fence, when well made, is moderately secure against cattle, and as cheap as any kind of fencing that we have. Still, cattle are liable to be injured by them, (especially where the uprights are too sparingly employed), often becoming entangled and thrown down.

I have had excellent wire fences put up at two shillings and ninepence per yard, the uprights being flat a quarter of an inch by an inch, and similar to those of the ordinary hurdle. Six wires form a fence three feet eight inches or four feet high, and the uprights should stand from three to four feet apart. The wires are generally in lengths of about thirty or forty feet, scarcely a quarter of an inch thick, and should be twisted securely together to connect them. The top bar should be about an inch and a quarter by half an inch, round at the top and flat underneath, and should be rivetted on to the top of all the uprights, in order to keep them true and firm.

This kind of fence has the advantage of being cheap, light, and good, and is not easily put out of shape. The top bar, by its size and figure, prevents the entanglement of cattle, as it is much readier seen by them than those made of wire only, without the top bar. Perhaps it would be still better to have the uprights round, or octagonal, of about three-quarters of an inch in diameter, standing four or five feet apart, with a top rail an inch broad and three-quarters thick, and rounded off.

Wire fencing, with the usual wooden uprights, is decidedly bad, for the wires are apt to become slack, and liable therefore to catch the legs of cattle; besides which, the posts or bearers are awkwardly heavy, as contrasted with those made of iron.

The Chain and Stone, I need hardly say, is unfitted for fencing purposes. The wonder is that it was ever introduced, for it is both useless and unsightly.

The Iron Hurdle is a useful kind of fence, as it can be conveniently moved where addition or deviation is thought desirable, but it has rather a temporary appearance.

The kind of fence I prefer, though more expensive than others, is one which we have lately introduced on various estates. It is composed of substantial and ornamental cast-iron uprights or columns, with octagonal panelled plinths of about three inches in diameter; the remaining part of the column, starting from the plinth, being of one dimension throughout, namely, two inches. At each bar above the plinth are squares, with the angles taken off and varied by moulding, and sockets in the centre of the square on each side the column project about an inch-and-a-half, (in addition to the hole formed through the columns), to receive the rods. The tops of the uprights are finished with a low cap, the uprights themselves standing six feet from each other, and being fixed in blocks of stone one foot to one foot six inches square, bevelled at the top, to allow the turf to grow over them. Where stone is scarce, the post may be cast with fangs, or, (what would be still better,) with a broad hollow base *(figure 26)*, ten inches deep by five broad at the top, and seven inches at the bottom, so as to be fastened in the earth in the usual way, by well ramming. All the rods must be round, seven-eighths of an inch in diameter, six in number, and the space betwixt every two rods should be seven inches. *(Figure 27.)* A fence of this kind is, in my opinion, in every respect superior to any other. It is both substantial and firm, and is most secure against cattle.

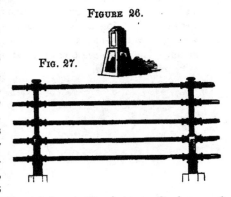

FIGURE 26.

FIG. 27.

At the same time, its line of demarcation between the lawn and pasture is just as strongly drawn as necessary, without either offending the eye by its harshness, or presenting too flimsy and unsubstantial an appearance.

Gilpin recommends, in preference to any other fence, a dwarf ornamental wall, relieved by pilasters at certain distances, shewing the wall on the side facing the house about three feet high, and on the park side four feet. This he considers a sufficient fence, except against deer, and he proposes a wire strung at the top as a protection against them. In most cases I think a fence of this kind would be very objectionable. A terrace wall or open balustrade may with propriety be employed, if in character with the house, and where it is thought necessary, the park or pasture should be brought sufficiently near to the house for the wall to appear as belonging to the latter; in that case, no other kind of fence could be so appropriate. Gilpin's wall might be allowable where the fall of ground in front of the house is so abrupt that it would not interfere with the view from the window or terrace walk; or in hollows, where the ground rises both ways, it might be not improperly introduced. I am at a loss to understand how Gilpin, with his refined taste in other respects, should have either projected or recommended it for other situations. The free flowing connection between the pasture and dress-grounds which that writer considers so objectionable, and to break which he would employ this kind of wall, seems to me (if it be well managed) quite accordant with true taste. But, if the grass in the park adjoining the lawn be of a coarse rough quality, it will necessarily require improving, by breaking up the ground, levelling and sowing it down again with proper seeds, and afterwards closely grazing it with sheep; and any rough parts the sheep may leave should be mown. The difference then, between the two grasses, will be so trifling as to be unobjectionable.

THE APPROACH.

The Approach, or Drive, to a residence of any pretensions, should start off at right angles from the public highway, not only because the gates and their appendages look best when uniform, and are instantaneous in their effect upon the sight, but because the entrance thus becomes equally suited to persons arriving in opposite directions. Diverging from the public road in this way also affords ample room for bold plantings on either side, which is highly important to a principal entrance.

I dissent altogether from the idea expressed by certain writers, namely, that the approach should be made in connection with some convenient turn in the public road, so as to leave it gradually and naturally; because, although the access would appear direct on one side, it would not do so on the other (*figure* 28), and because the plantings would have to be meagre on one side of the gate, when they should appear bold and massive upon both sides.

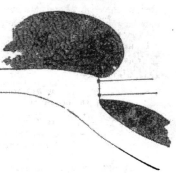

FIGURE 28.

I should decidedly take advantage of such a turn, if the position suited, and if I wished to leave the public road, so as to enter by a private lane before arriving at the principal gates. This would be desirable, especially where another road could be provided, to prevent persons going too far out of their way when coming from opposite directions; and it would also be in character. But this would not be suitable, as I have just shown, in the case of the principal approach.

Of private lanes like those referred to, I may take the opportunity of saying, that when they pass through the farm or domain, I should advise that they be of sufficient width, say fifteen to twenty yards, lined by neat, but not formal, cut hedges. Such hedges should not be planted on high embankments having deep ditches under them, but nearly level with the road. They might advantageously be fronted with groups and masses of roses, whins, brooms, hollies, and blackthorns. Honeysuckles might climb over the hawthorn or native maple. Trees, also, of various kinds, should aid in the decoration, having frequently large expanses of grass between them. At the same time it would be my endeavour to mask out all the field gates, as much as could be done conveniently. The grass of such lanes would be best kept in order by cattle feeding upon it, provided that the plants were sufficiently fenced until they were well grown.

. Whether the gates be entered from the public road or the private lane, the approach should invariably take a direct course for a distance of from ten to fifty yards, according to circumstances. *(See Park Plan.)* In any case, it would be decidedly wrong to curve immediately after entering: and, in its general course, notwithstanding the fondness shewn by some writers and critics of the day for deep and frequent curves, I think gentle and moderately long curves, as represented in the *Park Plan*, are more graceful and suitable than short bends, especially in grounds of gentle undulations. It is obvious that short bends are less convenient for carriage visiters, whose horses may be spirited and difficult to manage.

I cannot agree with Gilpin when he says—" An approach should appear as an unstudied road to the house." I still more decidedly dissent from Knight, who says,—

> " So let the Approach and Entrance to the place
> Display no glitter, and affect no grace."

I would rather reverse the counsel, thus,—

> So let the Approach and Entrance to the place
> Display all interest, elegance, and grace.

In fact, a road to a mansion is a highly picturesque and important object, and, when it takes a proper course, is not only beautiful in itself, but affords opportunities for the display of many charms which would otherwise be unseen. As De Ville expresses it :—" The paths are the ingenious guides of our steps, in shewing what ought to embellish the different points to which they lead."

I would not, however, have it understood, that in all cases the gentle curve is to be adopted: for where the ground is of an abrupt character, the curves must of necessity be more numerous and varied, in order to obtain the easiest and most pleasing course; yet even then they should be as gentle as possible.

Wherever it is wished to make a deviation in the approach, there must be evident reasons for it, such as deep hollows or considerable swells on the surface of the ground, or pools of water, or trees; and where these do not naturally exist, a reason must be suggested by the introduction of groups and masses of trees and bushes.

From whatever point of view the house is commanded, it must ever be remembered that the course of the road should be directed towards it, and never at any time seem to leave it whilst it is in view.

We find sometimes, in ancient places, that the approach from the public road is very short, probably passing through an avenue of stately trees without even entering the park at all. In some such cases, respect for antiquity will forbid any change. Other circumstances occasionally arise to prevent an approach passing through the most interesting portions of the park, such as very steep ground; the most suitable parts not falling in conveniently with the public road; or, indeed, the interposition of other property may prevent it. But when the approach can be carried through the most interesting parts of the estate, I should certainly so carry it, though contrary to the opinion of Gilpin, who says, "We often meet with the " approach studiously carried through the finest points of view, and thus "forestalling what ought to have been reserved for the windows or the " pleasure grounds." It is doubtless desirable that the best general views should be commanded from the windows; but should such happen to be caught on the way, their interest could scarcely be lessened by a casual glance. The prospect obtained in a drive, however varied, is often transitory; and although the composition is the same, it must unquestionably present a very different appearance as viewed from the windows; while the near inspection of objects afforded by a drive, such as trees or water, or groupings of small indigenous growths, the spotted deer or favourite horse, &c.,—even though these constitute portions only of the same scenery,—is desirable from the fact that they could never be seen from the windows with sufficient distinctness to be fully appreciated.

With regard to avenue roads, I own that, how much soever they may be in accordance with some tastes, they are not at all so with mine. They seem to frown on liberty, and to forbid the pure air of heaven to circulate freely. I admit that an avenue of stately trees is " ancestral," as Mrs. Hemans says, and noble and majestic ; but it has none of the stirring life within it of varied drives through light and airy expanses, where the sunshine is gloriously overhead, and where there is no gloom.

But I would not have the approach carried perceptibly out of the way for the sake of exploring scenery, nor brought so near the dwelling rooms as to disturb their privacy, or the repose of the pleasure ground. When, however, it can be done with propriety, and from a suitable distance, a view of the edifice ought occasionally to be obtained. Perhaps a near view of the house is generally best obtained when it possesses an entrance and two private fronts, by the approach being directed towards the angle of the house, (as represented in the *Villa Plan*), commanding one principal or private front and the entrance in perspective, and leaving the other front to be seen from the pleasure ground. We too often meet with seats distinguished for their fine architecture, yet entirely lost as to general effect, by the approach passing through a close avenue, or confined scenery, up to the very entrance. As the promenade or terrace walk is generally too near the house for those principal fronts to be properly inspected from it, architectural beauties are consequently lost, unless the spectator withdraws either to the lawn or into the park to obtain a view of them.

I would not, however, remove an avenue venerable by antiquity, with its mansion to correspond, if it did not materially interfere with the surrounding scenery, though not in accordance with what might be desired as in the best taste.

Avenues planted in the present century, and bordering carriage drives, remind one too strongly of the monotonous appearance of the telegraph-posts on a railway, or of the lamp-posts in Oxford-street.

Whilst on this subject, I may mention the impropriety of old avenues being replenished with young trees. By such a practice, we are ever attempting to build up what nature is pulling down before our eyes. Insignificant sprigs amongst noble trees are incongruous in the extreme. Even should they succeed in growth, by the time they are of moderate size other failures will have taken place, and so we shall always have a ragged, broken, and

111

offensive composition. Examples of this kind are to be found in Kensington Gardens; and still more signally in one of the carriage avenues at Wollaton Park, the seat of Lord Middleton. In such cases, I would much rather allow the trees to decline by degrees; and plant others outside, in connection with some of the best, so as eventually to form suitable groups and masses, in place of the avenue.

When the approach enters the dress ground, the gates should be concealed, as much as possible, by plantings. This cannot be done so completely when it enters (as I have just pointed out) in a direction towards the angle of the house, in consequence of the fence being generally too near the house to admit of it. But when the drive is directed towards the house, viewing the back part and the principal entrance perspectively, *(See Plan of Country Residence)*, the gate may be placed at any suitable distance, and the road pass thence through dress grounds of lawn and variously formed dug compartments, occupied by interesting shrubs and ornamental trees.

Although the dug compartments of this part, at first, exhibit form and order, they are eventually to become obliterated as the plants advance in growth, shewing only lawn, naturally varied by the outline of the plants.

The grass margins of the roads, in the narrowest parts, should not (except in very limited grounds) be less than three feet in breadth; but if wider, so much the better, that as the shrubs advance in growth, the edge-line of the margin may be subdued without the whole of the grass being covered, which is too often the case when we have to deal with the usual strips of a few inches. In no instance should an approach be decked with flowers, as they destroy that softly broken outline which it is desirable to preserve or to produce, and by being so placed give an idea of a limited extent of ground.

For villas generally, there should be left a space of gravel at the entrance sufficient for a carriage to turn in, say from ten to twenty yards in breadth, and of the form represented in the *Plan for a Country Residence*. This I consider preferable to a double road surrounding a plot of grass, excepting in situations where we can plant the farthest road entirely and naturally out by shrubs, without interfering with good views and free expanses of lawn; but the farthest curve must be carried to a considerable distance, and the extreme end be planted, in order to allow a large expanse of lawn between the planting and the mansion steps.

112

The approach to a palace ought unquestionably to enter a court, *(see Palace Plan)*, enclosed by walls in character architecturally with the edifice. There should also be proper lodges, rising higher than the walls. These, with the stables and any ornamental outbuildings partially presenting themselves embosomed in trees, would add extent and importance to the whole. Within the court, broad gravel roads should surround a plot or plots of lawn, grouped with shrubs and sculpture, for the purpose of accommodating carriages in waiting during their stay. There should be borders, too, of shrubs, to mask out the stable yard, with a few ornamental trees to give variety—without, however, entirely shutting out the stables. *(See Plan.)* Perhaps, in the case of a royal palace, where the approach is by a direct avenue, the enclosed front ought to be of grass, interspersed with rich shrubs, statuary, and fountains, and not all gravel, as at Buckingham Palace; and I should allow a greater extent than what is there, say sixty yards or more, in order to give an air of freedom, as well as to keep the public further from the windows. Then, in front of this, I would allow a breadth of forty or fifty yards of gravel, extending the whole length of the front, and as far beyond as is necessary for the convenience of military, carriages waiting, and spectators.

An approach should never run parallel with the public road from which it starts. Such an arrangement would not only cause useless expense, but indicate both bad taste and foolish display. It is far better to follow the public road, so as to be able to start directly from it, either through the kept ground or otherwise, taking care not to enter too near, and thus disturb the privacy of the residence by the gaze of the public.

Neither should we fall into another common error. I well remember an approach which had been studiously arranged with a view to increase its length as much as possible. It started from the turnpike road at one end of the estate, and passed through a newly planted park of scarcely any interest, for about three-quarters of a mile, having in view nearly the whole of the way the farm, kitchen gardens, and all the back premises. Its course was then directed past the principal living rooms to the entrance hall. Three sides of the edifice were by this very expensive process brought into view; but the grand object of the projector might have been accomplished by forming a drive, of about two hundred yards in length, from the same turnpike road.

The width of a carriage road should be from about ten to twenty feet. A very wide road is not particularly necessary in an open park; for, should two carriages meet, one of them can generally turn off a little on to the sward. But in dress grounds where the road is long, and two carriages may meet, eighteen feet will not be too wide.

The road should be well drained, and laid dry with rough stones or gravel, about five or six inches deep, or more, over which should be laid about three inches of well-broken gravel or stones, with an inch of fine gravel at the top. The surface of the road should have a fall from its centre of about an inch to the yard; and should be so arranged as to show the grass edgings not more than an inch higher than the road.

Gravel, especially in the dress ground, should always be kept smooth and firm, and neither hoed nor raked, but weeded by the hand, and often rolled a few hours after rain has fallen. Rolling in dry weather is more calculated to loosen than to fasten it. If not of a kind which sets well, a very slight covering of dry murly clay, or very small broken limestone, or scraplings, spread before the gravel is laid on, will be of service. Loose gravel, either on walks or roads, is decidedly objectionable.

LODGES AND GATES.

PORTERS' LODGES are essential to either country or villa residences; and although to some tastes they are rather objectionable, when the distance is short between them and the house, I should not hesitate to introduce them in all places where they can be concealed from the living rooms and private pleasure grounds. They are at all times a great protection against intruders, and highly convenient to callers, whether riding or driving, without a servant.

Lodges to live in should, as much as possible, partake of the character and style of the house to which they belong, except in localities where the ground is abrupt or romantic in the site chosen for a lodge; such rugged ground demands simplicity, rather than any attempt at grandeur, even when the edifice itself is imposing. In all cases care must be taken to guard against display in the entrance, so that the mind may not be led to expect more grandeur in the residence itself than really exists; otherwise the lodge would prove a false index to the mansion to which it is designed to direct.

Palaces or mansions require lodges and gates of corresponding pretensions with themselves; and I agree with Gilpin, who says, " The most noble " and most appropriate will be the arched gateway, when it is of sufficient " boldness to allow of the porter's lodge being formed within," similar to the arch bearing the statue of the Duke of Wellington in the Green Park. Gilpin's idea of a lodge is, in fact, far more in character for a baronial hall or palace than if the lodge were detached; and I think that a wall of corresponding height and character would give a better idea of strength and importance corresponding with the mansion to which it points or guides, than a low wall surmounted by palisades. Such gates should be placed at a moderate distance from the turnpike or village road,—say fifty or more yards, having a spacious lawn on either side of the carriage road, relieved by small groups of ornamental deciduous and evergreen trees, placed naturally at intervals over the grass, and separated from the plantations by walls corresponding with those connected with the lodge, and to which they are to be attached at right angles. These walls should branch off in curves up to the public road, and terminate with suitable piers, *(a, a)*, the distance between them being about one hundred yards. *(Figure 29.)* If thought proper, the approach may leave the public road as shewn by the dotted lines, instead of the straight one. If the gateway is of a Gothic character, then the gates should be of oak, or at least painted oak colour; but if the architecture is in the Grecian or Italian style, they should be of iron, richly ornamented.

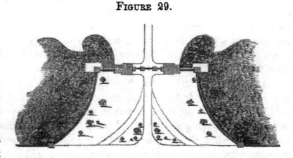

FIGURE 29.

A less pretending entrance than this will better suit houses or villas. To such, I think a detached lodge at the entrance more appropriate. It might be placed a few yards from the gates, but parallel with them and the carriage-road, keeping the latter quite straight till the lodge is past. The front of the lodge next to the approach should be a little in advance of the pillar at the end of the palisades *(figure 30, a)*, so that the porter may have a full view of the gates, and that the elevation of the lodge may be seen to the greatest advantage.

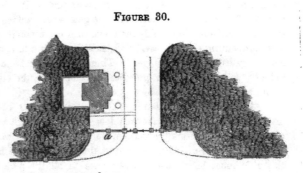

FIGURE 30.

In this respect, I differ from those who, through an excessive desire for simplicity, run into the opposite extreme, and would have the lodge so humble as to look meagre, and so secluded as to interfere with its usefulness. When the rise of the road, from the gates past the lodge, is rapid, a dwarf-terrace wall in front may be necessary to balance the elevation; and, in almost every case, its introduction is desirable. It need only be so high as to require two or three steps in ascent; and the dwarf wall may stand from twelve to eighteen inches above the level of the terrace walk, the breadth of the terrace itself being about six feet between the wall and the lodge, and either flagged or gravelled. If a space of nine or ten feet is allowed, three-feet flags may form the walk, in the centre of neat kept grass.

It is essential to observe that, in whatever style the lodge is executed, the entrance ought to be so managed as not to admit of any oversight into its rooms from the approach or public road—a thing too little attended to, and thereby exposing all within. A porch is seldom efficient, except there is both an outer and an inner door. Whether with or without a porch, a lobby is better, with an entrance to the rooms on one or each side.

Need I say a word on the neatness and order requisite in the occupants of such lodges? Their personal appearance is often indicative of what is to be expected beyond; and at least they should exemplify order and respectability.

The distance from the gates to the public road need not be so great as that which I have shewn to be necessary for a palace; and yet there must be a full expression of freedom given to every part of it. Perhaps from fifteen to thirty feet between the road and the gate would suffice in any case. The gates should be of iron, richly moulded, with corresponding palisades on each side, surmounting a neat dwarf wall, finishing from a to a, and with or without smaller gates for foot passengers. These walls must be in harmony with the lodges. A neat kept lawn, protected by chains, on the outside of the gates, would add to the general effect.

The fencing for the plantings about the gates to a considerable distance under the eye, (where the approach does not pass through a wood or plantation, but immediately enters the park), should be of iron or wire, such as I have recommended for dividing the kept grounds of the house from the park; and this rule must be observed in reference to all the park entrances. There should also be a free breadth of lawn between the drive and fence, of from six feet and upwards, according to the extent of the general design.

With regard to the lodges and gates of a residence near a town, they require a somewhat different arrangement. Not only have we to consider neatness of form, but to build so as to avoid a host of nuisances, which are there unfortunately too common. Nooks and recesses are to be studiously avoided; and instead of open gates, there should be doors, the posts flanked by a neatly dressed stone wall of an appropriate height, of the O-gee character; with the curve, however, so slight, that the gates may not recede from the straight line more than four feet. *(Figure 31.)* Indeed, I should consider this kind of

FIGURE 31.

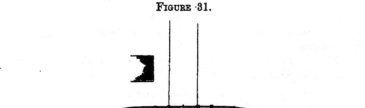

entrance very proper for a country villa, provided the gates were open instead of being closed, with or without palisades on each side, and the recesses a little deeper than the accompanying sketch.

If we compare this design with the concave entrances of earlier days *(fig. 32)*, we shall at once see that it is not liable to objection, as these were

FIGURE 32.

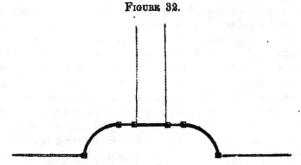

from their rectangular forms. But what was much worse,—the latter too often became the depôts for every kind of nuisance, besides affording lurking places for vicious and abandoned characters.

DRESS SCENERY.

I SHALL now treat upon scenery under distinct heads, and according to its special characteristics.

The creation and improvement of scenery are subjects of the highest interest to the Landscape Gardener.

> " What adds to Nature is an art
> That Nature makes."

I propose, therefore, to consider this part of the subject rather in detail.

By Dress Scenery, or kept grounds, I mean not only what is in the immediate vicinity of the house, but also that which is generally understood by " pleasure grounds." On the formation and arrangement of these I have already treated; but I wish further to observe, that whatever may be the natural character of the country which the house commands, whether picturesque, romantic, grand, beautiful, or rural, the mansion itself is a purely artificial object, and consequently the grounds immediately around it ought to partake of the same artificial character. To a refined taste the effect would be disagreeable, if, while the eye was at one moment gratified by the harmonious display of the objects within the drawing room, in the next rudeness and disorder were observed in the grounds. It seems, indeed, hardly necessary to insist upon the propriety of order and neatness being maintained about the house, as well as about those parts of the pleasure grounds which are appropriated to the display of ornamental trees, shrubs, and flowers in their natural beauty. It is this artificial character of the house as an object which renders its site, even amidst the most romantic scenery, a matter of primary consideration, not only with reference to comfort and convenience, but to taste: and yet, strange to say, some amongst the most eminent connoisseurs of painting have argued as if there was but one kind of beauty in natural scenery, namely, the picturesque. Thus

Knight, delighting in briars, docks, thistles, precipices, and unbeaten paths, inveighs with the utmost bitterness against close-mown lawn and nicely gravelled walks, exclaiming—

> " Curse on the shrubbery's insipid scenes
> Of tawdry fringe, encircling vapid greens."

And again—

> " Break their fell scythes, that would these beauties shave,
> And sink their iron rollers in the wave."

This writer is, however, answered by a close observer of the face of Nature, in terms which are most expressive,—

> " Hath Nature given us eyes
> To see the vaulted arch, and the rich crop
> Of sea and land; which can distinguish 'twixt
> The fiery orbs above, and the twin'd stones
> Upon the humble beach? And can we not
> Partition make, with spectacles so precious,
> 'Twixt foul and fair?"

Sir Uvedale Price, also, in his " Essays on the Picturesque," (in modern gardening), treats the professors of it with contempt and ridicule, denouncing them as " deformers," " shavers of nature," &c., and urges the adoption of pictorial scenery as the standard of natural beauty.

It is scarcely conceivable how men of such natural talent could so far lose themselves, and exhibit such a want of true taste, as to contend with such bitterness against art and order. Surely the abode of man is not to be associated with wildness and neglect, because neatness is considered by these writers as less suited to the pencil of the painter.

The reason of their denunciations may probably be found in the antagonism which they met with in such men as Brown and Repton, and other professors of Landscape Gardening of the same day, whose aim was to assist nature in the display of all her " fair proportions," without regard to pictorial imaginings. To my mind, Sir Uvedale Price and Mr. Knight were not only unsound in the arguments by which they attempted to support wild against cultivated nature, but the doggedness with which they maintained those arguments had a tendency to inculcate false principles as to forming and arranging home or dress scenery to the best effect.

Repton appears to have been of the same opinion as myself; for he says:—" But I am compelled by the duties of my profession to notice those " parts only which tend to vitiate the taste of the nation by introducing " false principles, by recommending negligences for ease, and slovenly weeds " for native beauty." If we, in fact, examine the matter a little more closely, we shall find that many objects which would be worth the study of a painter, and be highly pleasing as subjects for a picture, would be inadmissible into the home or even park scenery of a residence.

What would either Sir Uvedale Price or Mr. Knight have said to the introduction of a tawny weather-worn tent, pitched among wild bushes of thorns, whins, and brambles; a crazy cart and lanky half-starved horse, or an ass and panniers; a slovenly wood fire half formed, with an overhanging mess-pan, (which there would be no difficulty in fancying redolent of many abominations); a slovenly mother nursing her " puling" infant, amid the gambols of half a dozen ragged urchins of the same swarthy origin, into the home view of an otherwise excellent site? Or, suppose a grassy swell blended with mallows, docks, thistles, nettles, and brambles, on which rests the antiquated ivy-dressed cottage, with its appendages of cowhouse, piggeries, and hen roost,—here and there in the broken fence the stately elm, the sturdy oak, the reclining ash, associated with groups of native whin and ragged thorn, interwoven with the odoriferous honeysuckle and indigenous rambling rose,—a polled cow, which has just yielded the family beverage, with the smoking milk-pail cooling at the door, on which hangs pussy, partaking of its contents,—the half-dressed cottage dame, feeding the poultry, amongst which the muddy swine pokes himself in,—such would afford no mean subject for an artist's pencil, but would be perfectly out of keeping and highly offensive, if seen in reality in the dress grounds or the park of a mansion or other residence. But further, to shew the absurdity of attempting to make the paintings of great masters the standard of scenic improvement, I may observe that though, by the rules of their art, it is necessary for effect that some dark object should be introduced into the foreground of their picture, such as an old broken-paled fence, with a corresponding gate, or a tumble-down wall, or· a half-prostrate tree, probably a decayed stump, or a ragged thorn hedge, with a rail, here and there, resting on the surviving bushes; a heap of stones, partly covered with brambles or nettles; in short, anything that is wild or

121

uncouth—for which purpose unlimited license is allowed them critically; yet such liberties could neither be taken nor tolerated with actual dress scenery, however they may be in the ideal.

Again, a view to be represented on canvass is necessarily limited, and fine specimens of trees introduced into the foreground of a picture, in place of those usually there, would monopolize so much space as materially to interfere with the general effect; therefore, instead of the picture being furnished with " examples for our learning," it is embellished with skeleton trees, often out of the perpendicular, tufted with a few straggling branches. The professors of Landscape Gardening are, then, at issue with the Landscape Painter. They laugh at his deformities,—his rough grassy foreground, and his forced ideal effect of light and shade, as lessons to Landscapists; while he pours contempt upon their smooth shaven lawns, prim walks, beautiful shrubberies, and gay flowers.

Again, as paintings cannot afford correct examples, because the painter has not space in his limited picture for the introduction of groups and single trees, displaying their full beauty and true characters, are we to banish from the dress ground the majestic cedar, rising proudly above the earth, and stretching far and wide its arms to catch the invigorating breeze; the noble and elegant lime, pendulous and graceful; the deep-toned purple beech; the stately elm; the various pines, with their sombre shadows; or the pyramidal larch, sweeping the smooth lawn with the drooping spray of its recurvant branches? All these distinguish themselves, when fitly placed and freely grown, by their grace and loveliness. We ask, also, what has the painter to do with the gay parterre, the delightful flower garden,—the soul's delight of the majority of mankind? In what school, whether ancient or modern, are we to gather ideas of improvement in this department of our profession? It is, indeed, true, that an old academical master varied the monotony of his subjects with garden scenery; but he never intended to school gardeners, or to hold up his ideas of even the harmony of colours for their example.

But, because these picturesque enthusiasts would have us copy nature in her rudeness, are we to be deprived of the advantages of art to improve her? Is the gem to remain unpolished because it is a gem withal? Are we not to alter the form of the materials which she gives us, to our ideas of taste and use? Are we not to interfere, screen, divert, and convert, the raw material of the soil into the comfort of cultivation? Yes, we may say with Shenstone :—

> " 'Tis Nature here bids pleasing scenes arise,
> And wisely gives them Cynthia to revise,
> To veil each blemish, lighten every grace,
> Yet still preserve the lovely parent's face.
> How well the bard obeys, each valley tells;
> These lucid streams, gay meads and lonely cells,
> Where modest Art in silence lurks concealed;
> While Nature shines, so gracefully revealed,
> That she triumphant claims the total plan,
> And with fresh pride adopts the work of man."

Mr. Repton, whilst treating on the palace at Attingham, says, in opposition to Sir Uvedale Price's idea, that all improvement of scenery should be derived from the works of great painters :—

" I shall observe that at present there are very near the house some fragments of an old mill, brick arches, that make a charming study for the painter; the composition is not unlike a beautiful picture of Ruysdaal's at Attingham, which every man of taste must admire. Of this scene, which now exists, I have endeavoured to give a faint idea, which is represented by a sketch. Among the trees is seen part of the colonnade, that which joins the east wing to the body of the house. From the general character of this scenery, we cannot but suppose this to be a fragment of some ruined Grecian temple, and not part of a modern inhabited palace. Hence it is evident, that the mind cannot associate the ideas of elegance with neglect, or perfect repose and neatness with ruin and decay. Such objects, therefore, however picturesque in themselves, are incongruous and misplaced if near such a palace as Attingham."

After bringing forward other objects to shew the absurdity of taking pictures for our models of natural improvements, Mr. Repton remarks :—

" However I may respect the works of great masters in painting, and delight to look at Nature with a painter's eye, yet I shall never be induced to believe that the best Landscape Painter would be the best Landscape Gardener."

Towards the close of his letter to Sir Uvedale Price, the same writer says :—

" I shall conclude this long letter by an allusion to a work which it is impossible for you to admire more than I do. Mr. Burke, in his ' Essay on the Sublime and Beautiful,' observes that ' habit will make a man prefer the taste of tobacco to that of sugar, yet the world will never be brought to say that sugar is not sweet.' In like manner, both you and Mr. Knight are in the habit of admiring fine pictures, and both live amidst bold and picturesque scenery. This may have rendered you insensible to the beauty of those milder scenes which have charms for common observers. I will not arraign your taste, nor call it vitiated; but your palate certainly requires a degree of irritation rarely to be expected in garden scenery; and I trust the good sense and good taste of this country will never be led to despise the comfort of a gravel walk, the delicious fragrance of a shrubbery, the soul's delight of a wide-extended prospect, or a view down a steep hill, because they are all subjects incapable of being painted."

I may further quote the close of a letter to Mr. Repton, from William Windham, Esq., of Fellbrig, Norfolk, who, after shewing the unphilosophical system which Mr. Knight and Sir Uvedale Price seem to have set up, observes:—

"Places are not to be laid out with a view to their appearance in a picture, but to their uses, and the enjoyment of them in real life; and their conformity to those purposes is that which constitutes their beauty. With this view gravel walks and neat mown lawns, and in some situations straight alleys, fountains, terraces—and, for aught I know, parterres and cut hedges,—are in perfect good taste, and infinitely more conformable to the principles which form the bases of our pleasure in these instances, than the docks and thistles, and litter and disorder, that may make a much better figure in a picture."

No one admires nature more than I do, or has a more pleasurable interest in the various forms which she is ever presenting to mankind. My views are fully borne out by the language of the poet:—

> "Nature in every form is lovely still.
> I can admire to ecstacy, although
> I be not bower'd in a rustling grove,
> Tracing through flowery tufts some twinkling rill;
> Or, perch'd upon a green and sunny hill,
> Gazing upon the sylvanry below,
> And hearkening to the warbling beaks above.
> To me the wilderness of thorns and brambles,
> Beneath whose weeds the muddy runnel scrambles,—
> The bald, burnt moor,—the marsh's sedgy shallows,
> Where docks, bulrushes, waterflags, and mallows
> Choke the rank waste, alike can yield delight.
> A blade of silver hair-grass, nodding slowly
> In the soft wind;—the thistle's purple crown,
> The ferns, the rushes tall, and mosses lowly,
> A thorn, a weed, an insect, or a stone,
> Can thrill me with sensations exquisite—
> For all are exquisite, and every part
> Points to the Mighty Hand that fashioned it."

124

Let me not, then, be understood, from the foregoing remarks and quotations, to have no due appreciation of picturesque or natural scenery. What I contend for is, that wild scenery ought to be sought, rather than be always presented to the eye; it should never intrude upon the quietude which should pervade the dress grounds of a well-regulated residence, but should remain in reserve, so as to heighten, by contrast, the pleasurable feelings of the whole. The dress ground must always be assisted by art, if order and elegance are to be displayed, and if trees, shrubs, and flowers are to be exhibited in their natural form and beauty; and thus will all descriptions of scenery, though various in the extreme, afford the highest gratification to the sensitive mind, when viewed each in its proper sphere.

As, however, I have frequently observed examples of a taste regardless of congruity, and a vague notion that wild nature uninterfered with is beautiful, in places which ought to wear the most elegant dress and exhibit the most perfect repose; as, also, I have witnessed many instances of inharmonious mingling of rough and smooth, and of formality with the rude picturesque, I am constrained to dwell longer than I otherwise should on this part of the subject, and shew, by a few examples, what I consider to be great mistakes in scenic disposition.

Every one must have frequently seen climbing plants of various kinds trained, carelessly and without order, against beautiful and highly finished houses, and bushes planted at intervals, almost close to their walls. I have sometimes pleaded in vain against the introduction of these incongruities in connexion with newly finished mansions. A case in point exists at this time in Cumberland; where I hope, however, that I have succeeded in convincing my patron of the impropriety of disfiguring with climbers the fine architectural buildings he has raised with so much taste. Climbers are admissible, and even ornamental, on all buildings of small pretensions. They form a graceful appendage to cottage dwellings; and their pendent flowers add to the beauty and interest of such objects when trained with order and neatness, and when the appearance of wildness or neglect is scrupulously avoided. Ruins also, or dilapidated buildings, are proper objects to wear the natural careless and unstudied dress of the ivy, honeysuckle, rambling rose, and Virginia bower. To the ruined castle, the mouldering abbey, the time-worn and deserted manor house, these, with ferns and mosses, form embellishments of a high order, stamping on their walls the impression of time and antiquity. They seek such homes naturally, and cling to them with lasting fondness.

The introduction of rustic work into dress grounds and flower gardens is another example of the same vitiated taste. In such grounds there should be neither rustic chairs, seats, and arcades, nor wide tubs, nor raised beds bordered with stick-work for the growth of plants; but instead, vases, round wire baskets, or round beds edged with fancy iron-work, should be employed, with lattice-work for seats, arcades, &c. In place of rough rockeries of stones, wildly clad, there should be groups of handsome spar placed here and there, for the growth of simple yet elegant rock plants; thus keeping up a neatness corresponding with the smooth dressed lawn.

My views on this whole subject may perhaps be best illustrated by reference to one or two celebrated places. The first of these is Chatsworth, or "The Palace of the Peak," which, with its extensive grounds, has been generously thrown open by its noble owner to the examination of the public. I trust his Grace will pardon my taking the liberty to comment upon what I conceive to be certain incorrect associations to be found there. It is obvious that no expense has been spared in making both house and grounds at Chatsworth adapted for a princely residence, and consequently they will be naturally expected to present correct examples of good taste. The following remarks connected with them are advanced simply as lessons, to guard the inquiring mind against imbibing false principles.

To say nothing of the statuary room, the visiter passes through a conservatory fronted by a geometrical or classical flower garden, which is in full view from the windows of the mansion, and over which are scattered dressed ornamental stone columns. Now these neither appear as parts of any building, nor are they associated with any principal outline of an earlier structure. They seem, in fact, void of association,—modern pillars intro-duced for no other purpose than to support climbers, with which they are rudely clad; not the remains of a ruin which time, with its mouldering hand, had suited to these parasitic occupants.

Again, following a winding walk, we arrive at the foot of a large cascade, which exhibits both art and nature, not only in one, but in a series of views. From the summit of a considerable steep wooded bank, which abruptly bounds and shortens the view on the east side of the mansion, the fall is seen to commence, and it presents a very pretty and natural appearance for some distance down the steep, till lost to view. It reappears issuing from the end of a narrow aqueduct, which is carried on a common arched wall, over the end of which it glides in a formal strip, apparently almost perpendicularly. Once more it is lost, until seen flowing over a sort of temple or Swiss cottage, with an open door-way in the front, which, together with the overflow and the rising jets at its base, becomes almost enveloped in a confusion of foaming water, presenting a singular and (if the mind could be diverted from a sense of inharmonious composition) a not unpleasing effect. Lastly, the whole body of water passes over a considerable flight of architectural steps, at the bottom of which it disappears underground, and gives place to a considerable plain of fine kept lawn. In a line with the end of the fall stand two ornamental vases, one on either side, and there is also an assemblage of gay and brilliant flowering plants on each side, beneath forest trees blended with wild undergrowths of various kinds.

Now, to my taste, many of these features are objectionable, not because the effect is not in some cases pleasing, but because the associations are not in unison. The arched wall, for example, is too visibly intended for effect, and too devoid of architectural character, to class with the cottage and steps below, and of every thing in harmony with the natural commencement of the fall. Were we to allow the formal steps, they are never sufficiently covered with water to be effective. The abrupt disappearance also of the water under fine kept lawns, the combination of forest trees, wild undergrowths, and brilliant flowers,—art and nature thus bringing together gaiety and sombreness, order and wildness,—all this is, in my opinion, opposed to the dictates of good taste. Unquestionably neither artificial masonry nor formality should have shewn itself on the face of a steep so natural, and so suited to produce effect; neither should forest trees, with wild undergrowths, fine kept lawns, and cultivated flowers, have been thrown together under any circumstances whatever.

I have before said, that from the commencement to the first break, the appearance of this waterfall is natural and truly beautiful; and had the same style been carried out through its whole course, the effect would have been admirable. The fall should, I think, have been varied as much as possible;

for instance, now collected into a solid brawling mass, disappearing only to
be hereafter seen as a spreading sheet of silver ripple over broken or craggy
rocks; again dividing into various musical streamlets, and terminating at
length in a small pool; being lost to view amongst trees and bushes at a
proper level for the supply of the various fountains. If from this point the
picturesque and dress scenes had gradually blended into one another, the
effect would have been far more characteristic, and in better keeping than it
now is.

The group of jets on the south side of the house is judiciously placed
and pleasing, but insignificant. Others might have been properly introduced
in the classical gardens at the west front. But the oblong pond now in
these parts of the grounds is wholly objectionable, unless indeed a portion
of it were occupied by a massive group of fountains, forming a bold round
pool or basin of water, inclosed by corresponding masonry. I should certainly
occupy the rest of the space in this pond with richly varied groups of valuable
trees and shrubs, at the same time allowing the eye to range over the lawn in
proper parts, to the full extent of the kept ground, so as to catch also the
varied and beautiful scenery in the distance.

With regard to the grand jet, it is more calculated to surprise than to
excite permanent interest. To many it may appear a wonderful example of
the height to which water may be thrown; but even in producing this effect,
the column is forced too high for its substance. It consequently becomes
incapable of retaining its solidity, and is dispersed by the wind, deluging to
a considerable distance the dress ground about it, thereby destroying much
of its interest, and becoming in reality a nuisance. I cannot but repeat here
the opinion expressed in an earlier portion of this work, that no jet ought
ever to rise higher than it has power to remain solid, otherwise, instead of
falling in drops or bubbles, it is spread into mist or spray, and is liable to
be forced out of perpendicular with the least wind, thereby destroying the
effectiveness of the fountain, the form and regularity of which constitute its
main beauty, and preventing the musical sound of falling water, so delicious
at eventide.

I disapprove, moreover, of the harsh and characterless form of the base
from whence the grand jet rises. The water is seen to issue from a cast-iron
pipe, about eighteen inches above an unmeaning heap of large stones care-

lessly laid upon each other: two fan fountains, on either side of the parent pipe, also exhibit their pipes above the plain surface of the pond, completing a group totally at variance with either order or taste. Had jets risen out of small rocky cones, forming part of a natural-looking rocky island in the midst of a natural-looking lake, it would have been more in character than springing, as they do, from bare iron pipes associated with a stone-heap! The sculptor's art might surely have been more happily and tastefully employed, had it been intended to make the most of the advantages which this water power affords. The iron pipes, or heaps of stones, at all events should not have been allowed to appear.

Again, in following the walk through the wood towards the grand conservatory, some extensive artificial rock-work is seen. I think this has, generally, an agreeable and natural effect; its intricate outline, blended with natural wild growths, is excellent. In many cases, in fact, the stones are so well bedded as to be perfectly deceptive. But I disapprove of the paltry arches which span the walks. Such arches are never seen in nature, and ought never to have been introduced. Any attempt at arched rockery should be nothing short of subterraneous passages or caverns, in connexion with the most massive parts of the rock-work, and should be sufficiently crooked and elongated to prevent their being seen through from end to end.

The solid perpendicular parts or blocks of the rock are particularly well managed; in fact, the cemented parts almost defy detection. So admirably, indeed, is this done, that it seems a pity to expose the secret by which the little fall trickles from one of the blocks forming part of this rock-work. If the spectator examine it, he will find it to be some feet higher than that part of the hill which the rock faces, and to which it is attached, making it palpable that a pipe must be employed to raise the water over the stone, which is only some few feet in diameter, and consequently not sufficiently extensive to admit of any fissure from which a natural stream might issue. Consequently art is too visible for the visiter to be surprised; which must have been otherwise had the rock been larger, and the deception effected as at the dropping well at Knaresbro', where the idea is well carried out.

In the midst of this rockery at Chatsworth, a straight walk, of about twenty yards or more in length, passes through a sort of hollow or slack, and closes at each end in a flight of formal or dressed steps and stone walls. I cannot conceive of any reason for thus mingling the formal with the rude natural-like rockwork. If, by the latter, it is attempted to produce the effect of wild scenery, then these walls and steps of masonry, and straight walks, are not in keeping, but mar altogether the original intention. Moreover, to my mind, it is inconsistent with order and good taste for the rockery to terminate abruptly at the wall and archway by which the area to the grand conservatory is entered. It would, surely, have been much better for it to have terminated considerably short of this; and fifteen or twenty yards in length, at least, ought to have been employed in planting, on each side of a curved walk, so as to have formed a decided separation between the ornamental composition and the rude. Upon the whole, it is to be regretted that in such important places as Chatsworth, where expense is nothing to the attainment of perfection, true taste in composition is not more strictly observed, as it is in such situations that most is expected. They are, in fact, looked to for instruction and example, and the greater disappointment is experienced when any incongruity is exhibited.

I will add only one more example of what strikes me as objectionable at Chatsworth. It is that the plant-houses are placed in the kitchen garden, and thus not only too far from the house, but among the rougher specimens of the vegetable world. Perhaps, indeed, this may have been for contrast; certainly it has not a harmonious effect. There, among culinary productions, flourish exotics from every clime; and here a new building is erected expressly to display that new and rare plant, Victoria Regia, the wonder of the world. I own that the idea of associating flowers and vegetables is not confined to Chatsworth,—the practice is too common; but to present to the eye, at the same moment, such flowers and vegetables, is very objectionable. Whatever others may think, my taste would have been to make the plant-houses strictly ornamental, and to have placed them in connexion with the pleasure ground. The public should have had the option of visiting the kitchen garden, but I would have kept entirely separate the contemplation of both kinds of cultivation.

I have great pleasure in adding, however, that independent of these errors, (as I consider them), the general management of Chatsworth is admirable; and, although it is not equal to some domains for noble trees, the park and scenery around are highly interesting.

Scorsby Castle may be adduced as a second specimen of inharmonious arrangement. Interesting from its great antiquity, and being, by the liberality of the owner, thrown open to public resort, it is frequented by numberless visiters, which, I trust, will be a sufficient apology for the following remarks, illustrative of what I consider existing errors. Along the margin of the grounds flows the river Eden, at one time winding silently and gracefully along, at other times forcing its way in agitated torrents through a dell bounded by precipitous banks, which are clothed with trees and bushes richly fringing the margin of the passing stream, and producing most enchanting scenery; but, when traversing these grounds, which are principally laid out in the ancient style, that want of harmonious combination before noticed is at once observable. Two or three points may be specified in illustration.

In parts of these precipitous banks are caves and a boat-house, hewn out of the solid rock. When these were projected, I dare say it was with the idea, in some degree, of producing a natural effect; but in carrying out this idea, at considerable cost, the effect has been entirely lost. The caves, instead of having a natural appearance, are rooms formed out of the solid rock, of neatly tooled masonry both inside and out, and therefore utterly without their natural characteristic rudeness; whilst the damp and gloom inside render them useless as places of retirement, even under the most favourable circumstances. The boat-house is a double-roomed cell, in size about eighteen feet by twenty, and about seven feet high, tooled out of the rock, several yards above the level of, and at some distance from, the river; thus not only occupying an unnatural position, but rendering the housing of the boats a difficult as well as a tedious operation. The caves, if formed at all, ought to have been of the most broken rocky character, rude as if untouched by art; while the boat-house should have been a neat rustic structure, close to the waterside, spanning a small inlet of water, and having a landing place with convenient steps. Such a structure, tastefully arranged, would have added a pleasing feature to the scene.

Again, in another part is seen a limited flat surface at the foot of a steep bank, with a statue of Nelson in the middle of a small, round basin of water, which is supplied from a moderately high and natural-looking rocky yet scanty fall. Behind this, on the summit of the bank, is a small polished structure in imitation of a Grecian temple, through which the water passes, and falls trickling between it and the figure of Nelson, though some times more abundantly than at others, according to the state of the drainage of the land above, from which it appears to be derived.

Now, to me, the composition of these objects is most incongruous. There is such a mixture of the rough and smooth, of rude nature and polished art, all seen at once, and indeed closely connected. Why Nelson should have been placed on a pedestal in a basin of water, I am at a loss to imagine. Surely not because he was a sailor, and had achieved his fame upon the sea! To have carried out this idea more fully, one would have supposed he ought to have rested on a miniature ship, in the position which was most characteristic of him; but even this would have been toy-like and absurd.

Once again, in another part of the grounds stands a fine figure of Apollo, utterly unassociated with anything harmonizing with it, either in thought or action. Even the path which leads to the figure is so steep and wild, and indeed almost inaccessible, that the visiter would never be tempted to tread it, but for the expectation of finding at last something worthy of his search. No doubt, these grounds, a century ago, had a wide reputation, and even down to the present time, on leave days, are a place of frequent and fashionable resort for the good people of Carlisle. The views to be had in and about them are numerous and abundantly beautiful; but this affords the better field for artistic skill, which, properly employed, might incalculably enhance their beauties, besides both gratifying and improving the public taste in the contemplation and enjoyment of them.

I have thus endeavoured briefly to illustrate the inconsistency of amalgamating wild or picturesque rudeness with polished architecture, sculpture, and dress scenery; and I trust the hints given will be neither misinterpreted nor neglected. Our island beauties deserve the exercise of all art in their cultivation or display. England might then equal, if not exceed, the charms of most other lands, and travelled taste might learn at home what it had sought abroad in vain.

RURAL SCENERY.

WILD or Natural Scenery may be said to comprehend all the various forms of that which is wild and uncultivated. In the rural form, it is seldom calculated to inspire the mind with the highest pleasure; but its gentle variations of surface, and wooded thickets and hedge-rows, are rather calculated to produce calm and soothing meditation. The aim of the Landscapist would therefore be, after leaving the dress grounds, to provide recreative inducement, in the shape of dry walks, and necessary roads and drives, leading through woods and thickets, where these are to be met with; and where they are not, to form them, as well for profit as appearance. Their monotony should be broken by grassy glades, blended with patches of indigenous cowslip, primrose, wood anemone, bluebell, violet, orchids, honeysuckle, rambling rose, blackthorn, whin, heath, &c., which should be introduced in such varied groupings and masses as to prevent the least suspicion of artistic interference. It will further be important in grouping trees and low growths, wherever they can be seen from the walks, that their natural form and elegance should be fully displayed.

Neat rustic chairs, and covered seats formed of larch rods and poles, will be here in perfect keeping; and wherever a brook or streamlet intersects the walk, a neat bridge of the above materials will be proper.

Pools or lakes naturally introduced, I need not say, will be also quite in character; but after what has just been observed, I need not protest against the introduction of polished architectural structures, statuary, vases, urns, lattice or wire-work, or even rockeries. The last named would indeed be inadmissible, unless valleys were sunk and mounds thrown up so as to produce a varied and broken surface.

PICTURESQUE SCENERY.

PICTURESQUE SCENERY is abrupt, rude, and undulating. In the formation, therefore, of rides and drives, the artist must lay down a convenient as well as interesting course, that its salient points of scenery may be most easily observed, and produce the best effect. In walking from the dress grounds, the same attention will be required, with the exception that variations of the distant landscape may be made more readily accessible to the pedestrian, still commanding, however, the same objects as those for which the saddle or carriage visiter has further to travel. The aim of the designer must be to pass over the most charming parts; sometimes winding naturally round a hill, to gain the easiest access to its summit and obtain a prospect of the varied scenery below; sometimes taking an exploratory direction amongst rugged projections and dark recesses, amid thickets of heaths, brambles, bilberries, bluebells, anemones, primroses, and foxgloves, with the sturdy oak, ash, drooping elm, or native maple overhead, awaiting admiration and applause. If happily a brook or rivulet traverse the scene, the walk should, if possible, be directed to a convenient point for fording the brook by stepping stones; and taking a devious course on the opposite side, it should then ascend and descend abrupt and craggy steeps, leaving the spectator at leisure to contemplate and admire the natural beauties by which he is surrounded. At a suitable point, a rustic bridge spanning the water might not only be useful, but would add to the general interest. In secluded grounds of considerable extent, a cottage or two might be very properly introduced, built of untooled stone, and covered with wild but luxuriant growths. Rude seats ought also to be frequently met with, some open and some covered, so as to afford shelter from storms and rain; but all architectural display in these structures, and formality in the grounds, should be strictly avoided.

ROMANTIC SCENERY.

IN Romantic Scenery we have nature presented in the most rugged forms. The views, generally, are limited rather than extensive; lofty hills bound the landscape; broken precipitous banks also peep out at intervals from amongst tufts of trees and masses of indigenous low-growths. Or bold majestic rocks rear their towering heads and throw out shelfy projections, mantled with dangling creepers, pushing forth, perhaps, over a brawling cataract, or a foaming river that forces its agitated course over a rocky bed, rudely margined with bushes and native plants of minor growth, and where is seen the amphibious growth sheltering behind protruding points, or nestling in gloomy chasms and dripping caves. With such scenery the Landscape Gardener has but little to work upon in the way of enhancement. The hand of taste will scarcely venture to act; but whatever alterations may be necessary, should be in perfect unison with the character of the scene presented.

Should such scenery be without a natural cascade, any attempt to form one must be on a bold, and even gigantic scale. Advantage will have to be taken of some narrow parts of the river where rocky heights approximate, not only because these may be acted upon with the least expense, but because they will be most natural and appropriate. Massive blocks of stone, of several tons weight, may be firmly, though rudely, imbedded across, several yards in breadth, in connection with a firm wall of masonry, in order to present a compact body against the terrent which is to pass over them. The interstice left in the wall will require to be filled in with strong retentive puddle, so as to unite with the puddle under the newly-formed bank. This bank (which may be formed of any kind of rude materials) must be placed against the wall, sloping from it under the water, inasmuch as it bears and resists the pressure of water which will rest there before it flows over the fall. Stones will also have to be closely bedded over the puddle, resting upon the rock and the wall, so as to strengthen both, shewing, at the same time, as natural a front as possible on the fall side. *(Figure 33.)*

FIGURE 33.

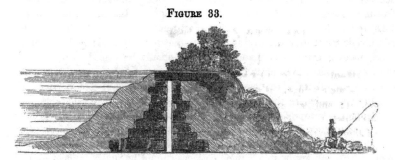

If this kind of scenery is at all barren, then planting will be essential, and, in this, nature must be strictly regarded and imitated. All kinds of ornamental trees and garden shrubs must be avoided; whilst what are planted in addition to the principal mass, must be thrown into large and small groups and thickets, leaving glades of grass blended with wild flowers, and, at intervals, patches of wild low-growths, as well as protruding rocks, to vary the scene. Occasionally, clusters and masses of larch would be characteristic in such scenery, especially if planted amongst rocky pyramids or steeps. Spruce silver and Scotch firs sparingly introduced would also be proper; but the trees most generally introduced should be the Wych and English elms, oaks, ashes, and undergrowths of thorns, maples, blackthorns, hazels, dogwood, hollies, yews, whins, brooms, honeysuckles, hedge roses, bilberries, &c. Alders, birch, and various kinds of willows and spruce firs, may occasionally share in the assemblage and combination with the blackthorn, ling, ferns, bilberries, and dogroses, which are well suited for fringing the margin of the river.

Walks and tracks must be formed in apparently the most casual and desultory manner and pleasing course. Where the grounds are steep, there should be unpretending paths winding obliquely round the sides to the summit; otherwise, they should be occasionally in easy flats, sufficiently wide to admit of small assemblages of parties, but without artistic finish, and sufficiently drained to be quite dry at all seasons.

Throughout the entire development of the design, the artist must ever aim to entrap, as it were, the attention, by continual peeps at the principal scenery of the neighbourhood or place, from every available point of view. Openings should be made, without any appearance of design, by cutting down trees and bushes wherever a pleasing object would present itself to the view. Here, huts for shelter and resting places ought to be erected; and rude open seats, made of trunks and branches of trees, should be placed at the top of every steep ascent, in order to accommodate all parties who may wish to avail themselves of them. Dry caves, with seats inside, would also be in good keeping; and, where this kind of scenery is extensive, a comfortable and convenient, yet unpretending, cottage would be by no means inappropriate, as fatigued parties might there find the means of supplying themselves with refreshments, and the pedestrian obtain somewhat of a change from the theme of his solitary ramble. Such cottages should be rudely built of stone, thatched, and only one story high, so as to have the appearance of age, and altogether correspond with the general character of the scenery.

Over any water, even if fordable, yet liable to be swollen by floods, a bridge of rustic wood-work or stone would heighten the effect. If of the latter material, several arches would be more characteristic than one or two of larger span; and whether many or few, both arches and battlements should be simple, that when they have become grey by time, they may more completely correspond with surrounding objects. I have sometimes noticed in such scenery as this, in localities suitably enough selected, groups of figures of banditti or other startling objects, or perhaps a hermit in his cave; but I could neither recommend efforts to effect such surprises, nor admire them when effected. They are more grotesque than anything else, and are wholly alien from the thoughts naturally engendered by a contemplation of the operations of Creative goodness and power.

PARK· SCENERY.

PARK SCENERY is that which is attached to a country residence—commonly so called,—and is composed of wood, water, and pasture ground, so arranged and cultivated as to combine benefit and comfort with pleasurable interest, whether viewed from the windows of the residence or from other points. It constitutes, in fact, the medium between mere pleasure ground and agricultural, or that of wild and distant scenery. Here, then, the aim of the Landscapist is to combine utility, harmony, and beauty. A park, indeed, is an important appendage to an edifice of any pretensions. Even a villa, with but a few acres of land attached to it, should have them so managed as to assume a park-like appearance to the fullest extent, by the introduction of graceful and stately trees, over smooth green pasturage, animated with cattle. It is desirable to point out in detail what constitutes scenery of this character, and the mode by which the effect is to be obtained.

And, first, as to draining. I need scarcely specify this as an essential preliminary to all other measures. In wet lands in particular, without effective drainage in the first instance, all other steps would be comparatively useless. Then, all sudden hills and hollows, ridges and furrows, require to be brought to a regularly even surface by the plough and harrow; and, when freed from weeds, must be laid down again with grasses of fine herbage.

The "approach" to the house must be an object of primary interest, and should present an aspect (as I have before shewn) as agreeable as possible to the visiter. The road should be firm, smooth, and dry, and wind gently through the most interesting part of the park, as far as it can be conveniently carried, and without producing an unnecessarily circuitous route, for the sake, as it were, of a lengthened drive.

Gravel walks, leading to objects such as a church, a prospect tower, or a lake, following a varied and winding course, occasionally lost to view, would be in character. But care should be taken that no more roads or walks than

T

are necessary should present themselves, as that would destroy the quietness of the lawn. The pasture should in no case present a coarse or neglected appearance. It should be entirely free from weeds and coarse tufts of grass; and should be very closely grazed by sheep and deer, to give it the closeness and evenness of a lawn, without its polish, so to speak.

Water is a highly important element in the composition of Park Scenery, and nothing is more fascinating than a lake or river, seen with its margin adorned with sylvan dress, reflected on its glassy surface, and at length disappearing in the distant landscape. Such an object ought to be a primary feature in the view from the dwelling-rooms, or from principal parts of the pleasure ground, where the locality will admit.

As I have already treated upon water, it will be sufficient here to mention, that when a lake or river is to form an object in a park of gentle undulations and even surface, the margin of the water must not present a rough or neglected appearance. When, however, the lake or river is bounded by abrupt points or rocky steeps, a corresponding wildness of appearance in the dress of their margin must be attempted. But let it be remembered that, in every case, slovenly weeds, which only spread over and disfigure the surface of the water, and are often seen on stagnant ponds, must be carefully removed.

Appropriately neat and orderly kept cottages for keepers, shepherds, or others employed on the land, scattered over extensive estates, are objects of beauty, and materially add to the landscape. They should be embosomed in clumps of trees, and only very partially seen; their blue smoke, as it curls among the branches, indicating the locality to visiters, and affording a useful hint also to midnight depredators.

A church is a highly important feature, most picturesque when partially concealed by trees and shrubs.

Ornamental sheds for cattle may also be made pleasing as well as useful objects in the general composition, if not too glaringly exposed.

Trees are always indispensable objects in scenery: indeed, they are the essence of a true landscape. Scenery unadorned by trees is like a beautiful bird stripped of its plumage, or like a sea without an object to relieve its monotony; creation is there, but it is without its usual charms. In spring, when their buds are bursting, we watch them, and recall the incidents of a year which has passed since last we saw them opening into life. In summer, when the green leaves are expanded, and their blossoms exhale sweet odours, how we rejoice in the fragrance with which the air is charged! And in the autumn, when the changeful foliage displays every lovely hue, how vividly does each falling leaf remind us of the shortness and uncertainty of life—

> " Thus, one by one, the faded leaves
> Fall with each slight autumnal breeze,
> And great and small drop silently
> Beneath the sear and withered trees.
> E'en when the brightest stars are flinging,
> In dewy light, o'er hill and dale,
> Farewells to that sweet bower, where singing,
> Sat in sweet spring the nightingale;
> 'Tis then that more than ever, Death
> Lurks in that pure and softest light,
> And, mourning, with its balmy breath
> Sighs o'er the wild work of the night.
> And thus 'tis human leaves will fall;
> The gentlest wind can lay them low.
> Young, old, gay, sad, the great, the small,
> Now sportive move, fall lifeless now;
> And never more that earth shall see
> Bright eyes, fair cheeks, or flower or tree."

TREES SUITABLE FOR PARK SCENERY.

BEFORE I proceed to consider "Plantations," and the arrangement of trees and bushes in Park Scenery, it may be proper to name a few, and make a few remarks upon each kind of tree peculiarly suitable for this sort of embellishment; of which the oak, ash, beech, sycamore, English, Scotch, or Wych elm, with some others, are examples. These just enumerated constitute the prominent dress of English scenery; and, as they also form the most useful timber which our country produces, they ought to be considered primarily, not only in forming new plantations, but in regulating old ones, and also in hedge-row cultivation.

I wish it to be particularly understood, that trees of each kind should occasionally form groups and masses, independent of any other species'; and, at other times, be associated with different kinds, so as to produce variety of form and shade. The density of a forest of oaks, or any other trees, should be here and there relieved by groups and masses of some or all the principal trees before named, as well as groups of larch, Spanish chesnut, birch, silver fir, spruce and Scotch fir, and pines of more recent introduction.

The Common Oak *(Quercus pedunculata)* is a tree of slow growth, but, when matured, is most majestic and noble in its form and general appearance. Dark masculine limbs, and sturdy crooked branches, render it the most picturesque of our indigenous trees, and justify its name of "The King of the Forest." It should constitute a general leading feature in Park Scenery, forming masses and groups of itself; in other cases, the relief above spoken of may be well given by an intermingling of the beech, English elm, Scotch elm, Turkey oak, and externally by the thorn, the alder, and the maple. I do not mean by this that all these kinds of trees should appear in one group; but that variety should be secured by the use of one or other species, not only in this case, but in connection with other kinds.

The Common Ash *(Fraxinus excelsior)* is a tall, quick-growing, ovated tree, of a light, elegant, and often (when old) of a pendent form. It is valuable in scenery, though wearing its summer dress for a very short period, the shortest, perhaps, of all trees; while its numerous and fibrous roots grow so near the surface as to be highly injurious to pasturage or cultivated land: it ought, therefore, to be sparingly introduced. Being a tall grower, it is suited to occupy the centre of a group, of which oaks, wych elms, horse chesnuts, &c., form the mass. Since it does not suffer materially from exposure, it may advantageously be employed in bleak high grounds as a means of shelter; and as it thrives better in shallow soils than most other trees, it is well adapted for planting in craggy or rocky places.

> " The Ash asks not a depth of fruitful mould,
> But (like frugality) on little means
> It thrives; and high o'er creviced ruins spreads
> Its ample shade, or on the naked rock
> That nods in air, with graceful limbs depends."—BIDLAKE.

The Beech, *(Fagus sylvatica),* for the first few years after being planted, grows but slowly; but, when well established, becomes a lofty and noble smooth-barked tree, stretching its gigantic arms far and wide, with their long branches adorned with feathery spray. This is another of the class of trees well calculated to form groups and masses of themselves; but it may be advantageously mixed with the purple and fern-leaved beech, the spruce fir, and the birch, none of which, however, should be planted so near as to interfere with the free spreading of its branches. If the purple beech be introduced into a group, it should occupy, as nearly as possible, the centre front, in order to avoid a one-sided effect, which, by its dark colour, it would be likely to have were it otherwise placed.

The Wych or Scotch Elm *(Ulmus montana)* is a quick-growing, round-headed tree. While young it is rather ugly, but on attaining full growth it proves one of the noblest and most elegant of trees. Its smooth majestic limbs, clustered with drooping branches, and terminating in massive twigs, produce an effect of light and shade so striking that the observer cannot but admire. Its general appearance is so commanding, that while we admit the old English oak to be " The King of the Forest," we are insensibly led to give him in the Scotch elm a partner worthy of his royal race, and crown it " The

Queen of the Forest." This tree groups well with the English elm, one or two of the latter forming the centre; or two or three larches, with a Turkey oak, may form another centre. Care must be taken to give to the wych elm sufficient room, not only to develop its growth, but to shew its form without interference. It will of itself also serve for groups and masses of a first-rate character.

The English Elm, *(Ulmus campestris)*, of which there are several varieties, is generally of a quick growth, and tall, having one upright trunk, with a few short ramified arms. It is more ovated than round-headed. The rough, or Cork-barked kind, makes a handsome tree; but the quantity of suckers it throws up is adverse to its use. The smooth-barked variety is equally handsome, a more rapid grower, and, therefore, generally to be preferred. It may be had at the nurseries under the name of "The Grafted English Elm." It is grafted on the Wych elm, by which its growth is promoted. I know of no tree which assumes an ornamental character so soon as the English elm. It is, therefore, especially adapted to new sites altogether destitute or deficient of trees. Its dark stiff limbs, short clustered branches, and thick-set spray, or massive twigs, produce this peculiar and pleasing appearance, while the tree is but yet young. It has also the valuable property of retaining its leaves till late in the autumn. In many parts of Staffordshire, I have noticed it in quite a green foliage as late in the year as November. In association with other varieties of the same family, but which had put on their autumnal tints earlier, it produced a beautiful and striking effect. But whether in leaf or out, whether young or old, the English elm is at all times, and in all seasons, a pleasing object, exceedingly picturesque and interesting; it ought, in fact, to be freely introduced into all Park Scenery in masses and groups, some of the groups being varied on their outside with birch, cut-leaved birch, cut-leaved hornbeam, maple, thorn, and occasionally with the larch and spruce fir, the two latter taking a central position.

The Sycamore *(Acer pseudo-platanus)* is a quick-growing, and, perhaps, the most sturdy and hardy tree we have; and therefore most suitable for bleak situations. It is not, however, of so pleasing a character when stripped of its foliage as some other trees, unless when very old, its branches being generally too equally dispersed and terminating somewhat bluntly, so as to give it a formal appearance. But when in healthy foliage, it is a fine tree, more especially when its branches and twigs assemble in tiers or massive groups, as we sometimes see them; the effect of light and shade is then peculiarly striking. One great drawback from the value of the sycamore is its liability to be attacked by the *aphis*, or green fly. It rarely happens that it is not infected every season by a large species of that family; and I have occasionally seen whole plantations nearly stripped of their foliage by this pest, which, by piercing the leaves, extracts the sap, and destroys them. From this circumstance, a vulgar notion has arisen that its drooping unhealthy appearance is caused by lightning. In exposed situations the sycamore is a valuable tree: it is firm and immovable by winds, and therefore particularly useful from the shelter it affords. It looks well in the centre of a few oaks, horse chesnuts, or occidental plane trees, or at the outside of groups of English elms or Turkey oaks.

A few of the most interesting subordinate trees, or such as ought only to be specially introduced to give variety to a scene, rather than constitute the principal or prominent features of a landscape, may here be mentioned.

The Mountain Ash *(Pyrus aucuparia)* is a hardy, stiff, low, and formal tree, and therefore unfit to be introduced, except for the variety which it offers in its beautiful foliage and bright coral berries, which, in the autumn, are very effective. A few may be associated externally with the acacia, or ash; or may take the centre of groups of thorn or maple.

The Common Acacia, or Locust Tree, *(Robinia pseudo-acacia)*, is a lofty open tree, of quick growth. When divested of foliage, its general aspect is not very interesting, its naked arms being long and over-grown; but its beautiful light pinnate foliage, and clustered, pinky, pea-like flowers, make it desirable for occasional introduction. Very exposed situations should not be chosen, as its brittle limbs are very apt to be broken by violent winds. It may take the centre of others to which it is nearly allied, as follows:—Robinia microphilla, and Robinia umbraculifera (the umbrella-headed robinia), —a very ornamental tree, with dense, umbrageous, dome-like head, and few large branches.

The Birch *(Betula)*. Of the white or common Birch, *(B. alba)*, of which there are two varieties, both having white-barked trunks, one is pendulous, the other more upright. They are both light and elegant in form. Coleridge calls the birch "Most beautiful of forest trees, the Lady of the

Woods." The pendulous variety is especially graceful, having slender drooping branches, densely clustered with small spray, or twigs, which produce light and shade, elegance and beauty, scarcely to be surpassed by any other tree, more especially when divested of its foliage. It is indigenous amongst rocks in the Highlands of Scotland,—

> " Where weeps the Birch, with silver bark
> And long dishevelled hair."

These two varieties may be grouped with the American birch and the cut-leaved birch, (the American taking the centre); also with the Gleditschia triacanthos, and crimson and double pink thorns, which being placed on the outside, besides blending well with the group, are all proper associates.

The Cut-leaved Birch *(Betula lacinata)* is a particularly elegant tree, of similar habit to the common weeping birch, but with uniformly deep serrated leaves. It may be associated with that just named, and may take the centre of a group of hemlock spruces, Babylonian willows, rosemary-leaved willows, &c.

The Paper Birch *(Betula papyracea)* is also an elegant tree, of somewhat rapid growth; its leaves of a rather larger size than the common birch. This tree sheds a thin paper-like bark in the summer months, which gives the stem at that time a singularly ragged appearance. It should take the centre of the various birches to which I have referred.

Of the Beeches, the purple-leaved *(Fagus sylvatica purpurea)* is a large, quick-growing tree, perhaps equal in vigour and size to the common beech, of which it is a variety. Loudon says that " there was a tree of this kind at Envilla, sixty feet high, covering a surface ninety feet in diameter." It is striking and particularly handsome; but, on account of its deep colour, and the strong contrast which it forms with other trees, it is precluded from a too general introduction. It is suitable, however, for the centre of a group of common, or of the fern-leaved beeches, or of limes.

The Cut-leaved Beech *(Fagus incisa)* is a vigorous growing tree, with elegant, narrow, serrated leaves, having regular tiers of branches, thickly set with feathery spray. Its form is stiffer and more upright than that of the common beech, but it is very handsome. It is well suited to form the centre of a mass of common birches and oaks, cut-leaved hornbeams, or alders, or, indeed, to blend with others of its own family.

The Spanish or Sweet Chesnut *(Castanea vesca)* is a stately, tall, and round-headed tree, with beautiful bright green serrated and oblong leaves. Its clustered spiky blossoms (though of a dead yellow green) have a peculiarly pleasing appearance in July and August, and the tree is not less interesting in the autumn, when studded with its spiny fruit. There are some immense trees of this kind in Edgbaston Park, the seat of Lord Calthorp, where I saw them at the close of July, 1848, looking particularly grand and majestic. They ought to be far more frequently introduced than at present.

The Horse Chesnut *(Æsculus hippocastanum)* is a robust, round-headed tree, with large palmated leaves, and spiky cream-coloured flowers. It is beautiful when in blossom and full of foliage, but, except when aged, its general appearance is stiff and formal, especially when stripped of its summer dress. It is, therefore, comparatively uninteresting in general scenery. This may also be said of the scarlet and yellow varieties—the former beautiful for its scarlet blossoms, and the latter for its different foliage; consequently, all the varieties may share in forming groups occasionally in connection with the sycamore and the Western plane tree, with pleasing effect.

The Cedar of Lebanon *(Cedrus Libani)* is one of the most noble and picturesque evergreen trees we have. One which was measured in the memorial groups on the snowy heights of Lebanon, was of the extraordinary dimensions of thirty-six feet six inches in girth, and thirty-seven yards in the spread of its boughs. At six yards from the ground it was divided into five limbs, each equal to a large tree. From some of the most recent accounts, we learn that only very few of these splendid and interesting trees now exist in their native locality. Lamartine names seven, which, he says, " from their massiveness can be presumed contemporaries of the Biblical era." In addition to the remarkably picturesque beauty of this tree, its scriptural associations invest it with peculiar interest. Loudon suggests the propriety of planting it in whole forests, for the sake of producing an imposing effect. In this opinion, however, I differ from him. As the Cedar of Lebanon is an evergreen, and of formal habits, there would be too much sameness of effect and too great depth of colour. Still a few masses, and large and small groups, thrown into extensively wooded scenery, would be striking, particularly if some were varied by the introduction of a few larches, silver firs, and pines of sorts ; and in large masses a few of most of these kinds might be introduced, grouped in kinds. Groups of the cedar, placed in various parts of the park in sudden openings, would be startling, as well as highly pleasing, to the beholder. In a group of five or six, I would plant two as near to each other as four feet, and the rest at various distances of from fifteen to forty feet apart. A group of eight or nine of these trees, with a larch or two in the middle, and a spruce fir, silver fir, or Pinus excelsa, blended in the group, some of the cedars taking the outside, would have a very imposing effect: or an interesting group might be formed of one cedar of Lebanon and two or three of the Cedrus deodara, the cedar of Lebanon taking the centre.

The *Cedrus deodara* is a noble evergreen tree, not so stiff in its habits as its relative, but more elegant and pendent, and, perhaps, if anything, a freer grower. This tree should also be placed in groups where it can be readily seen. Three or four, with a larch, or silver or spruce fir in the centre, would form a pleasing object; or they would form beautiful groups of themselves. Two or three hemlock-spruces, also, would group well with this cedar, if placed on the outside, and so as not to interfere with its elegant form.

The Common Wild Cherry *(Cerasus sylvestris)* and the double blossomed Cherry, are beautiful showy trees when in bloom. They may be associated with the cut-leaved hornbeam, maple, holly, and thorn. The wild cherry, being a rapid growing tree, and taller than the others, should take the centre.

The Three-thorned Acacia *(Gleditschia triacanthos)* is a pretty, low-growing tree, with pinnated or acacia-like foliage, though rather smaller and more thickly set, and therefore more delicate and beautiful. It is, however, too tender for very exposed situations. It might take the outside of the mountain ash, thorn, or cut-leaved beech.

The Common Holly *(Ilex aquifolium)* is a most beautiful, low, evergreen, native tree. It grows low, but its coral berries in winter, and its deep-green glossy leaves at all seasons, give it a pleasing appearance. There is a smoother-leaved kind, of much quicker growth, which is particularly worthy of introduction. These form an appropriate group with the green hedge-hog variety, and may take the outside of the evergreen oak, thorn, maple, or alder; or a pine may occupy the centre of a group of three or four,—and, in fact, the common holly blends well in a mass of almost any kind of trees. It is, also, particularly useful in forming thickets with the thorn, blackthorn, and native whin, in Park Scenery.

The Larch, *(Larix Europæ)*, when old, is a highly beautiful tree, which no kind of scenery ought to be without; yet its formality forbids its very extensive introduction. In a park, it should mainly assist in forming groups. A few together, rising out of masses of almost every kind of trees, but especially of firs, would look well. It may form the principal in a group with two or three of any of the following :—the alder, birch, thorn, hemlock-spruce, or spruce fir. The larch is well adapted for planting on the sides of rocky or craggy steeps, or mountain sides, which are particularly enriched by its spiral form ; and its groups and masses may be varied advantageously with spruce, silver, and other firs.

The Maple *(Acer)*. Of this tree, there are several interesting kinds ; for instance, the Norway maple *(Acer platanoides)* ; the snake-barked *(Acer striatum)* ; the long-leaved *(Acer macrophyllum)* ; the sugar maple *(Acer saccharinum)*. These are all well-shaped, low trees, adapted to form the outside of a group of Wych elms, or the outer circle of single trees of the English elm, sycamore, or horse chesnut.

The Turkey, or Mossy Cupped Oak, *(Quercus cerris)*, is a fine, tall, quick growing tree, of which there are several varieties, differing in the indentation of their foliage, all suitable for diversifying the form of a plantation, which would, otherwise, be likely to grow too equal in height. They may be advantageously planted either in masses or in wooded scenery, or to take the centre of a group of most other kinds of trees.

There are several kinds of American Oaks, having large, handsome foliage, of various tints during the autumn months,—scarlet, red, and brown, and which group exceedingly well either with the variegated Turkey oak, or handsome sub-evergreen kinds, as Turner's, Luccomb, and Fulham oaks ; or by themselves, or with the Turkey, and occasionally with the evergreen oak intermingled.

The Common Lime *(Tilia Europæ)* is a handsome, gigantic tree, of which there are several varieties, having similar habits. Sometimes we see old limes beautifully pendent, their branches sweeping the ground, and sometimes presenting a peculiar appearance, very different from any other tree.

There are several majestic trees of this kind in Edgbaston Park, the trunks of which, as well as the base of the branches, are closely set with small twigs, giving to their muscular limbs, when devoid of foliage, a singularly dense appearance. Limes should form groups of themselves, or they may be planted in the centre of groups of maples, or mingled with the English elm.

The Common Hornbeam *(Carpinus betulus)* is a pleasingly massive twigged tree, as is also the cut-leaved variety, which is particularly handsome. Either of them may be associated with the English elm, Turkey oak, or beech, or form occasional groups of their own family.

The Hemlock-Spruce *(Abies Canadensis)* is a most graceful and elegant, low, evergreen tree ;, and groups admirably with a larch in the centre, or with a cut-leaved birch, or spruce fir, or cut-leaved beech.

The Pine family is a most striking and interesting one. The species are numerous and distinctly marked. The Scotch pine, *(Pinus sylvestris)*, although much despised when young, is a most noble tree when old, especially if it has had freedom of growth. Its ramified limbs and clustering branches, with their dense foliage, though of a sombre character, render it imposing and picturesque, and the effects of light and shade which it presents are peculiarly striking. The Pinus excelsa is a magnificent, rapid growing tree, having long, light, silvery foliage, similar to the Weymouth pine. Both, indeed, are very handsome, and group well with the Scotch fir, and others of the more interesting kinds of the same family. Into the centre of such groups, the silver fir, the larch, and the spruce, should occasionally be thrown ; and the common oak, the alder, and the English elm, also introduced. While, however, a few of the fir tribe are indispensable for the sake of beauty and effect, yet, in consequence of their dense sombre appearance, very few groups, and especially masses of them, should appear in a park.

The Common Black and White Spruce Firs *(Abies nigra et alba)* are pleasingly formed trees, and may, occasionally, with others of the family, be well grouped with the larch, silver, or Balm of Gilead fir; or they may be effectively mingled in a group of larches alone.

The Silver Fir *(Picea pectinata)* is a very handsome, smooth-barked, formal tree, having tiers of horizontal branches, densely covered with light green, silvery foliage, stretching away in symmetrical order. It should, by all means, contribute to the beauty of a park. In addition to some family groups, a few may be planted in the centre of any groups of the pine family; and two or three would be in harmony with the fern-leaved beech, or the larch.

The Common Thorn *(Cratœgus oxyacantha)* is a highly beautiful, low-growing, shrubby tree, remarkable for its white odoriferous blossoms. Its densely set, though rather confused twigs, and its dark handsome outline, render it worthy the attention of every planter. There are several varieties of this family. The single scarlet, *(C. O. punicea)*, and double scarlet, *(C. O. punicea flora plena)*, are truly beautiful. The C. grandiflora is a highly desirable kind, displaying fine white large blossoms, and is of quick growth. The deep cut-leaved (Tanacetifolia) Douglasii, and several other species, are particularly desirable. This interesting family ought, indeed, to be far more extensively introduced into Park Scenery and pleasure grounds generally, grouped in varieties, and having thrown in amongst them now and then the double-blossomed cherry, birch, and alder. In fact, almost any tree may be employed as an associate.

There are numerous kinds of Willows, some of which are very elegant and beautiful. The *Salix Babylonica* and *Salix crispa* are pendent, and peculiarly elegant. The latter is a singular and pleasing variety, as are also the black *(Salix nigra)*, and white-leaved *(Salix alba)*. All are needful for damp ground planting at the side of water.

The Common Yew *(Taxus baccata)* is a well-known, low, evergreen, hardy tree, and forms a fine object grouped with the thorn, whin, or holly. It masks out well any disagreeable object in the landscape, or breaks or varies the lawn. It is also a fine undergrowth, equal to the common holly.

Numerous other rare and beautiful trees might be named; but having specified such as I consider likely to be generally useful and interesting, and which would at the same time form a good collection, it is needless, therefore, to extend this portion of my work.

THE OUTLINE OF PLANTATIONS.

THIS is a subject of more than ordinary interest, inasmuch as two evils now prevail, against both of which it is necessary to guard. These are insipidity and formality. The maintenance of round, ovated, lumpy forms in clumps, and of tame zigzag curves in plantations generally, is attended by such unpicturesque effects, that I cannot too strongly impress the importance of right views on the subject. In all such outlines, whether the plantations be in groups, masses, or forests, forcible irregularities are important requisites. They are to be effected only by deep recesses, and very prominent projections of bold and pointed forms, (as will be noticed by reference to Sketches and Plans), generally avoiding mere indentations or little curves, which are comparatively monotonous and feeble. Still it may occasionally be desirable to break long-continued sweeping curves with those of less extent, or the disadvantage of monotony is even here perceptible. The lumpy ovals, round clumps, and graceful curves, so generally introduced in the days of Brown, so strenuously recommended by Sir H. Stewart in his "Planter's Guide," and so frequently to be met with, are greatly to be deprecated. They are far too formal and unlike nature, and our best efforts to break such existing clumps into natural or irregular forms, rarely succeed without a great sacrifice of trees.

THE ARRANGEMENT AND GROUPING OF TREES.

I PROCEED to show what seem to me the style and arrangement of Plantations best adapted to combine natural beauty with force and variety. At the outset, I beg to refer the reader to the designations given to various characters of plantings at page 49, in order that subsequent remarks may be better understood.

I scarcely need observe, that ground consisting of gentle undulations and abrupt falls is much more pleasing, and affords greater scope for planting with a view to the picturesque and beautiful in Landscape Scenery, than flat plains. In the former, the eye catches more variety of form, both in planting and pasture, as well as of depth and force in the undulating surface or aerial line of planting. But as we cannot command a varied surface in all domains, it may be well to show how each is capable of producing pleasing effects, and be acted upon to the greatest advantage. In every case, whether in flat or undulating ground, there must be woods or leading massive plantations as principals; and the mansion should have the chief plantations about it, for effect as well as shelter. To develop these principals, they must, in the first place, be accompanied by smaller masses and larger groups, so arranged that the length of each group or mass shall be parallel with the principal, and, although detached, yet be so placed as to seem a part of it. These parts, again, require softening down with smaller groups and single trees, (the single trees never being planted so straggling as to appear isolated), arranged so as to produce natural and various effects of light and shade, and avoid every appearance of heaviness. *(See General Plans.)*

An extensive plantation or wood is much improved by glades of various extent, *(see Palace Plan)*, which destroy its monotony. On flat tame ground, where a portion of such glades is too low for the eye to fall upon it over the trees, in order that there may be no waste of land, it may be furnished with coppice wood; but in the case of high undulating ground, the effect will be considerably enhanced by permitting the eye to fall upon glades of grass, varied with patches of ling, or whin, or other low growths.

In a park, occasionally some of the plantings should form thickets by the introduction of whins, thorns, hollies, rambling roses, blackthorns, and honeysuckles, so as entirely to conceal the lawn or pasture from view, and thus to create intricacy, variety, and force in the expression, which open masses and groups do not fully effect.

Parks are commonly belted, with a view to shut out either the public road or the boundary fence. To my mind, a continuity of belting in the boundary of a park, unless its breadth be strikingly varied, is highly objectionable. If the boundary, of whatever nature, be not sufficiently distant to be inoffensive to the eye without a belt, the continued appearance of screen planting must be avoided in the arrangement as much as possible. A good deal may be done to accomplish this by judicious planting. About the entrance the belt should be generally massive, and in other parts bold projections should occur, of from thirty to one hundred yards in extent, according to the locality and to the magnitude of the place. Of course, a small park must not be over-balanced with planting, but should have just enough to destroy the formality of the belt, and thus to give an appearance, if possible, of more extent of park than there is in reality. The belt must, of course, be of various breadths; and, that these variations may appear the more striking, groups of different sizes ought to be planted ten or twenty yards, or even more, in advance of the prominent parts. (*Fig.* 34.) The narrowest parts of the belt ought never to be less than ten yards wide, to complete a block. Where it is possible to let the eye range beyond the boundary without falling upon disagreeable objects, I would propose a varied strip of shrubby growth, just

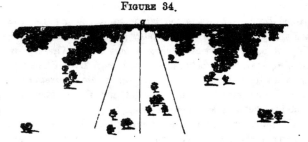

FIGURE 34.

153

sufficient to hide the fence and shut out the public. The extremities of this broad hedge, (if I may so call it), should be joined by the narrow parts of the planting or belt. It may be composed of whins, thorns, blackthorns, and wild roses, planted in groups, of kinds naturally blending together, shewing various breadths of from one to three yards, with a natural varied outline next the park *(a)*. Whilst such a hedge would conceal the fence, and afford a sufficient protection against the public gaze, it would permit the eye to range beyond; thereby, to all appearance, adding extent to the domain. These breaks, or range outlets, should be of various extent, from ten to twenty, or even one hundred yards. The wider spaces will require breaking by small groups of trees, some near and others at a considerable distance, avoiding everything like formality. In this way, freedom and extent of view will be secured. It is true that the eye may, in the distance, rest upon fields of different shades, here and there catching a glimpse of the labourer with his team; and, though such objects may not be considered quite in harmony with the scenery of a richly varied park, yet the mind, ever conscious of liberty, prefers scenes like these, to being confined within a limited tract, however beautiful.

Beltings, employed in the boundaries between the home farm and the park, should be similarly treated, exactly for the same causes.

Where, however, the boundary of a park comprises the whole domain, and disagreeable objects present themselves beyond, instead of the varied hedge, the narrow parts of the planting may be continuous, and its screen-like appearance broken by a mass, or groups, of trees and bushes, placed considerably nearer to the point of view than the projecting or broader part of the belt. The whole depth of bay will thus not be destroyed or filled up, and the eye will have liberty to range over the pasture as much as possible, between the mass or groups, and the projections of the belt.

A domain composed of tame flat scenery requires the greatest judgment and care in the formation of new plantations, and the grouping and adjusting of existing woods or plantations, and hedgerow trees. I have already shown that there must be plantations in a domain acting as principals. In forming these, it is most important to group them in kinds, as recommended in a previous chapter on planting in the vicinity of the superstructure, (page 51); and if this style of planting be more appropriate

x

in any one kind of ground than in others, it is when the surface is flat, because different kinds of trees vary so much, not only in their early growth, but in the height which they attain at maturity. Grouping in kinds produces force in the variety of surface, whilst the system of mingling produces only an indented surface, almost wholly destitute of expression. The oak and the grafted elm, the Spanish and the horse chesnut, the ash and the thorn, the beech and the lime, the sycamore and the maple, the wych elm and the holly, the Turkey and the English oak, the larch and the thorn, the silver fir and the Scotch pine, the spruce fir and the alder, all contrast effectually.

But to guard against misunderstanding, let me repeat what I mean by grouping in kinds. In massive plantations there should be twenty, thirty, or fifty oaks (according to extent), ten or twenty English elms, thirty or forty Spanish chesnuts, five horse chesnuts, twenty ashes, five or six birches, and so on of each species, together, but blending naturally into each other, keeping low-growing kinds next to a group of tall ones, so that the greatest variety and brokenness of surface may be produced. The most useful kinds of trees should always compose the largest masses. A few small groups of Lombardy poplars or larches, rising out of a mass that would otherwise present a uniform surface, will be effective in varying it. It must also be remembered that when the least rising ground presents itself in the planting sites, there the tallest growing trees ought to be planted; and next to these, where it is necessary to plant, those of a more dwarfish habit must be employed; while in other parts that are flat or level, it will be necessary at one time to assemble together tall trees, and at another lower growing kinds. In this way an undulating surface will be produced, while the mingled system would be all monotony and evenness, affording the eye neither change nor delight. A park of flat surface must never be crowded with masses nor scattered trees. This would limit the view and destroy variety. The groups and masses there required to enliven the landscape must be fewer than in bold scenery, and so arranged as to leave peeps of pasture for the eye to rest upon when looking from the house, and otherwise command as much extent as may be, without falling too abruptly on the boundary line. These openings or vistas ought not to appear of precisely equal breadth through their whole extent, but should produce an impression of intricacy and variety, by being arranged obliquely and diversely, as well as directly.

155

Nature, in adjusting her sylvan dress to the earth's varied surface, seems to act on an opposite plan from that adopted by the Landscape Gardener, and sanctioned by the lover of landscape beauties. She has chosen quiet dells and valleys as best fitted to the healthy production, as well as profitableness, of trees, without any special regard to mere scenic effect; whilst Art, in her arrangements, studies more the latter object, and to give expression and beauty by a variety of surface. One of the most pleasing results produced by planting, either in a park or elsewhere, is that of being thus enabled to diversify the surface of the surrounding country. The principle has been long established, and fully borne out by examples presenting themselves in abundance in hilly countries. The hills there, in many instances, are richly wooded from their base, the plantations climbing boldly and naturally to various heights, sometimes even over the summits. When seen either from below or from other hills, with a rich valley interposing, these noble examples of wooded scenery are most imposing.

Then, in planting a park, or in general scenery having a varied surface or hilly character, it must be our aim to decorate the hills rather than the flats or valleys, and this especially in grounds of gentle undulation; as the former course adds to the force of existing undulations, while the latter detracts from it. I would not, however, be understood to say that there is little beauty in a wooded valley, or that such scenery is never to be planted. Far from it: a richly wooded vale, in which pasture land and water appear, and which is animated by cattle, when seen from an eminence, often presents a scene truly beautiful and cheering. This may be said, with great truth, of the vale of the Thames, as viewed from Richmond Hill; but, while I confess its beauties, I still think not only that the trees are too numerous, but that the groups and masses are not so happily associated as they might have been, and that the eye does not rest wholly without confusion on the expanse of lawn there presented.

The remarks I have made in speaking of a park of flat surface, with regard to the formation of principal plantings, to seem and actually to be connected with the superstructure, with smaller masses and groups so placed as to appear to proceed from them, and yet form broken parts, applies equally to a park of varied surface. The general rule here will be to plant on rising ground and not in valleys, except some object require it. In planting on

x 2

rising ground, it is of consequence that the masses or large groups should commence with the broadest part downwards, whether at the base or higher up the steep; the broader part of the hill being more in harmony with the broad part of the mass, would consequently have a more natural appearance than a narrow part of a mass would do, were it seen descending the hill. In these massive plantings, promontories should present themselves climbing the hill considerably in advance of others; or, if the hill be conical, the highest may seemingly take the centre, and the next in height follow on each side, varying in form and some little in height, but not too much. The other projections may then vary, so as to appear less formal. This would harmonize best with the formal cone. *(Figure 35.)* In other cases, the deepest bay

Figure 35.

may appear the most central; otherwise, as circumstances require. The projector should always bear in mind the characteristics of natural beauty, and by no means allow the projecting portions of the wood to appear to finish on the hill side at the same height. A decidedly varied outline in the planting must appear; for any defects in an elevated position are readily perceived. Where it is considered proper to plant a hill side generally for

157

effect, varied breaks or unplanted parts, at intervals, would add to the variety of surface produced by the grouping of trees in kinds, and the charming influences of contrasted light and shade would be much heightened. The crown or summit of a hill should never be planted without its seeming to proceed from a larger mass on the hill side below. A solitary clump, or, in other words, a round cap of trees, such as we sometimes see in mountainous districts, on the summit of a conical hill, is so utterly unpicturesque, that there is little fear of such examples being copied in the nineteenth century.

Correct grouping is one of the first principles of Landscaping. Massive plantings, dissociated from groups of trees and bushes, would appear stiff, heavy, unnatural, and totally devoid of interest to the painter. In associating groups with masses, the best and most natural effect, and that which gives the greatest expression, is generally attained by first placing the largest group or cluster in advance, and pretty near to a projection of the mass; and then smaller ones about these again. Thus the depth of bay in the mass is augmented, and the projection also increased. A few small groups of low-growing trees placed in the bays at intervals, make the depth more intricate. Care must be taken, however, in the arrangement, not to lessen this depth, nor to fill the bay too much. A mass of trees, even not exceeding half an acre in extent, placed in a park independently of the wood or principal plantation, under command of a bird's-eye view, would require several larger and smaller groups to proceed, as it were, from it by degrees. A broken, loose appearance, producing effective light and shade, would thus be attained, and afford much greater beauty than the same mass would do dissociated from other trees, were its outline ever so varied. The mass itself ought not to appear one dense body, but should have its monotony broken by parts being left unplanted.

In planting a park, and adjusting existing trees therein, I may first mention that it is important that the kept ground should be linked easily and naturally with it, by placing groups of trees and bushes, of the same relation or character as those in the kept ground, on the park side of the division fence, so as to appear parts of one mass or group. This will prevent a sudden break between the two scenes. When hedge-rows are so numerous as to produce a generally monotonous wooded appearance, a sufficient number must be taken down to let the eye occasionally glance through free and open spaces, and to constitute an assemblage of masses and groups with those that are left. We see hedge-row trees in many parks so left as to shew the line where the hedges existed previously to their being cleared to form the park-like appearance: and sometimes, especially when seen from an eminence, the breadth of the former fields may be clearly traced. When trees are scarce, and the dress of the landscape is a good deal dependent upon hedge-row timber, this evil is often difficult to remedy, especially if the lines are straight. It is, however, best effected by cutting down bushes and trees, so as to leave various spaces without them, *(fig. 36)*, and thereby throw those which are left necessarily into groups. Such of the hedge-row trees, (or even others, as large as can be transplanted), should also be placed from two to a few yards from the line, alternately on each side of it, and as much as possible in association with those left in the line, in preference to young trees, which would be many years in producing the necessary effect.

The greatest caution is required in the assemblage of trees and bushes, that irregularity of breadth may be preserved in the glades or pastures, and that the dotting system may be strictly avoided. I allude not only to the vapid manner of dotting a lawn over with single trees and bushes, and which is so frequently met with, but to an error not the less to be deprecated, namely, that of spotting groups (if I may be allowed the expression) equally all over a surface, thus frittering away repose, and nowhere showing broad and varied expanses of lawn, which are so eminently to be desired. I have been often obliged, before leaving a place, to urge this point upon gentlemen who have done me the honour to consult me; there being such a wonderful propensity to fill up

into equal parts the larger and freer expanses of lawn, which I have studiously left for effect's sake.

I scarcely need mention, that the rarest and most interesting kinds of trees and bushes ought to appear nearest to the road, walk, or mansion, as they might otherwise be overlooked. A group must at one time be composed of plants of one kind, and at another of various kinds, as I have pointed out in the chapter descriptive of trees.

In the arrangement of trees at the time of planting or thinning, two principles require to be respected, namely—firstly, always to maintain a balance in the composition; and secondly, that there should be form and variety in the groups themselves. On taking a cursory view of Park Scenery, an unsightly group may not appear objectionable; but it becomes so when the eye frequently falls or dwells upon it.

What is meant by maintaining balance I may thus explain. In a group, and especially in a small one, the centre should appear the highest. For example: a group of three trees *(fig.* 1*)* would be much more pleasing than if the lowest were placed in the centre *(fig.* 2*)*. Again; three trees of different heights, so as to appear like steps, one above another, forming a line, or nearly so, either at equal distances or otherwise *(fig.* 5*)*, would be much less beautiful than if arranged as in *fig.* 4. So is the wry group *(fig.* 7*)* highly improved in *fig.* 8. Again; the striking transition of character between a spruce or a larch, and a round-headed tree *(fig.* 10*)*, is improved by keeping the spiral tree central *(fig.* 11*)*. The same may be said of the union of a spiral with a flame-shaped tree, as the Lombardy poplar; *fig.* 16 is out of keeping compared with *fig.* 17. *Fig.* 19 is far more in unison with two spruce firs, as they there appear, than if they were planted on the outside of the poplar, on account of their deep tone. Or a group of spruce firs, or larch *(fig.* 20*)*, with a silver fir, or Cedar of Lebanon, is more in character than if either of the latter took one side. *Fig.* 13 is injured by the small spruce fir, and highly improved in *fig.* 14. A group of five trees, or more, with one or two .tall ones placed near together and pretty central, though some may have crooked stems, yet, if they rise pretty perpendicularly, produce an agreeable and natural effect *(fig.* 3*)*.

An effective and balanced group may be made of seven or eight trees, or more, if two of them be placed only a foot or two apart; a third, three or four feet further off; and the rest at various distances, say from five to thirty feet, the taller ones appearing midway, similar to the two larches represented at *fig.* 9 ; but if one or two tall trees appeared on one side, this balance would be no longer maintained.

A large or massive group composed of various trees, and of various heights and distances, with the most striking character blended inside, would produce an assemblage of varied outline and of natural loveliness *(fig.* 21*)*; but if a single tree only, of striking character, were placed on one side of such a group, (as, for instance, a Cedar of Lebanon, Scotch fir, spruce fir, larch, or purple beech,) the balance of beauty would be instantly destroyed.

A group of Scotch firs, or other pines, spruce, or evergreens of any kind, having a larch, elm, birch, or some other deciduous tree on one side, would be objectionable ; but place these judiciously inside, and the effect will be good. Where two trees only are planted together, they should invariably be of one kind, or so nearly allied to each other as not to appear very different, either in form or colour. Nothing, in the association of trees, can be more defective, or offensive to the sight, than two of decidedly opposite characters. The ramified arms of the sycamore could never be made to blend happily with the delicate birch *(fig.* 12*)*, or the ash with the Scotch fir, the horse chesnut with the larch or narrow poplar *(fig.* 16*)*, or the round-headed lime with the spruce fir *(fig.* 10*)*. Both the planting and thinning, therefore, of ornamental trees, require the attention of a skilful hand. The form and varieties of a group, or groups, must be of different degrees. When two only are planted, they should be placed at least so close together as to intermingle their branches *(fig.* 15*)*; but the best effect is produced when two are placed as near to each other as, to all appearance, to form but one tree, as represented in the Wych elm *(fig.* 6*)* and the beech *(fig.* 18*)*. I have frequently seen the alder, with two or three stems starting from one base, produce a most beautiful and striking appearance. A group of several trees always produces the best effect when two or three of them stand close together, or nearly so, at their base, pretty central in the group, and two or three more within a few feet of them. In this way we produce force of expression alike in the stems and heads, and give a principal to the group. Extent and variety of form are also secured by spreading out the rest, and varying their distances. In a large group or mass, two or more of such principals would be necessary. (See figure below.) In no case should a group be formed by trees placed at equal distances. *Fig.* 37 represents ground plans of a mass and group, with their original outline, and the dots inside shew the position of the adopted plants as they are to remain when thinned and regulated, and the fence removed. A bush

FIGURE 37.

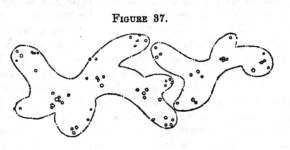

or two of thorns, hollies, blackthorns, whin, or maples, added to the principals (as I have termed them) of some of the groups, would provide variety, and assist much in giving that solidity to the association we wish to secure. Occasional bushes would also be quite appropriate, if connected occasionally with straggling trees. In the placing of groups and masses, their position should always appear to range lengthways with the carriage road or walks, or their relative plantings, (as shewn in the *Park Plan)*, as it would be quite discordant to start with the ends at right angles from them. By a judicious arrangement of trees and bushes, we attain the full effect of light and shade, as well as elegance and picturesque beauty; whilst in the proper assemblage of trees, free, bold, and varied breadths in the glades are produced, and as a whole, a combination of extent, importance, and grandeur, is effected.

It is unanimously allowed that a Park is an important and striking appendage to a residence. I cannot, therefore, leave this subject without again impressing upon my readers the importance of its composition. The pasture should be freed from coarse tufts of grass, and everything which tends to the appearance even of disorder. There must be no slovenly fences, no dead or broken branches left upon the trees to disfigure them. All tumble-down trees must be discarded, and roads and walks must be kept orderly and in their original form. Of course I do not refer to specimens of venerable declining trees; neither do I mean that a stunted tree, when it has lost its true character, and is covered with ivy, thickly crowned with its winter blossoms, should be removed. Nor have I in view the wild rambling rose, weaving itself into the rigid thorn; nor the native woodbine, entwining itself on the stem of the maple, and reaching to its very summit, its odoriferous blossoms filling the air with sweet perfumes.

What I have said on the creation or dress of scenery, may seem to be an attempt at fostering art and formality at the expense of nature. But it is not so: at least my intention has been otherwise. I am desirous only to establish a system most calculated to produce true beauty in Park Scenery, and therefore to follow nature. But in cultivated ground, wildness is not beauty; and although such affords the greatest pleasure in its proper place, it becomes perplexing and tiresome when misplaced; whilst a true balance of composition, conveying a just idea of colour, position, and variety, and a true admixture of animate and inanimate nature, afford never-palling gratification.

PROSPECT SCENERY; OR SCENERY BEYOND THE PARK.

THERE seems an inherent love of prospect in the human mind, and a wish to explore to the utmost whatever is extensive in scenery. When, however, points are so distant as to present objects dimly, the eye becomes perplexed and the mind dissatisfied. But, when scenery consists of bold or gentle undulations, studded with villages, hamlets, towns, churches, windmills, woods, and groups of trees,—water, animated nature, and the ever-varying light and shade lending their effective aid,—a picture is presented which never fails to charm the soul, and fill the contemplative mind with delight.

When extensive scenery is under control and susceptible of improvement, judicious planting is most important, and the first step to be attended to. This is particularly necessary outside the park, in order to present a continuity of rich wooded connection beyond the pale, and in such a manner that the actual limits of the park may not be apparent. If a public road passes along the park boundary dividing it from other parts of the domain, this end may be secured by planting masses and groups of trees near the road, on the opposite side, and at various distances from it.

Although the fields beyond present various shades of agricultural produce, it will be important to extend and give a oneness of character to the whole domain, by forming hedge-row trees, at intervals, into groups, as well as by adding various sized forest masses and groups, taking principally, for convenience, the junction of fences. At the same time, though existing fences may in part serve to protect the planting, they must only be so much employed as to present a well varied outline. In some parts it will be necessary to have groups in the fields, apart from the hedge-rows; but this should be sparingly done, as it would impede cultivation, except in high ground which cannot conveniently be put under the plough. The extreme boundary of the estate should be wooded, but by no means so as to represent a belt, or any line of demarcation suggesting that there the domain terminates.

Mountainous regions very commonly justify help in dressing judiciously the bold swelling hill, the towering peak, and the grassy vale. The utmost variety and effect will be produced by only planting a few of the hill sides. Economy would, moreover, teach us that those should be left which are the most fertile, and those planted which in some degree would be otherwise barren. In such planting we may advantageously commence with the principal body at the base, and rise naturally up the mount with deep and broken outlines, as high as it may be thought that trees will grow. In addition to a varied outline, the most massive parts should have their sameness broken by the occasional appearance of vacant spots. Some of the most contracted parts or channels between the mountain, that afford little or no flat surface, may very properly be planted, uniting the plantations ascending the mountain on each side into one. The bold hills or swells, and flats, should be varied with groups and masses, so as to combine with the more remote wooded mountains; but it must be remembered not to plant too much the slacks where the swells are gentle, as that would lessen the contrast produced by the undulations, and produce too much of a level. In the case of a space between two hills *(fig. 38, a)*, rising above lower swells which form and front their base, the

FIGURE 38.

lower one should be kept free from trees fronting the opening *a*, to let the eye fall upon the dark valley and woody mountain which may appear beyond, thereby producing extent and forcible variety in light and shade.

TREES BEST SUITED TO FORM THE AERIAL LINE.

THE round-headed and ovated trees are unquestionably best adapted to form the sky or aerial line, or to crown the summit of a hill. Their convex outline particularly harmonizes with the concave or arched canopy of the heavens. I will name a few which are generally under our notice in English scenery.

The Mountain or Wych Elm is the most elegant, when aged, and is one of the best for the purpose.

The English Elm is particularly striking when viewed before the horizon. Its dark upright trunk, stiff dark arms and clustered branches, and its thick-set spray, contrasted with the light of the sky seen through its foliage, produces a more pleasing effect than perhaps any other tree.

The Beech, with its noble extended arms, and light feathery twigs, is well adapted, and truly elegant in its outline.

The Birch is very elegant when seen in this position, especially if it be of the weeping kind, and particularly if the top only catches the horizon, and the greatest portion of the trunk is backed by a hill. The trunk, being white, however, and seldom of noble stature, its importance is in some degree lessened, and consequently its introduction ought not to be so general.

The Oak is very appropriate. Its picturesque character is then clearly presented.

The Sycamore, when stripped of its foliage, presents a stiff, blunt appearance, except when the tree is of a good age, and its branches are formed into divisions or tiers, and clustered twigs: it has then a fine effect. But such a tree in full foliage is truly grand.

An aged Ash is suitable, from its lightness and elegance.

The Lime is a well-formed tree for the purpose, but scarcely varied enough in the distribution of its branches to produce striking effects of light and shade; still it is not objectionable.

The Alder, being dark, with assembled twigs and branches thrown into horizontal tiers, as we often find them branching from one, two, or more trunks, is a beautiful object falling upon the horizon; indeed, an aged specimen is much to be admired.

The Horse Chesnut, although its dome-like head is calculated to harmonize with the sky-line, is so very stiff and monotonous in its general character, especially when stripped of its foliage, as not to be considered very appropriate.

The Mountain Ash is objectionable for a similar reason.

The Scotch or Mountain Pine, when old, is a fine, natural-formed, noble, picturesque tree; but it is of a very sombre character, and therefore too heavy to meet the horizon. In other situations, especially when backed by rising ground, by other trees, or by buildings, or when seen on bold or abrupt ground backed by hills of greater height, it is a fine object.

Pointed or spiral trees are inharmonious with the aerial line, and seldom, therefore, afford subjects suited to the artist's pencil. Amongst these are the Larch, Spruce Fir, Silver Fir, Cypress, Red Cedar, and the Lombardy Poplar.

The Larch, Spruce and Silver Fir, and others of similar character, are well suited to share the dress of pyramidal scenes, and also to climb the sides of hills and broken rocky heights, provided their spiry points are overshadowed by the various precipices or hills rising above them. They are in character when associated with buildings, especially those of the Gothic style; also on flats or gentle rising ground, when trees or higher ground intervene to prevent their points catching the horizon.

The Red Cedar and the upright Cypress are best suited to low situations, taking part in a group of low shrubby trees, or forming a group of themselves, and associated with Gothic buildings, or in hollows, blending amongst mounds and pyramids. These observations also apply to the Lombardy Poplar, which, nevertheless, accords well with the pinnacles of churches, or looks well in groups when seen rising out of a mass of buildings, or out of a massive wood, so as not to catch the sky-line. But scattered about as solitary trees, or grown in rows, it has never a happy effect. Occasional groups of three or four, or more, rising out of a plain, and viewed from an elevated position, so as not to fall upon the horizon, are generally very effective in such scenery.

THE MANAGEMENT OF ORNAMENTAL TREES AND SCREEN

PLANTATIONS.

THERE is so much neglect of, and such an objection to, cutting down or giving timely thinning to plantations, (that the true forms of trees, and the beauty of scenery, may be preserved,) that I am induced to lay down the following brief directions, in the hope that they may have the effect of influencing proprietors to turn their attention more fully to so important a subject.

First, then, I would recommend that choice be made of such trees as are likely to remain where they are planted, and that they should be marked slightly with white paint, in order to prevent their being taken down at the time of thinning. On each successive occasion of that kind, (which should be once in every two or three years for thriving plantations,) a few of the lower branches of these trees should be removed, until a clear stem is formed of from five to eight feet in height. The pendent kinds, such as the Wych elm, beech, lime, &c., should be trimmed to the longest stem; and formal upright kinds, such as the horse chesnut, sycamore, mountain ash, &c., to the shortest stem; taking care always to shorten such branches as appear to outgrow the rest, for, if left unchecked, they would throw the tree out of its proper balance, and thus deform it.

Second. Lop off from other trees all branches that intrude, and cut down, as occasion may require, such of the trees as appear to crowd the adopted plants; by which means the plants will have room to grow, and to form large and massive branches, adapted to be both useful and ornamental. A single tree, even, will thus eventually afford a screen almost equal to a hundred neglected or mismanaged skeletons. I do not mean that ornamental plantations should be so thinned as to leave the trees standing at equal distances, as in forests; but so that, after being properly thinned, they may still appear to be thrown together in different sized groups; and although some of them might, for effect's sake, be kept near together,—indeed, so near as in some cases to touch one another, still they would become fine and ornamental, provided sufficient space were kept clear for them to throw out their branches freely, so as to give variety and richness to the landscape.

Instead, however, of receiving timely attention in thinning and pruning, we generally find plantations neglected for the space of fifteen or twenty years, sometimes even for longer periods; and that, too, although the trees were planted at first at no greater distance than three or four feet from each other. Such mismanagement must necessarily cause the branches to decay, and the trees to be little better than naked poles, ill adapted to form a screen or ornament to the scenery amid which they are placed. We must guard against the common bad practice of thinning a crowded plantation by stripping every tree alike of its branches, as an excuse for thinning, without cutting down, until it is too late for any of them ever to assume their proper character and beauty, and answer the end required.

The general practice of introducing nurse plants, (as they are termed), into plantations, seldom answers the purpose intended, and simply from a want of early attention. The Italian poplar and the larch, for instance, are of such rapid growth, that in four or five years they will overpower and materially injure almost every other kind of tree, particularly the oak and the beech; consequently, at that period, care should be taken to afford the latter room, by lopping off the branches of some of the nurse plants, and cutting down others, as the case may require.

The Black Italian Poplar should never be introduced, either as a nurse plant, for shelter, or otherwise, except with a full determination upon its final removal; for it never commands admiration at any period of its growth: when young, it does not harmonize with other trees, and as it advances in growth it presents long naked limbs, and becomes disproportionate, top-heavy, and at length so overbalanced as invariably to lean sideways, and frequently to become nearly prostrate. It is to be seen blemishing our English scenery in almost every part. I have frequently alluded publicly to this tree, as well as to the poplar family generally, and not in vain, for much has been already done in ridding us of them. I know none of the poplar family worthy of introduction into scenery, (with the exception of the Lombardy, upon which I have given my opinion in a former chapter). The interest created by their catkin blossoms for a few days in a year is, I think, counterbalanced by the litter produced as they fall from the tree.

FENCES FOR PARK AND FOREST PLANTATIONS.

NEITHER walls nor hedges should ever be used as fences to masses or clumps in Park Scenery. The stiff, marked line or barrier which they produce, is highly objectionable; and if once put up, their removal in due time is seldom attended to. Temporary fences are the best: the intention being, that in ten or fifteen years, or when it is supposed the trees have attained sufficient growth not to be injured by cattle, these barriers shall be wholly removed, and the whole ground among them thrown into one range. The wire fence, named in a previous chapter, for dividing the park and the dress grounds, would be the most useful. Cheaper and lighter wire may be had, but, as already observed, playful cattle are liable to entangle their legs in the wires. The iron hurdle is a very suitable fence, being moveable at will; the small-sized ones, three feet three inches in height, and six feet in length, if well made, (at a cost of about two shillings or two shillings and threepence per yard,) are quite sufficient, and last long when kept well painted. The Scotch fencing may be employed when materials are on the spot, and not to buy; but, as it is not very durable, if it has to be purchased, the iron or wire fencing is the cheapest. The Scotch fencing is composed of larch rods, of about two or three inches in diameter, driven into the ground about six inches apart, and standing about three feet six inches in height. A half-rounded rod is nailed on the top of the stakes, with the flat side downward, binding the whole firmly together.

Posts and rails, though a rough fence, are preferable to the stiff hedge, wall, or palings; but wire and iron fencings are so moderate in price and so durable, that no other argument is needed to enforce the propriety of their adoption in preference.

General plantations or woods are best fenced by dwarf walls or hedges. A wall, about three feet or three feet six inches high, is the better of the two. At a distance, and when the stones have become stained and moss-grown,

z

they may be said to be in harmony, particularly in woods, and more especially when, here and there, clusters of whins, blackthorns, rambling roses, honeysuckles, ferns, &c., are found growing out of them, with other shrubs scattered in advance. If hedges are used, they should be frequently well cut, in order to prevent their growing thin, as well as to prevent their interfering with the natural outline of the trees. At the best, from the overhanging of the trees, the hedge is liable, in the course of time, to be so injured as no longer to constitute a sufficient fence. In any case, it must never be allowed to grow too high, and thus to lessen the expansion and beauty of the trees for the sake of the hedge appearing wild or natural. Examples of this are too frequent.

Single trees may be cheaply and neatly protected from horses and cows by driving strong larch and other stakes into the ground, from two to three feet apart, all round the tree, about three feet six inches from it, and four and a half feet high, a half-round larch coping being nailed on the tops of the stakes, to bind them together. They will require a second rail on the outside of the stakes, about a foot below, in order to prevent the cattle getting their heads under the top bar or coping. A still better fence may be formed of the above stakes and coping, with the addition of three lines of wire nailed a foot apart, tight and firm, to them. A still more lasting fence would be made with iron uprights, and two or three horizontal wires stretched firm round the uprights. When plants are small, to keep off sheep, four or five lines of wire may be employed. But, perhaps, the cheapest and readiest mode of guarding a single tree, and one which is recommended by its simple neatness, is to drive four strong larch stakes firmly into the ground, each stake being fifteen inches from the tree, four feet six inches high, and so placed, as regards the tree, that when two rods are nailed on the top of the stakes they may just clear its stem, as represented at *figure* 39, *a*. These two rods, which may be about two inches in diameter, must be cut down the middle, and be six feet six inches in length, that they may each project

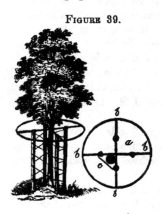

FIGURE 39.

two feet beyond the stakes. At the extremity of these rods, a hoop of wire, not less than the eighth of an inch in thickness, and forming a circle of six feet six inches in diameter, must be fastened on with a small staple, *b b b b*, completing the fence. Or, in place of wire, a strong hoop of proper dimensions, such as are used for hooping large tubs, would answer the purpose, and last a long time with painting. But No. 2 wire would only cost about one penny per yard, and would be preferable. The stakes being pretty near to the tree, prevent sheep from rubbing against it, and the wire hoop keeps off larger cattle; and if a short bar be nailed on at *c*, forming a triangle, a complete stay to the tree is provided against boisterous winds. Tow, short hay, or some convenient material, should be filled in to prevent the tree being chafed. In the case of small, low trees, it will only be necessary to nail two or three lines of small rods round the stakes, to keep the sheep from gnawing the young wood. In most instances, in Park Scenery, there is always a considerable necessity for the introduction of single trees, and, consequently, the cheapest fence, consistent with neatness, is a consideration. I have, therefore, invented the one in question, as meeting all requirements. There are very complete tree guards made of iron, averaging about twelve or fifteen shillings each; but one of this kind might be made much cheaper, and perhaps as useful, by four uprights bent so as to throw the top part three feet from the tree, and one foot from the bottom of it. On the top of these should be rivetted a half inch by a quarter rod; a round quarter rod should next be run through the uprights about a foot below, and a third a foot from the bottom, making the circle firm in two halves, (fastened to each other by small wire), so as to be moved conveniently, and placed round the tree firmly.

z 2

THE TIME OF PLANTING TREES, WITH A FEW

CAUTIONARY DIRECTIONS.

FOR evergreen and tender shrubs—indeed, for almost any kind of shrubs—autumn and spring are the best times for planting. In autumn, the natural state of the young wood will, perhaps, be the best guide to the planter in commencing his operations, say about the end of September or the beginning of October. The exact time, of course, will vary according to the season and different localities, whether the young wood is or is not matured, or the weather is hot and droughty; as, even with daily waterings, the shrubs would not only be liable to great injury by the scorching sun and winds, but the ground itself would also be hard and dry, and thereby render their removal from the nursery more difficult and unsafe. However, autumn planting should not be too long deferred, since the only advantage gained by it is that the plants have sufficient time to form new fibres before winter. If, therefore, they are not planted soon enough to make sufficient progress before that time, spring planting is the best.

Winter planting (except for forest trees) I consider the worst season of any. Of course, extensive forest planting will not be carried out without taking the winter months with others. In such cases, the plants, being hardy and generally small, are less liable to be rocked about and injured by boisterous winds. Moreover, in extensive plantings, there is a less degree of danger in the gloomy months in moving the plants from place to place, and in the general operations, than in bright droughty weather. Therefore, under such circumstances, we may consider from the fall of the leaf to the end of February the best season for extensive forest planting.

As a general rule, I prefer spring planting for ornamental trees and shrubs, to every other period; for those planted in the autumn have to contend with, and to bear the pressure and rocking of, boisterous gales, which strain the newly-formed fibres, and, by leaving the earth open round the stem, expose the young roots to the liability of frosts.

Ornamental planting is, therefore, generally most successfully accomplished in the spring months. I hold this opinion not theoretically, but from general observation, and would, consequently, suggest the adoption of the following practice. As soon as the plants are matured in growth in the autumn, (if the weather permits), they should be procured from the nurseries, and should be well protected from wind and sun during the process of taking up, and in their journey. They should then be carefully laid in the earth, in some sheltered spot near to where they are to be planted, thinly, in rows,—say three, six, or more inches from plant to plant, and about twelve inches or more from row to row, just as the size of the plants may seem to require,— covering the roots with fine soil, somewhat deeper than what they were in when growing in the nursery. The whole operations should be performed just as if they were permanently planted, excepting that they will protect themselves better if they are laid so that the tops may incline a little, rather than stand perpendicularly. In the case of more tender plants, the earth between the rows should be thinly covered with leaves or straw. I say thinly, for too much covering would be likely to rot and injure delicate plants.

Some persons object to the system of laying plants in the earth preparatory to planting, on account of the losses commonly sustained thereby ; and I am not surprised at the objection, for the careless manner in which they are generally put in, sometimes in clusters, and often just as they arrive from the nurseries, tied up in bundles, makes it scarcely possible that any should live. The earth, in many such cases, never touches the roots, and they thus lie so open as to be destroyed by air, frost, or mould, or perhaps by all combined. The method I have proposed of securing the plants in the autumn, will be found advantageous, inasmuch as many of them will form fibres between the time of being taken up and that of planting, and which, if planted in moist weather, will lay hold of the earth at once. Even should it not be convenient to obtain the plants so early as autumn, by their being secured and carefully laid in before droughty weather in the spring, a great advantage is gained over their being brought from the nurseries at a time when they would be exposed to drought, both in the process of taking them up, and in their conveyance. A lengthened exposure to sun and air is most prejudicial to their vitality.

174

It scarcely need be said that, if possible, the ground should be prepared by good digging or trenching, sufficiently early to ensure its being well pulverized during frosts preparatory to planting; and when the soil is of a cold clayey nature, it would be much improved by a moderate quantity of small stones being laid at the bottom of the trench; or moderately fine coal ashes would be valuable. I consider it a mistaken notion (as generally practised) to clear lands, as much as possible, of all stones, (except where neatness is a chief consideration). Trees, and indeed vegetation generally, seem to be in their element when their fibres are nestling amongst stones. At the beginning of April, or rather as soon as the buds of the shrubs or trees appear pretty well swollen, plant as the weather suits, that is, in quite gloomy and showery weather; always minding in the process not to allow the roots to be too long exposed to a dry atmosphere. Perhaps the best mode of preventing this will be, that the person employed to arrange the plants for the planters should be closely followed by an assistant. Thus, after the plant is laid down to be ready, the assistant may with his spade throw a little soil upon the roots, as they lie, until the planters who follow can plant them.

In ornamental planting, I consider it better for the person who arranges the plants to lay the roots at the exact point where the tree is to be planted, rather than have holes previously made, (I am speaking in reference to young plants). The latter course often leads to mistakes as to the proper position of the shrubs, especially about the front of the plantings. In all cases it is quite necessary that spacious holes or pits be made, to admit of the roots being freely spread out, first covering them with fine soil, instead of lumpy soil, as it may happen,—a thing too much practised. It may be proper to speak of the common practice of fastening the plants by indiscriminate hard treading. Sometimes we observe men ramming the earth about the roots with their feet as if to fasten a gate post; and whether the plants are delicate or robust, it is all the same. Of course every plant should have the soil pretty firmly pressed about the roots, so as to fasten it sufficiently, and the earth should nowhere lie hollow about them; but this should be done with care and discrimination. A plant with a ball of earth attached to it should by no means be trampled or pressed hard near to the stem, or over the ball of earth; because, although it may be deposited, and covered with soil, and out of sight, if the ball be broken underground, it is as injurious to the plant as if it had been done previous to planting. With such plants, the earth should be more especially and carefully pressed round the outside of the ball; or, when plants are placed in the ground with balls of earth which have been a long time in pots, the balls should be rather broken all round before they are planted: otherwise the fibrous roots may become so matted within the ball, as not to be able to extricate themselves, and the plants will be retarded in their growth.

Both trees and bushes may be planted with great safety when the buds are nearly expanded, especially in damp gloomy weather, but not without the check being greater than if planted a little earlier; certainly, however, with better success than late in the autumn or in winter. It will be found of the greatest moment to water freely such plants as have been removed in the spring months. This should take place at least twice a week, should the weather prove droughty, till they are safely established, say four or six waterings, or more. There are many kinds of rare plants kept in pots, which in cases of need may be planted in June, indeed at any time, without risk of death; but the month of May is preferable to a later date. One great advantage of having the plants lying in the earth at hand, (as I have described above), is, that the most congenial weather can thus be seized upon for planting them.

The planter should be particular always to have the trees and shrubs taken up with as many fibrous roots as possible; and while I impress the importance of this, it will be still more important to warn against the unnatural practice of dubbing the roots, so generally pursued previous to planting. Common sense teaches us that to divest a plant of its healthy roots, is depriving it of vital organs, through the medium of which its principal support is derived.

SEA-SIDE PLANTING.

IT is generally allowed to be very difficult to get trees and shrubs to grow, much more flourish, on many parts of the sea coast, and thus afford any degree of interest and satisfaction. But while admitting the difficulty, I am persuaded that, with attention and care, their growth may be greatly promoted, as I propose to shew from two cases that have come under my observation; one on the eastern, and the other on the western coast. The difficulty arises, it is thought, from the injurious effects of the sea spray falling upon trees; but this, in my opinion, is very doubtful.

About fourteen years ago, I was engaged to fix the site of a marine villa on the eastern coast, and to lay out the grounds. The ground is in general flat, with little variation. Between the edifice and the sea there is a space of about one hundred and sixty yards; the flat extends about one hundred and twenty yards, to a point about one hundred feet above the level of the sea; the rest forms a steep bank, sloping rapidly down to the sands. The nature of the ground is very stiff, with a clayey bottom, but well drained. Among other things, I arranged a plantation of trees and shrubs from the house down to the sands. It was planted in the usual way, with trees from three to four years old, set about four feet apart. Two years after planting, half the trees at least were dead, and the rest had made scarcely any progress. The whole was replanted very thickly, the trees not being more than from one to two feet apart. I visited the place about two years afterwards, and found above half alive, though very little improved. The young shoots were mostly dead, and the rest dying; but on my visit to the spot about seven years after, I found, from the shelter the trees had afforded each other, by being thickly planted, many of them had attained the height of twelve feet. Among these were the Wych elm, willow, sycamore, common ash, and a solitary occidental plane, (which was well sheltered by other trees), the whole having made shoots that year from two to three feet long; the Turkey oak, larch, lime, mountain ash, horse chesnut and laburnum, had attained the height of from eight to ten feet; the spruce and Balm of Gilead firs were healthy, and making fine shoots. Such of the shrubs, also, both deciduous and evergreen, as had survived, are now thriving well; a manifest proof that the mischief the plants had previously sustained was to be attributed more to their exposure to the north and north-east winds beating upon the coast, than to the sea spray. I found some of the trees, although within ten yards of the reach of the tide, growing very freely on parts of the sloping bank, wherever the soil was moderately free, and they were not so fully exposed to the violence of the winds, in consequence of the current taking the higher level; and, at the same distance from the sea, I observed strawberries really flourishing, which, I was informed, had been planted five years, and had produced abundantly. I may also mention, as corroborative of my opinion, that the trees on the bank sloping down to the sea at Scarborough thrive remarkably well, wherever they are at all sheltered from sweeping winds.

Since, then, it is evident that shelter is of the utmost importance to young plantations on the sea coast, I would recommend, in the first place, that the ground be very thickly planted, keeping the black spruce, Austrian pine, sycamore, Wych elm, common elder, and the willow, on the bleak sides. In the next place, in the most exposed parts, I would have poles (not pleasing objects, but expedients,) fixed firmly in the ground, and interwoven with good hay or straw ropes, three or four inches apart; and in other parts, such as inner clumps or plantings, the usual hurdles, made of hazel or other coppice rods, would be found very serviceable. These were extensively used at a new place I laid out on the western coast, about half a mile from the sea, in a situation a good deal exposed to the west wind. Protected in this way, the trees and shrubs in general succeeded well; and when the hurdles, &c., were removed in the spring of the second and third years afterwards, they appeared to sustain no injury. I would just notice, that great caution must be observed in thinning plantations in such localities. It is best to commence by lopping off the branches of those trees that are to be ultimately removed; then, in a year or two, remove them altogether. This method will prevent the adopted plants from being too suddenly exposed, and will gradually inure them to greater severities.

A A

REMOVING LARGE TREES.

THIS is a subject well worthy of attention, and especially from those who are making improvements, where present effect is expedient, and where the change in the position of a favourite tree or shrub is necessary. I remember that attempts of this kind used to be made upwards of fifty years ago, with trees from thirty to forty feet in height; and there are accounts of the practice even before that time, but certainly with much less success and facility than subsequently. Within the last forty years a good deal has been written on this subject, proving its practicability. Sir H. Stewart, fifteen or twenty years ago, brought before the public a very elaborate work, affording useful information on the subject. Many other papers have also appeared in various periodicals, but not of equal value in point of general information. However, as some of my readers may not possess the requisite knowledge, it may be proper to lay down a few useful, though brief, directions for the process.

First, then, we are to make choice of trees or shrubs not already crowded amongst others; not only because they are less tender and better formed, but because they can be more easily taken up with good roots, and more easily removed; our great aim being to secure to them in their removal a sufficient extent of good fibrous roots. This is best obtained by first throwing out a trench round the tree, about twelve or fifteen inches wide, and sufficiently deep to enable us to cut through the principal roots at a proper distance from the trunk, and undermine and loosen the soil between the roots with a pickaxe, so as in the end to leave the tree more than half taken up. Perhaps a tree with a bole ten or twelve inches in diameter near to its base, should have the trench made five to six feet from the trunk all round; that is, to leave roots which would measure across, from outside to outside, about ten or twelve feet, or even more. If this is done in winter or early in spring, and the trench is then covered in again slightly, the tree will form numerous small fibres, which will, with care, provide for a safe removal by the next planting season. Probably the least labour would be to cover the trench or excavation with stubble, litter, or straw: I have no doubt that the fibres would form under such a covering. A tree of the same magnitude, removed without this preparation, would require to be taken up with a greater extent of roots, in order to secure to it a sufficiency of those fibres to imbibe the elements adapted to produce health and growth.

Trees may be transplanted from the fall of the leaf till the beginning of spring; and it will be necessary to make the proposed receptacles for them deep enough to allow the roots, when planted, to be a few inches lower than when in their former locality. Previous to planting the tree, the pit should be trenched two or three spade-depths; then, at a proper depth, a bed of fine loose broken soil should be laid all over the hole, to receive the first pushings of the fibres, and the pit should be considerably wider than the roots may seem to require, to allow plenty of loose earth for the young roots to penetrate in and lay hold freely. Trees of considerable size will need a large machine, *(fig. 40)*, the wheels of which should be from eight to ten feet in diameter. It should have also a strong axle-tree, and a long pole sufficiently strong to lift up the tree from its bed, and bear it to its new destination. In transporting a tree, these wheels must be placed as near to the root as possible. Then, after fastening the pole and tree together, while it is perpendicular, another cord should be fastened to the end of the pole, by which the tree will be drawn prostrate. This being done, horses should be yoked to the machine on the root side of the tree, in order to remove it to its new destination. While the tree is in this position, if the top is considerably too heavy or large for the roots to support, a branch here and there may be taken away; but by no means more than would preserve, to all appearance, its original

FIGURE 40.

size and handsome form. We should never, as some do, dub a tree so much as nearly to divest it of its branches, supposing that the roots curtailed by the process of taking up are inadequate to support the vitality of its top; for this is to a great degree erroneous. It is true that the roots are not capable of imbibing sufficient support for the first year or two, to produce much growth in the top; but if the tree survives, the leaves which it produces, as well as the roots, become ultimately equal for its conservation. They form, in fact, lungs of the tree; absorbing, as well as evaporating organs, necessary to its health and growth. To cut off, therefore, such means of vitality from a tree while in this delicate position, would prevent the necessary free motion of its sap. However, were we to admit that the dubbed tree would make greater shoots, and those sooner than one with its top undubbed, for the first year or two, many years would be required for its original dimensions and beauty to be regained,—if, indeed that were ever done; whereas, by the process which I have mentioned, it retains nearly its full size, and in two or three years, a well-managed tree would become so established as to grow freely and increase in size and beauty. The tree being raised perpendicularly, its roots and fibres are then to be regulated and put in order by the hand, and covered by degrees with fine soil, which is to be worked in amongst the roots carefully with an appropriate stick, so that the roots do not lie hollow. To accomplish this more effectually, when the roots are more than half covered, the whole must be well drenched with water, the tree being moved or rocked a little at the same time, to allow the puddle to mix and fill in amongst the roots. About this stage of the process, before all the earth is filled in, in order to prevent boisterous winds disturbing the roots and pressing the tree out of its perpendicular, it is a good plan to fasten the roots down in three or four places by means of a strong stick, about two feet long, laid across them near to their extremities, and kept in its place with strong hooked sticks at each end, until the stick bends with the pressure, rather than otherwise. *(Fig.* 41, *a.)* The next day after watering, or when it may be considered that the water previously applied is absorbed, the soil should be filled in and trodden moderately and firmly down. In finishing, the levelling should be left to appear to be a very gentle swell, to represent the natural raising of the ground by the roots of the tree, as is general. But this artificial swell must have a slight hollow at its top near the tree, for the convenience of holding water during the process of watering. At the close of this operation, a good soaking of water by several pailfuls at a time is essential, which must be followed up once or twice a week during the months of April and May, or even longer, if the weather is very droughty. But even in slightly rainy weather, extensive watering is necessary once a week, at least in the months of April and May; for slight rains do nothing more than refresh the leaves and branches. If these directions are attended to, very few failures will ensue.

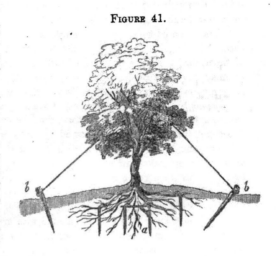

FIGURE 41.

When it is inconvenient, or where the number of trees to be removed is not sufficient to warrant the expense of a machine as thus described, a mason's truck, or a low wherry, drawn by a horse, will be found very useful. A pulley will, however, be necessary to rear and fix the tree upon the truck, in which position it must be steadied by labourers, with the assistance of ropes. Trees of three or four inches in diameter may be transported to a short distance readily, by six or eight men, having strong, yet not heavy, poles, sufficiently long for two or three men on each side of the tree to carry it. The pole, when the tree is prostrate, should be placed underneath it and close to the roots, fastened there by cords, so as not to allow it to slip about; and mats, or cloths, should be placed between the poles and the tree, to prevent its bark being bruised. Other men will be required to assist with the top part of the tree. Of course, the tree must be carried horizontally with its roots first. As the successful removal of large trees depends principally upon

182

their having the essential requisites, it may not be improper again to point them out. First, then, the tree is to possess good, fibrous, and spacious roots; second, fine broken soil must be blended amongst the roots; third, it is to be supplied with copious waterings; and, fourth, it must be well stayed in its new locality against boisterous winds.

Transplanted trees, not sufficiently large to be out of danger from cattle without fencing, may be very completely stayed by placing a rod on each side of them, nearly close to the tree, of sufficient length so that each end of the rod may rest upon the fencing, and be made fast by nails; or, if the fence is of iron, wire will be necessary to fasten these cross bars, which are again to be crossed by short pieces, forming a square pretty close to the tree; this square is to be filled with hay or straw, that the tree may be kept from chafing. Trees not thus fenced may be stayed by three or four cords tied round the bole near the top of the tree, and fastened pretty tightly by string obliquely, to short strong stakes, driven into the ground a few yards from the tree, and leaning from it, in order to provide a more secure fastening for the cords. (*Figure* 41 *b b*).

By a strict adherence to the foregoing recommendations, large trees and shrubs of most kinds may be transplanted with great success; and, certainly, in grounds unadorned with trees, nothing can be more pleasing than the immediate and striking effects which may be produced in this way. I have just visited a place I laid out fifteen years ago, (Bolton Hall, near Doncaster,) where several large trees were removed, the trunks of which were from half a yard to two feet in diameter, and most of them are doing well. I particularly noticed a Wych elm, (a fine spreading tree, having a trunk two feet in diameter near to the ground,) which had made shoots this year half a yard long. The other trees were Spanish chesnuts, oaks, elms, and beeches.

TOWN GARDENS.

Town Gardens are those which skirt a town, and are usually of small extent, generally, indeed, occupying only the front of the house. Unquestionably, such gardens are best laid out in the formal style. It is absurd to make the least attempt to imitate rude nature in such places where the eye easily falls upon the square boundary, and on every other point at once.

I have given a sketch, *(Plate* 1, *figure* 1,) as an example of what I consider best for a place of this kind, when it may not be thought necessary to drive up to the door; and another shewing a carriage drive *(Plate* 1, *figure* 2 *)*. Gardens such as these ought to be composed of fine turf, and should be furnished with handsome low trees and interesting shrubs,—not planted indiscriminately with all kinds of large shrubs. Forest trees are out of the question. I will name a few that I think the most suitable low trees for a smoky atmosphere; such are double and single crimson thorns, snake-barked maple, various weeping trees, cut-leaved birch, red cedar, Hemlock-spruce, double blossomed cherry, Cotoneaster frigida, hollies of sorts, laburnums, snowy mespilus, Gleditschia triacanthos, Araucaria imbricata, and Cedrus deodara. Though the two last-named attain to a large size in their native country, there will be no danger, in these localities, of their becoming too large for many years, indeed, for a century to come. Amongst the evergreen shrubs which stand smoke best, are the Aucuba japonica, Rhododendron ponticum, Irish yew and Irish juniper, arborvitæ, Erica stricta, multiflora, and carnea, box, laurustine, variegated hollies, Phillyrea ilex, Phillyrea angustifolia and oppositifolia, Arbutus regia, and Mahonia aquifolium. Deciduous flowering shrubs, in consequence of shedding their leaves in autumn, are not so liable to be injured by smoke as evergreens are; therefore, the deciduous plants ought to be the more largely employed, not forgetting the spring and autumnal roses, fuchsias, red and white mezereons, the white, red, and double ribes, Weigelia rosea, Spirea salicifolia, Douglasii, Lyndleyana and areafolia. Hollyhocks and dahlias ought to take part in decorating the shrubbery; and pinks, sweet-williams, piccotees, carnations, pansies, Alpine auriculas, columbines, antirhinums, polyanthuses, double primroses of various colours, wallflowers, with various other gay and odoriferous flowering plants and annuals, must be especially employed for decorating and embellishing the flower beds.

Climbers for walls will be necessary, such as white and yellow jasmine, not forgetting Jasminum nudiflora, Amie vibert, Fellenberg, ruga and Thorsbiana roses, Pyrus Japonica, long blowing and other honeysuckles, pyracantha (white and red berried), Wistaria consequan, Clematis azurea florida and Seiboldii, and Cotoneaster microphilla.

EXPLANATION OF PLATE I.

IDEAL PLAN FOR TOWN GARDENS.

FIGURE 1.

A. House.

B. Terrace.

C, C. Two styles of shrub borders, shewn purposely for choice. Whichever is chosen, it is to represent both sides of the garden alike. The four circles, D, D, D, D, are intended for rich flowers, surrounded with wire baskets. The other four beds are also for flowers; the remainder of the plot to be composed of fine lawn. The four small squares, E, E, E, E, are situations for sculpture, or fancy wire plant supporters.

FIGURE 2.

A. House.

B. Terrace.

C, C, C. Shrubs, fronted with flowers.

D. Dial.

E. Sculpture.

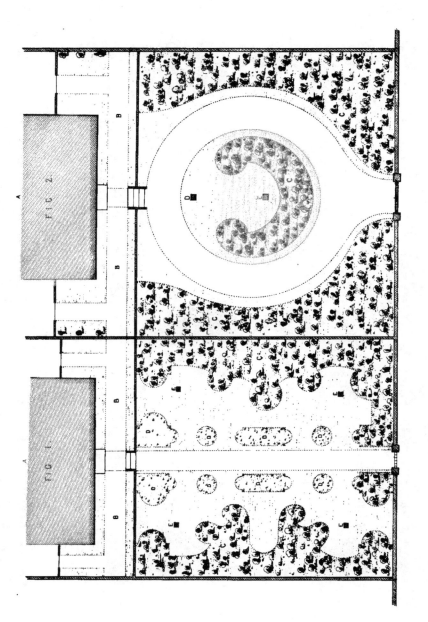

Plan for Town Gardens.

EXPLANATION OF PLATE II.

IDEAL PLAN FOR A VILLA RESIDENCE UPON AN ACRE OF GROUND.

1. House.
2. Yard.
3. Stables.
4. Clothes yard, through which passes the back road to the house.
5. Vegetable garden.
6. Geometrical flower garden.
7. Sculpture.
8. Covered seat.
9. Greenhouse.
10. Dial.

The beds are intended to be planted principally with good kinds of shrubs, and the belting or boundary with ornamental trees and shrubs.

Plate 2

Plan for a Villa Residence.

1 ACRE

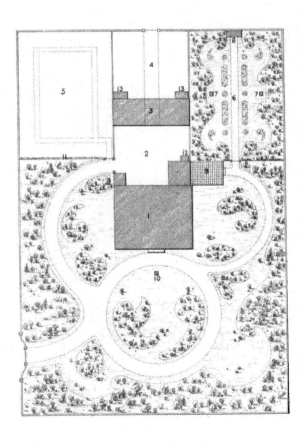

EXPLANATION OF PLATE III.

IDEAL PLAN FOR A VILLA RESIDENCE UPON FOUR ACRES OF GROUND.

A. House.
B. Kitchen yard.
C. Stable yard.
D. Stables.
E. Cattle yard and cart shed.
F. Clothes yard.
G. Back road.
H. Kitchen garden.
I. Forcing-houses.
J. Lodge.
K. Round basket-work for flowers.
L. Fountain.
M. Aviary.
N. Covered seat.
O. Greenhouse, with verandah attached at each end for greenhouse plants in the summer.
P, P. English or modern flower garden.
Q. Small pond.
R. Paddock, grouped with trees, and shewing the manner of assembling trees for producing natural beauty.
S. Rivulet.

All the dotted beds are intended for flowers. The other beds are for shrubs, blended with smooth lawn. The boundary planting is proposed to be of trees and shrubs of the most pleasing and useful kinds.

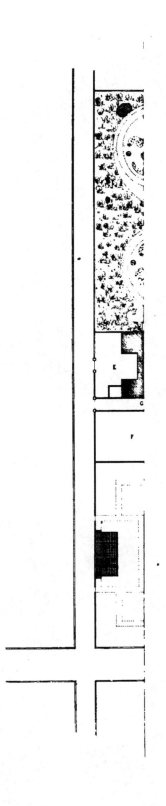

SUBURBAN VILLAS.

Plate 2 is an ideal plan of about an acre of land, not strictly uniform, yet for the most part formal. Being too small to justify fully an attempt at the natural or modern style, and being supposed to possess a site a good deal exposed to the gaze of the public, it will be necessary to plant a sufficient portion of the belt with hardy evergreen shrubs, such as common laurels, laurustine, Aucuba japonica, variegated hollies, phillyreas, allaturnus, best evergreen privet, box-leaved privet, &c., and front these with rich flowering and evergreen shrubs. In order to obtain both variety and shelter, we may in the same belt plant low-growing ornamental trees, which will not only help to exclude the public view, or to shut out any disagreeable object, but will also give variety of surface. If large trees are absolutely required, the following bear a smoky atmosphere moderately well:—the Wych and English elm, lime, cut-leaved beech, cut-leaved hornbeam; but the horse chesnut, mountain ash, poplar, sycamore, common ash, and birch, are generally ragged, and thrive ill in a smoky atmosphere. A collection of good kinds of shrubs ought to occupy the various beds represented as shrub-masses in the plate; also suitable kinds should form light groups on the lawn as grass plants. It is of consequence that the plants in such small places should not be allowed to be overgrown or too much crowded. The narrowest margin of grass may, in confined grounds, between the beds and walks, be fifteen or eighteen inches broad. Such small places being constantly under the eye, the greatest nicety of keeping is essential; for instance, smooth-cropped lawns, clean smooth walks, true and graceful curves, showing even, though very shallow, edgings, of not more than an inch deep. Further interest and beauty must be supplied by sculpture, round beds bordered with iron or wire, neat trellised seats, wire plant-supporters, and other garden ornaments. Above all, a provision of gay floral productions should be studiously presented throughout the season; and in order to this, two or three successions of annuals should be introduced.

B B

Plate 3 is an ideal plan of about four acres of land, proposed for a suburban villa, parsonage, or small country residence, with about two acres of it appropriated to pasture land, and the remainder to pleasure ground, vegetable garden, and other conveniences. In the arrangement of these grounds the modern style is kept in view, as much as the extent of ground will admit. Such sites must never be overplanted with large growing common trees, to the exclusion of a good and pleasing collection of ornamental trees and shrubs, as that would lessen the interest which ought ever to be held out as inviting the citizen from his busy haunts, to change his toil for that enjoyment of the beauties of nature which a richly decorated garden is so calculated to afford. Due regard must be paid to secure privacy by masking out the public view by planting. Even where distant views are desirable, and where evergreen shrubs would be sufficient to shut out the gaze of the public without trees, their introduction in this way, occasionally, would not only preserve desirable views, but also vary and heighten the landscape. The hints I have already given on planting in Park Scenery will apply also to this subject; but, of course, all must be on a proportionately smaller scale.

THE KITCHEN GARDEN.

It would seem almost unnecessary to treat at all on Vegetable Gardens, as the laying out of them is well understood by gardeners generally, all agreeing that straight lines and parallel forms are more suitable for the arrangement of their crops than crooked lines. I may observe, however, that the Vegetable Garden ought not to be at a considerable distance from the house, except a proper locality does not present itself nearer. When it is half a mile or more distant, as in many instances, the supply of the house with vegetables is effected with great inconvenience. At the same time, strict regard must be paid to its being so placed as to be concealed, as much as possible, from the general landscape. The gardens which are laid down on the *General Plan* in this work, are placed at as short a distance as should be allowed, for a proper disposal of the rest of the ground; the size laid down would, also, only in very few instances be large enough; therefore, any greater extent required should be added backwards, or further from the house.

It may be useful to observe, that good drainage is of the highest importance to the health and flavour of both fruit and vegetables, especially in clayey or strong land. When such is the nature of the land, a principal drain should be laid in all the walks, considerably below the undisturbed subsoil, with necessary branch drains all over the garden, and especially in the borders between the walks and the wall, in order to keep the soil in as pure a state as possible for the roots of the wall trees. Further, when the bottom of these borders below the subsoil is of clay, in addition to the drains, the most useful and effective means to prevent the roots of vines, and other fruit trees, penetrating into the clay—in fact, to preserve them in a healthy state—is, to spread a thin covering of stones, or gravel, from an inch to three inches deep, all over the clay, then to cover the whole with lime, or lime-craps, sufficient to fill all the crevices, and afterwards to brush it in with a little water, so that, the whole being made firm and even, with a gentle fall from the wall, no water from excessive rains may settle in pools. This not only prevents the roots from penetrating into the cold clay, but keeps them in a warmer and more congenial element, whilst the trees are in every respect healthier, and produce better flavoured fruit. If this plan be considered too expensive, the next best method is to flag, or stone, below the subsoil in the above manner, five or six feet square, and then to plant the tree in a proper depth of soil, from eighteen inches or more. This will give a turn to the roots, and make them less liable to enter the clay, which is very prejudicial to them. Quicksandy bottoms require the same treatment.

It is necessary to guard against planting fruit trees too numerously in other parts of the Vegetable Garden. They should be limited to such a number as will admit of a free circulation of air. A suitable place, not far distant from the kitchen garden, should be selected for an orchard, to supply the deficiency in the garden, paving the bottom as above. I think (though it is not a matter of paramount importance) that gardens should be kept clear of any arrangement calculated to produce an untidy appearance,—such as forcing-pits; and that sea-kale and rhubarb, which require forcing with manure or litter, should be found in places entirely set apart for that purpose. The principal forcing houses should, of course, be in the principal garden.

A FEW OBSERVATIONS ON VILLAGES.

THE owners of hamlets and villages should give earnest attention to their neatness, picturesque beauty, and general appearance, as well as to the comfort of the occupiers, especially those of the poorer classes, since,— independent of higher considerations,—a well-managed village adds much to the importance and beauty of a domain. To my mind, a really rural village is one of the most pleasing objects, especially when the cottages have not too much of a street-like appearance, but stand in groups, with fields here and there interspersed, with now and then clusters of trees and neatly clipped hedges, and clean firm roads and gravelled paths close to and on each side of the road. No open drains, offices, or rubbish heaps, should be any where visible. Cottages should be kept in comfortable repair, neat in their external appearance, and by all means the occupiers should be urged to cleanliness and order within. Roses and other climbing plants, neatly and uniformly trained to the cottage walls, give an idea also of management and respect-ability; and I would therefore recommend proprietors to put up in front of every cottage, for the protection of such plants, a simple but neat palisade, from about three feet to three feet six inches high, and at a distance of about three feet from the cottage front. If the cottages are old, perhaps a corresponding dwarf wall, two feet six inches high, might be better; or larch rods of similar height, two to three inches in diameter, fixed upright, three or four inches apart, with a half one nailed on the top, the round side upwards, and stained or painted oak colour, would be quite in character. I should in no instance allow more front garden to appear, as such, unless the greatest order is kept, without which the beauty which we wish a village to present would be lessened. This three feet of garden should be fully occupied with flowers, such as stocks, pinks, pansies, tulips, wallflowers, mignonette, &c. The principal garden ought to be behind the house, for which, perhaps, each cottager should be allowed from five hundred yards to a quarter of an acre, as a general average, for vegetables, fruit, and flowers.

It would also be well if each cottage could be provided with pigsties, and tanks for collecting drainage for tillage. If, too, sufficient land could be allowed to support a cow, it would be a considerable privilege. The gardens in the first instance, I think, ought to be laid out by the owners' gardeners, or some competent person, and necessary fences and fruit trees introduced, under condition that the form of the grounds and the position of the trees should be always maintained. This would be far better both for landlord and tenant than for the tenant to pursue his own plans, as, on the latter plan, with every change of tenant a change in the garden would be the result, and discord and confusion would arise. I think also that the proprietors' gardeners should be allowed to pay a visit to each garden two or three times a year, that they might give a few general instructions, with which, and with the help of the Cottage Garden Book, the cottager might (if he is only willing) manage very well. I am the more anxious about this practical assistance being given in the first instance, because, if the breaking up and formation of a new garden were left entirely to the untutored cottager, the result would most likely be that his produce would not repay his labour, and he would, in time, dislike what ought to have proved both a profit and a pleasure; at least, he would follow it with slovenliness and neglect. Thus, the objects of his having a garden would be frustrated, namely, affording him pecuniary assistance in the best form, preventing the waste of time at a public-house, and leading to the devotion of his leisure hours to pursuits which are most healthy, rational, and interesting, and calculated to increase the union, happiness, and pleasurable recreation of his whole family.

One or two horticultural shows in a year in a village, or among a number of adjoining villages, would be likely to create great interest, and to stimulate the cottagers to vie with each other in the growth of the best productions.

I would very respectfully ask the lady of the village to co-operate with the pastor, by paying occasional visits to cheer and encourage the cottagers, and giving them both temporal and spiritual advice. Such attention and watchfulness will not fail to win the affection and respect of the villagers to their superiors. I took the liberty, some fifteen years ago, to suggest publicly similar views, which I had afterwards the pleasure of witnessing carried into practice. In one instance where I had the honour of paying a visit to a family in Westmoreland, I found a neat, clean village, trained with roses and other climbing plants, the church-yard wall, outside, covered with ivy, mingling with monthly roses, &c.; the lady of the village engaged in dressing and pruning some of the plants, and her gardener in training them. This lady's own grounds were rich in plants, and in the finest keeping; and I learnt before I left, that her kindness to the villagers had won their warmest attachment and esteem.

I may mention another case, where I was consulted a short time afterwards by a clergyman in Lincolnshire, who had three small parishes under his care, and who was revered by all his parishioners. He had a complete medicine chest in his house, and in going round among his poorer brethren, when he found them a little ailing, they were assisted with simple medicine, when it was not thought necessary to call in the aid of a medical man. During my stay I went with my clerical friend through his parishes, and it was highly gratifying to see with what pleasure the people received the visit of their kind pastor. As it was his wish in some degree to carry out my views, by inculcating a style of order and neatness, and cultivating a taste for gardening amongst his cottagers, he lost no time in distributing various climbing plants for their cottages, and fruit trees of the best kinds to such as were provided with gardens. Many of the work-people possessed a small portion of land, and kept a cow; and I remember well, on one of my visits, he observed, that nearly the whole of his flock appeared so comfortable that their circumstances were really enviable. I have since had the pleasure to visit the same gentleman, who has left his former charge, and is watching with equal zeal over another in a rural parish in Nottinghamshire. It is true that this liberal and kind-hearted pastor had the pecuniary means of doing what it is much to be regretted that many good and pious clergymen wish to do, but cannot to the same extent; but every clergyman can do a little, at least, in the way of counsel and advice.

A plot of ground, in every village, should be set apart for athletic games and other innocent amusements. It would also be most desirable if water could be introduced at one end of the plot, and be planted out from the gaze of the public, so as to afford baths and swimming ponds, and also winter recreations on the ice. The water should not be more than three or four feet deep, to prevent accidents.

Schools for the education of the poorer classes are now becoming so general, that it is scarcely necessary to refer to that subject. Of course, no village can be complete without a school, and no perfection of schools can be maintained without the superintending visits of the heads of the village. I cannot help speaking of one instance of the paternal care I am so anxious to see general, irrelevant as it may be to the subject of Landscape Gardening. In one instance, where I was called in to improve an extensive domain in Cumberland, my patron and his lady were very benevolent, and turned their attention particularly to the education of the children of the poor. In addition to the general appendages to the mansion, there were erected, at a convenient distance from it, ornamental and comfortable cottages for the married servants; two separate schools, one for boys and the other for girls, which were used both as day and Sunday schools; also a cottage each for the master and mistress of the schools; and, in addition to these, I fixed the site for a neat lodge for the back approach. These, together with the dairy and farm buildings, presented the appearance of a neat picturesque village or hamlet mingled with trees, which both added extent, variety, and importance to the estate, and formed, with the mansion, a very complete whole. In these schools the day boys receive more than ordinary education, and are in due time provided with suitable places. Such as wish to be gardeners are practically educated in the gentleman's own gardens, where the range of glass is immense, as well as the grounds extensive. The girls are taught, in addition to general education, every kind of needlework, with the necessary routine best fitted to prepare them for respectable places, which are (if possible) provided for them also. To these schools the ladies pay frequent visits, and assist there on Sundays. At certain times, both the Sunday and day scholars have festivals, or holidays, when they are regaled with buns, tea, &c., and are also permitted to walk in the pleasure grounds, and look into the plant and forcing houses. I had the pleasure to be present on one of these occasions. In the afternoon, the children were assembled together on the terrace and regaled in the manner above noticed; hints and appropriate advice, and encouragement, being also given by their benefactor. He endeavoured to impress upon their young minds the importance of honesty, loyalty, obedience to parents, employers, and benefactors, but, above all things, to make the Bible their study and guide. The neat and clean appearance of the children, and their orderly behaviour, were very gratifying. We were cheered by the singing of their little hymns, and, at dismissal, they all joined in singing the national anthem, which they did with spirit and cheerfulness.

PUBLIC PARKS CONNECTED WITH LARGE TOWNS.

PUBLIC PARKS for large towns are of very great importance to persons whose occupations compel them to dwell in a smoky and impure atmosphere. They are, indeed, almost necessary; and they ought to be of sufficient extent to afford a spacious promenade, to have a great variety of pleasure ground, and to present, if not a complete, at least a judicious collection of attractive kinds of trees, shrubs, and flowers, varied with lawn, arranged in the best possible manner and most attractive style.

An Arboretum, upon the principle of that at Derby, would also be highly attractive, as well as instructive. When the extent of ground is of sufficient magnitude, room must also be afforded for various athletic games, and for other amusements, as at Manchester. In forming the three parks at Manchester, (which we had the privilege of designing), the committee particularly wished us to arrange our plans so as to offer convenience for as many varieties of games as possible. In order, therefore, to make the most of the ground we had to operate upon, we designed the pleasure ground as near as practicable to the skirts of the plot, and then took advantage of every nook or recess which was to spare for the different play-grounds,—for archery, quoit alley, skittle ground, bowling green, climbing poles, gymnasium, marbles, see-saws, &c., for males; and see-saws, balls, skipping rope, the Graces, &c., for females. A general play-ground was formed in the centre of the whole plot, of about twelve or fifteen acres, for cricket, knor and spell, leaping poles, football, and foot races, &c., and also for the additional purpose of large public meetings. These plans, with but a few exceptions, were generally approved and acted upon. One exception I think it necessary to mention, because the omission very much deteriorated our general arrangements; and the committee would not have permitted it had their funds been larger. I allude to an inner fence of wire, by which it was intended to divide the

c c

pleasure grounds from the open area or general play ground, so that the grass might be kept short by letting in sheep at hours when the ground was otherwise unoccupied. This I consider the cheapest way of keeping in order so large a space. Such a fence would also have been useful in preventing the formation of tracks in order to gain the shortest access to any particular spot. Of such tracks there were soon many, in addition to the walks originally laid down, and which, I understand, has resulted in many additional walks being made, whereby the boldness and freedom of the whole has been to a great extent destroyed. I mention this to prevent similar errors.

It is much to be regretted that nowhere amongst our public parks in England, or in any part of her Majesty's dominions, are there to be found general good specimens of the English style of Landscape Gardening, even in places where there has been ample scope to admit of the finest examples. Our metropolitan parks are amongst the worst of all. Where lies the blame? Surely it cannot be said that this has happened for want of artistic skill, while we have had a Repton, a Gilpin, and a Loudon. Had their taste and talent been called into action, such barbarous productions as we see in these national parks would not have presented themselves. It requires no great skill to detect that the arrangement of the three metropolitan public parks, where much might have been expected, namely, Hyde Park, Regent's Park, and the Green Park, has not been guided by an experienced hand.

Of these parks, it can only be said that they are open and healthy places of resort for the public, who may choose to leave the confined streets and alleys of the metropolis, to resort to them. But it appears to me that such praise is far less than they might have merited. London is the grand emporium of the world, to which people from all parts and all nations resort, and who naturally expect great things there; consequently, in the parks of London ought to be exhibited the chief model of the English style of Landscape Gardening, not only as a pattern for her Majesty's subjects to copy, but to put to silence the censure of other nations. In illustration of this, I may mention that a very severe criticism was passed upon the English style of Landscape Gardening generally, by a German tourist, in the pages of the *Gardeners' Magazine*, vol. vi., page 31, and it fell to my lot to vindicate it in a succeeding number of the same volume, page 611. But if these parks had been the only objects of his censure, and I had been called upon to establish the proposition, that true taste was displayed in them, I must unquestionably have failed in the attempt.

Without entering into any detail of the faults existing in the parks of London, (which, by the way, would be too voluminous for this work), I may be permitted to urge the propriety of their being remodelled, so as to exhibit, as fully and completely as possible, the modern or English style of Landscape Gardening. For example: there might be shewn the proper position and naturally varied outline of principal plantings; the style of planting each kind of trees in groups and masses; the different forms and sizes of groups and masses, with the manner in which they, as well as the trees, should be associated. The water now in the parks should be formed into imitative lakes, river, and rivulets, having their margins naturally varied and fringed at intervals with plants, and their banks occasionally grouped with trees and bushes, with islands here and there introduced, so as to produce intricacy and variety,—at one time allowing the water to be closely approached, at another preventing it by groups of trees and shrubs.

I would, by no means, allow the indecent practice of open bathing in these waters; provision ought to be made for that purpose elsewhere.

Spacious winding drives and rides should be there. Besides dress grounds with bold, graceful, and easily curved walks, there ought to be shrubberies or masses of shrubs, without any appearance of earthy parts, but with varied outlines produced by their natural growth blending with varied expanses of lawn, and associated with clusters and single bushes and trees, so as generally to bring out prominent bends, and to effect deeper bays. There should also be covered and open seats, sculpture, fountains, plant-houses, and all necessary garden structures. A general flower garden, composed of elegantly formed beds both of shrubs and flowers, harmoniously dispersed over lawn, and varied with small groups of some of the most striking and beautiful shrubs, would also be most pleasing. A rosarium, American and rock garden, botanic garden, aquarium, and an arboretum, as complete as possible—so arranged as to be studied in regular order, even by strangers, without their being confused or perplexed—would be highly useful. Lastly, all the various kinds of plants should be distinctly named, their native country, with the time of their introduction into this country, being also stated.

I would particularly advise the appropriation of spaces (under restrictions) for innocent athletic games, in addition to the open park necessarily required for more extensive games and recreations, and military exercise. Great caution would, however, be necessary, that none of these provisions should interfere with the composition and beauty of the general landscape, and that throughout there should be a unity and harmony preserved.

MISCELLANEOUS.

Shrubs suitable as Undergrowths for Thickening Plantations.

It is the opinion of many persons that plants under other trees do not thrive, because of the drip from those trees; and hence arises the common phrase, "They cannot bear the drip." To me this appears a misconception. I think that the success or non-success of plants introduced under trees ought more to be attributed, sometimes, to a want of light and heat to accelerate and mature their growth, and sometimes (even in the case of plants that will bear the shade), to want of a strict preparation of the soil previous to their being planted. In most cases, the existing roots absorb nearly all the nutriment which the soil can give, and thereby impoverish it so much as to leave the new plants no opportunity to do more than just live, or live in sickness. In order, therefore, to promote their success, in the first place, spacious pits, from two to six feet wide, and about half a yard deep, (according to circumstances), must be made, to disturb or clear away the existing roots and fibres. Then a moderate quantity of good soil or decaying sods must be added; and it will be a further advantage if a little humus of decayed leaves or manure, or both, can be supplied, which would establish the plants fully. By the way, all ornamental plantings, especially those cleared of all fallen leaves, ought occasionally to be manured. The following kinds will be found generally to flourish pretty well, except the overhanging trees are very much crowded, which ought not to be, for the sake of ornament and effect, (as I have remarked in the chapter on the management of ornamental trees). The yew, common holly, and smooth-leaved holly, are invaluable for this purpose, and, indeed, so are the variegated kinds for front situations. The common and Portugal laurels, best evergreen and box-leaved privet, Daphne pontica, Butcher's broom, box in varieties, English juniper, mahonia aquifolia, repens, and other varieties, whins, brooms, hemlock-spruce, and the rhododendron ponticum, are highly desirable for forming thickets and for varying the scene. I remember, upwards of forty years ago, noticing magnificent bushes of the latter, growing freely in the shade, in the woods at Kenwood, the seat of the Earl of Mansfield. Among the deciduous shrubs are the red dogwood, silver and gold striped elder, nuts, blackthorns, and the Dundee rambling roses. Woodbine and Virginian bower, borne up by some neighbouring bush or tree, are particularly pleasing. Vinca minor, of varieties, and Vinca major, are valuable plants for covering bare ground under trees in pleasure grounds; and in such situations they serve as a bordering for walks. Also the common ling and other heaths, Gaultheria shallon, and crowberries, may be employed for the same purpose.

CLIMBING PLANTS.

First, I may mention the following as very suitable for clinging to old buildings, with little or no assistance, both with a view to produce effect, and also for covering walls, in order to destroy their glaring appearance :—Irish ivy, small-leaved silver-striped ivy, and gold-striped Irish giant ivy, palmate-leaved and common small-leaved Virginian creeper; Bignonia radicans, and Bignonia radicans major.

Next, those suitable for trellis work and walls, but requiring to be trained, are,—Clematis azurea grandiflora, Clematis flamula, Clematis florida, Clematis florida pleno, Clematis bicolor, Eccremocarpus scabra, Lycium barbarum, Lycium ruthenicum, Catalpa syringifolia, Wistaria consequana, Jasminum nudiflorum, Wallachiana, and the white jasmine, Passiflora cœrulea, honeysuckles of sorts, Fellemberg, Amie vibert, Thorsbiana, and other perpetual roses.

PLANTS FOR BEAUTIFYING TREES WHICH ARE NOT OF THEMSELVES PLEASING OBJECTS.

The double Ayrshire and Thorsbiana roses, varieties of honeysuckles, Virginian bower, sweet-scented clematis, cut-leaved ivy, small leaved and silver ivy, are pleasing objects climbing round the stems and branches of old crooked trees, not handsome of themselves. But let it be noticed, that ivy pressing and grasping straight-stemmed trees of all ages, exhibiting puny tops, and gasping for life, (as we often see it in woods), is neither natural in its effect, nor pleasing, but much the reverse. On the other hand, when we see it stealing over and taking possession of the trunk and branches of an old, time-worn tree, the special character of which is gone, and thus presenting to view a varied ivy tree, studded with its tufted blossoms, we have an object most pleasing and picturesque.

Compost for Plants.

Perhaps I ought to name the kind of compost suitable to be used in planting young plants in situations where the soil is not naturally good. I believe nothing is more suitable for the growth of plants, generally, than sods, taken from a loose or kind loamy pasture, an inch to two inches thick, and laid on a heap to decay. This compost would be usable after lying twelve months, but would be equally good for several years; and if the sod is taken from light land, and mixed with decaying leaves of equal quantity, with the addition of one-eighth of river sand, such a compost would be a good substitute for peat soil for the growth of rhododendrons, heaths, and many other plants commonly called bog plants, especially if a little real peat was first put around the roots, to start their growth. The above compost, in either case, would be improved by the addition of a moderate quantity of decayed stable manure.

To Protect Tender Plants.

Beds of tender plants, such as monthly roses, may be protected from severe weather by pricking in amongst them short branches of whins, or different kinds of firs, especially the spruce and silver, or with common heaths. Small single plants, also, may be secured against the inclemency of the weather by three or four branches being set round each plant. These retain their greenness pretty well all winter, and do not appear disagreeable,—at least, not nearly so much as when the plants are bound round with matting, or covered with basket work in the usual way.

To Destroy Weeds in Walks.

When walks become by any means so neglected as to be overrun with mosses and small grasses, or other weeds, too tedious to hand-weed, they may be destroyed by pouring upon them a moderate quantity of boiling water from a watering-pan and rose, or a barrel fixed upon wheels, letting the water through a tap into a tube the whole breadth of the walk, or nearly so, pierced with holes, so as to allow it to fall freely all over the walk, without injuring the boundaries or borders of grass. It is useless to employ other ingredients, under the idea that they may render the remedy more efficacious, for weeds cannot survive the application of boiling water.

To Destroy Worms.

Worms throw up their casts on both lawns and walks. This may be prevented by occasional applications of lime-water, composed of lime slacked until it falls, just as is done by builders. A spadeful of this, mixed with ten gallons of water, stirred well together for about ten minutes or more, will be effective for their destruction, if poured on the parts freely in the spring or in the autumn; or it may be applied at other times, in damp or showery weather, when worms are near the surface. The water then fails not to reach them. The lime will keep for months if the air be excluded from it, which may be done by the use of tubs, or otherwise; but it becomes useless when exposed for a while to the atmosphere.

EXPLANATION OF PLATES.

PLATE V.—IDEAL PLAN OF A COUNTRY RESIDENCE,

ATTEMPTING TO DELINEATE THE TRUE ENGLISH OR NATURAL STYLE OF LAYING-OUT PLEASURE GROUNDS.

This being drawn upon a scale too large for the Park to be attached, I have given a detached plan, Plate VI., which will shew the style I recommend for the arrangement of a Park.

1. House.
2. Kitchen yard and outbuildings.
3. Stable yard.
4. Stables.
5. Clothes, or laundry yard.
6. Conservatory, or plant houses adapted for a winter promenade.
7. Reading-room, museum, or plant house.
8. Shed and fire-place.
9, 9. Terrace,—the wall of which to be decorated with vases, sculpture, &c.
10. Small paddock, which may be appropriated to play grounds.
11. Aviary, or menagerie, with yard attached.
12. Swimming pond, with dressing rooms.
13. Covered seat in wooded scenery.
14. Lodge and entrance gates.
15, 15. Back entrance gates.
16. Stack yard.
17. Farm.
18. Ice-house.
19, 19. Gardener's and under-gardener's house.
20. Forcing-pit and reserve garden.
21, 21. Compost ground.
22. Forcing houses and shed.
23, 23, 23. Walls enclosing vegetable garden, bounded by borders for wall trees and vegetables, &c.
24. Botanic garden.
25. Arboretum on lawn, in the gardenesque style.

26. Covered seat.
27. Rockery, or rock garden.
28. Rude covered seat.
29. Greenhouse, with wings of lattice work attached, in which to place plants in summer, the whole fronted by a dwarf terrace wall, decorated with vases, sculpture, &c.
30. Fountain.
31, 31, 31. General flower garden.
32. Group, or mass garden.
33. Florist garden; or the whole to be employed as a General Flower Garden, and the round beds for groups and masses of bedding plants.
34. Beds for American plants, or such as require peat soil.
35, 35. Ornamental seats.   The dots at the junctions of the walks denote situations for sculpture.   Places for light, elegant, open seats are represented by oblong marks on the sides of the walks.

PLATE VI.—IDEAL PLAN DELINEATING
THE MODERN OR ENGLISH STYLE OF LAYING OUT A PARK,
SUITABLE FOR A COUNTRY RESIDENCE,—Plate V.

36. Hut for aquatic animals.
37, 37, 37. Bridges.
38. Covered open seat.
39. Rustic covered seat.
40. Boat-house.
41. Jet, issuing out of a rocky base in the lake.
42. Lake, interspersed with islands.
43. Waterfall and rockwork.
44. Entrance gates and lodge.
45. Boundary fence, fronted with low-growths, not intended to grow higher than the wall, but just to shut out the public gaze, yet allow the eye to range beyond; and to assist in destroying the boundary, or belted appearance.

PLATE VII.—DESIGN FOR PALACE OR MANSION GROUNDS.

This plan being too extensive to admit of a Park being attached, Plate VI. is intended to suffice to show the style recommended.

1. Palace.
2. Court, composed of lawn, gravel, shrubs, and sculpture.
3, 3. Porter's lodges, with arched gateways.
4, 4, 4. Shrubs, intended to hide the stable yard from view, with a few ornamental low trees added, in order to vary the surface line, and prevent a full exposure of the stables, but not to shut them out altogether.

203

5. Stable yard.
6. Stables.
7. Carpenter's yard, &c.
8. Kitchen yard, &c.
9. Clothes yard.
10. Terrace, with small beds on lawn, proposed to be edged round with terra cotta, and strong wire basket work, to be adorned with the richest and most beautiful flowers from the reserve garden or plant houses, when in bloom.
11. Terrace wall, or balustrades, to be ornamented with vases, urns, and varied sculpture.
12. Conservatory,—to be entered from one of the living rooms, and proposed to be used as a promenade in unfavourable weather, having a centre walk for that purpose.
13. Winter garden, with a plant house, in which early flowering plants are to be kept; or, if Figure 12 be employed and considered sufficient, this site may be appropriated to an arcade, the sides of which should be formed with open archways and handsome trellised pilasters, trained with creepers. Patterns for the garden are shewn upon a larger scale at Figure 4.
14. Play ground, in which is to be a gymnasium.
15. Baths and swimming pond.
16. Compartments for choice rhododendrons and azalias.
17. Common rhododendrons, and other low American trees.
18. Lawn, varied with masses of shrubs and single bushes.
19. Tower, reading-room, or museum, placed in the midst of a formal rosarium, in which four different patterns of beds are shewn for dwarf roses blended with lawn, on which are to be placed standards, represented by dots. Whichever pattern may be chosen, it would be more characteristic to keep the whole garden of the same figure ;—the different designs are given merely for choice.
20. Florist compartment.
21. Compartment for small American plants, and other kinds requiring peat soil.
22, 22. Compartment for herbaceous or perennial flowers, varied with shrub masses and bushes.
23. Mass or group garden.
24. Fountain.
25. Plant house.
26. Compartment for greenhouse plants in summer time, the fronts of which are to be composed of handsome pilasters of lattice work, with arched openings. The whole to be neatly trained with pretty climbing plants.
27. Aviary, surrounded with lawn, studded with bird cages, &c., and wire devices for supporting flowers.
28. Covered seats.
29, 29. Rivulet, which may be employed for the growth of aquatic plants, and for exhibiting gold and silver fish. The bottom to be bedded with white sandy gravel.
30. Menagerie, surrounded by circular walks and grass.
31. Open seats.
32. Principal stove and sheds.

33. Vegetable garden, enclosed by fruit walls, with borders both inside and out.
34. Pineries and other forcing compartments.
35, 35. Dwarf fruit trees, intermixed with filberts.
36. Gardeners' houses.
37. Compost ground, &c.
38. Forest walk, which may command specimens of the rarer and ornamental trees.
39, 39. Boundary fence between the park and pleasure ground.
40. Lodge.
41. Pinetum, upon lawn, introducing now and then groups of trees of a different character, in order to vary its monotony, and soften the dense, sombre tone which would otherwise present itself. It will also be necessary to blend a few of the pines into the adjoining forest planting, in order that the transition between the two may not be too great.
42. Rustic seat.
43, 43, 43. Forest walking ground.

NG THE GENERAL ARRA

COUNTRY RESIDENC

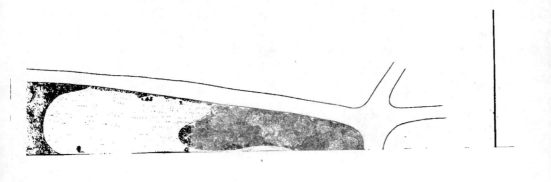

LIST OF SUBSCRIBERS.

His Grace the Duke of Norfolk, Arundel Castle, Sussex.
His Grace the Archbishop of York, Bishopthorpe, near York.
The Right Honourable the Earl of Carlisle, Castle Howard, Yorkshire.
The Right Honourable Earl Fitzwilliam, Wentworth Park, Yorkshire.
The Right Honourable the Earl of Effingham, The Grange, Yorkshire.
The Right Honourable the Earl of Dartmouth, Sandwell Park, Staffordshire.
The Right Honourable Lord Calthorpe, Ampton Park, Suffolk.
The Right Honourable Lord Feversham, Duncombe Park, Yorkshire.
The Right Honourable Lord Panmure, Dunkeld Park, Scotland.
The Rev. John Dodson, Littledale, near Lancaster.
William Beckett, Esq., M.P., Kirkstall Grange, near Leeds.
William Williams Brown, Esq., Allerton Hall, near Leeds.
Arthur Lupton, Esq., Newton Hall, near Leeds.
Sir George Goodman, Knt., M.P., Roundhay, near Leeds.
Thomas William Tottie, Esq., Beech Grove, near Leeds.
David Cooper, Esq., Shadwell Grange, near Leeds.
T. P. Teale, Esq., Leeds.
Joseph Teale, Esq., Leeds.
John Upton, Esq., Brompton, near London.
Michael Stocks, Esq., Catherine House, near Halifax.
Charles Yates, Esq., Birmingham.
James Sanderson, Esq., Endcliffe Cottage, Sheffield.
Frederick Thynne, Esq., Westminster, London.
The Rev. C. A. Hulbert, Slaithwaite, near Huddersfield.
Hamer Stansfeld, Esq., Burley Grange, near Otley.
William Smith Dickinson, Esq., Pannal, near Harrogate.
Charles Brook, Esq., Healey House, near Huddersfield.
Charles Brook, Jun., Esq., Wood Cottage, Meltham, near Huddersfield.
The Honourable Mr. Gough, Perry Hall, near Birmingham.
Benjamin Hemsworth, Esq., Monk Fryston Hall, near Ferrybridge.
W. Andrews, Esq., Bradford.
Robert Dymond, Esq., M.D, Bolton Hall, near Doncaster.
W. W. Bagshawe, Esq., The Oaks, near Sheffield.
Daniel Peckover, Esq., Wood Hall, near Bradford.

206

J. Rogers, Esq., Abbeydale, near Sheffield.
Henry Forbes, Esq., Harrogate.
Robert Milligan, Esq., M.P., Acacia, near Bradford.
Titus Salt, Esq., Crow Nest, near Bradford.
W. Murgatroyd, Esq., Bank Field, near Bingley.
B. B. Popplewell, Esq., Beacon Hill, near Ilkley.
The Rev. H. B. Smyth, Thornes Parsonage, near Wakefield.
J. Riley, Esq., Birkby, near Huddersfield.
Thomas Firth, Esq., Toothill.
Bentley Shaw, Esq., Wood Field House, near Huddersfield.
Joseph Hirst, Esq., Wilshaw, near Huddersfield.
Thomas Horsfall, Esq., Burley Hall, near Otley.
W. P. Milner, Esq., Attercliffe, near Sheffield.
Wilson Overend, Esq., Sheffield.
T. W. Watson, Esq., Sheffield.
J. T. Fisher, Esq., Marsden.
Sydney Norris, Esq., Fixby Park.
Richard Hurst, Esq., Mirfield.
Messrs. Batt and Rutley, London.
Joseph Dent, Esq., Ribstone Park, near Wetherby.
W. W. Walker, Esq., Bolling Hall, near Bradford.
Edward Waud, Esq., Manston Hall, near Leeds.
James Hamerton, Esq., Hellifield Peel, near Skipton.
Wm. Tipping, Esq., Bank Hall, near Clitheroe.
Thomas Nelson, Esq., Carlisle.
Alderman Sidney, London.
W. J. Horn, Esq., Carr House, near Sheffield.
William Aldam, Jun., Esq., Frickley Hall, near Doncaster.
William Jacomb, Esq., Mold Green, near Huddersfield.
A. Wilson, Esq., Pitsmoor, near Sheffield.
John Brooke, Esq., Armitage Bridge.
John Crossley, Esq., Halifax.
Edward Akroyd, Esq., Denton Park, near Otley.
William Leigh Brook, Esq., Meltham Hall, near Huddersfield.
John Waterhouse, Esq., Well Head, near Halifax.
John Fullerton, Esq., Thryberg Park, near Rotherham.
Joseph Robert Atkinson, Esq., Elmwood House, Leeds.
The Venerable Archdeacon Musgrave, Halifax.
Henry Akroyd, Esq., Halifax.
George Wilson, Esq., Prinlaws, Fife, Scotland.
Alexander Lawson, Esq., Burnturk, Scotland.
George Higham, Esq., Brighouse, (2 copies).
George Rogers, Esq., Priestley Green, near Halifax.
D. B. Mouncey, Esq., Hillham Hall, near Ferrybridge.
Samuel Waterhouse, Esq., Green Hays, near Halifax.

207

Mrs. John Allen, Huddersfield.
Bernard Hartley, Esq., Allangate, near Halifax.
James Stansfeld, Esq., Halifax.
Charles Norris, Esq., Wood Hall, near Halifax.
Thomas Varley, Esq., Edgerton House, near Huddersfield.
B. B. Taylor, Esq., York House, near Huddersfield.
William Haigh, Esq., The Shay, near Halifax.
E. L. Betts, Esq., Preston Hall, near Maidstone, Kent.
Robert Baker, Esq., Manston, near Leeds.
Robert John Bentley, Esq., Finningley Park, near Bawtry.
William Robinson, Esq., Settle.
John Dixon, Esq., Knells, near Carlisle.
G. G. Tetley, Esq., Daisy Hill, near Bradford.
Messrs. Henderson and Son, Pine Apple Place, near London.
William Butcher, Esq., Glossop Road, near Sheffield.
F. W. T. Vernon Wentworth, Esq., Wentworth Castle, Yorkshire.
Robert Younge, Esq., Grey Stones, near Sheffield.
Corden Thompson, Esq., M.D., Sheffield.
William Jeffcock, Esq., High Hazels, near Sheffield.
William Martin, Esq., Undercliffe, near Bradford.
John Jeats Thexton, Esq., Ashton House, Milnthorpe, near Lancaster.
William M. Brown, Esq., Leeds.
Joshua Pollard, Esq., Scarr Hill, near Bradford.
Mrs. Bentley, Esholt House, near Leeds.
Malcolm Ross, Esq., Manchester.
Sir John Potter, Knt., Buile Hill, Manchester.
William Fairbairn, Esq., Manchester.
J. Tindale, Esq., Rose Villa, near Huddersfield.
Robert Barnes, Esq., Brookside, Manchester.
Charles Gascoigne Maclea, Esq., Blenheim Terrace, Leeds.
William Greenwood, Esq., Wood House, near Ilkley.
Anthony Titley, Esq., Hill Top, Headingley, near Leeds.
P. W. Passavant, Esq., Knowsthorpe, near Leeds.
William Henry Rawson, Esq., Hill House, Sowerby, near Halifax.
R. E. Payne, Esq., Roundhay, near Leeds.
Frederick Baines, Esq., St. Ann's, Burley, near Leeds.
Captain Spong, R.N., Maidstone, Kent.
James Holdforth, Esq., Burley Hill, Leeds.
John Skelton, Esq., Moor Allerton, near Leeds.
Robert Hudson, Esq., Acacia Villa, Roundhay.
P. Davis Cooke, Esq., Gwysane, Mold, Flintshire.
William Beverley, Esq., St. Ann's, Burley, near Leeds.
John Horsfall, Esq., Bolton Royd, Bradford.
Thomas Brooke, Esq., Northgate House, Honley, near Huddersfield.
R. H. Singleton, Esq., Springfield Lodge, near Leeds.

John Rhodes, Esq., Potternewton House, near Leeds.
Charles Bousfield, Esq., Roundhay, near Leeds.
Thomas Skelton, Esq., Headingley, near Leeds.
William Meynell, Esq., Little Woodhouse, Leeds.
Joshua Fielden, Esq., Stansfield Hall, Todmorden.
E. J. Maude, Esq., The Old Hall, Knowsthorpe, near Leeds.
Edmund Maude, Esq., Potternewton, near Leeds.
Edward J. Teale, Esq., Woodhouse-lane, Leeds.
William Hey, Esq., Roundhay, near Leeds.
Lionel Knowles, Esq., Gomersal, near Leeds.
Edward Wilkinson, Esq., Winmoor Lodge, near Leeds.
John G. Sugden, Esq., Steeton Hall, near Keighley.
William Reinhardt, Esq., Leeds.
T. P. Crosland, Esq., Gledholt, near Huddersfield.
Wm. Singleton, Esq., Park Place, Leeds.
Joseph Ogden March, Esq., Beech Grove, Leeds.
John Heaton, Esq., St. John's Cottage, near Leeds.
Edwin Eddison, Esq., Headingley, near Leeds.
William M. Maude, Esq., Knowsthorpe Hall, near Leeds.
John Sykes, Esq., Headingley Hill, near Leeds.
William Gott, Esq., Spring Bank, Harrogate.
The Rev. J. A. Rhodes, Roundhay, near Leeds.
John Wilkinson, Esq., Gledhow Mount, Potternewton.
John Wilson, Esq., Roundhay, near Leeds.
Thomas Wilks Lord, Esq., Bridgefield-place, near Leeds.
Richard Harrison, Esq., Woodlesford House, near Leeds.
Messrs. Perkin and Backhouse, Leeds.
John Ripley, Esq., Cowper Villa, near Leeds.
Samuel Hammond, Esq., Bridgefield-place, near Leeds.
Major Spong, Boley Hill, Rochester, Kent.
Dr. Ramsbottom, Huddersfield.
John Calverley, Esq., Oulton Park, near Leeds.
Edward Rawson, Esq., Ash Grove, near Halifax.
George Hayward, Esq., Headingley.

EDWARD BAINES AND SONS, PRINTERS, LEEDS.

CPSIA information can be obtained
at www.ICGtesting.com
Printed in the USA
LVHW081503201121
703970LV00010B/233